School of Divinity

Gardner-Webb University
School of Divinity

This book donated
by

Also available

VOL I THEMES OF BIBLICAL THEOLOGY

VOL III ECUMENICITY AND RENEWAL

Twentieth Century Theology in the Making

II The Theological Dialogue: Issues and Resources

EDITED BY JAROSLAV PELIKAN

TRANSLATED BY R. A. WILSON

Harper & Row, Publishers
New York, Evanston, San Francisco, London

*This translation is a selection from the second
edition of* Die Religion in Geschichte und Gegenwart
*published by J. C. B. Mohr (Paul Siebeck)
in Tübingen 1927-1932*

Contents

Contents

Contents

Contents

8

Contents

Contents

Contents

Contents

Contents

Contents

Acknowledgements

Scripture quotations from the Revised Standard Version of the Bible, copyrighted 1946 and 1952 by the Division of Christian Education of the National Council of the Churches of Christ in the United States of America, are used by permission.

General Introduction

An encyclopedia can be a piece of high-level hack work, warming over and serving up the conventional wisdom, factual or not, contained in previous works of reference— or it can be an active partner in creative scholarship, giving thinkers at the growing edge of research an opportunity to state the results of that research for the non-technical reader and to correlate their results with the work of men in related fields.

A splendid example of the second type of encyclopedia is *Die Religion in Geschichte und Gegenwart,* a multi-volume reference work on religion and theology. Its first edition was published by J. C. B. Mohr (Paul Siebeck) in Tübingen from 1909 to 1913; the second edition from 1927 to 1932; the third edition from 1956 to 1962. Thus its first edition was published in the German Empire, the second in the Weimar Republic, the third in the German Federal Republic; there was no new edition during either of the World Wars or during the Third Reich.

More even than the vicissitudes of the German people and State over the past half-century, it is the scarcely less turbulent changes in German Protestant theology that are reflected in the successive editions of the *R.G.G.* When the first volume of the first edition appeared in 1909, Paul Tillich and Karl Barth had just completed their schooling, and Rudolf Bultmann was still a graduate student. When the last volume of the third edition appeared in 1962, all three were emeriti, and they and their colleagues had meanwhile changed the shape of theology so drastically that every major article had been radically revised as the result of their work.

The second edition of the *R.G.G.*, therefore, occupies a special place in the making of twentieth-century theology. For here many of the men who redrew the theological map have set down their thought on the key issues of theology. Most of them wrote full-length books on those issues. While some of the books have been translated into English, others have not. As a result, the articles in this edition provide a unique wealth of material, from which the selections in these three volumes have been made.

These selections are based on the conjunction of several criteria: the issues that have, since *R.G.G.*[2], become or continued to be dominant in theological discussion; the men who wrote for *R.G.G.*[2] who have shaped the development of twentieth-century theology; the resources that have been drawn upon for that development. In many cases, the article by *the* man on *the* issue in *R.G.G.*[2] is the best available summary of his position; practically all of them appear here in English for the first time. Thus here, and perhaps nowhere else, the present-day reader may study Paul Tillich on *Myth and Mythology* and on *Revelation*, Rudolf Bultmann on *Gospels* and on *Paul*, Friedrich Heiler on *Catholicism*, Paul Althaus on *Eschatology*, Nathan Søderblom on *Union Movements*, Adolf Haernack on *Origen*, and many other seminal thinkers of the twentieth century on the questions which have made them important, but which have also shaped us and our time.

Each volume is supplied with a brief introduction both to the men and to the movements it sets forth, and with a bibliography of works in English pertinent to both. But these have been deliberately held to a minimum, in order to permit the material to speak for itself.

J. P.

Introduction to Volume II

As a theological and philosophical term 'dialogue' is, of course, older than Christianity; it may be even older than Plato. Very early in Christian history, however, the dialogue became a genre of literature for demonstrating the superiority of Christian theology to Jewish and pagan thought. The subsequent role of various philosophical systems in the development of Christian theology shows that even when it was dogmatic in its claims, theology continued to be dialogic in its method—often more dialogic than it was prepared to acknowledge.

Nevertheless, theological dialogue as an integral factor of the theologian's work has come to acquire a special meaning in the modern setting of theology, viz., in theology since the Enlightenment, and an increasing prominence in this century. In fact, like 'encounter' and 'commitment' before it and like 'charisma' after it, 'dialogue' threatens to become a twentieth-century cliché. Whatever term we use, however, it is one of the most important marks of the contemporary theologian that he has learned to listen seriously to other thinkers and scholars. More perhaps than at any earlier time in the history of Christian thought, the full range of secular disciplines can be seen at work in the forming of theological judgements. Ironically, this change has come just at the time when communication in the other direction—from theology to the secular disciplines—seemed to be at or near an all-time low. Perhaps as a result, theology during the twentieth century has tended to give the impression of being so desperately in need of dialogue with other disciplines and with 'the modern world' as to ignore the continuing dialogue with its own heritage. Although apologetics has been called, in a phrase made familiar by Emil Brunner, 'the other task of theology' alongside the dogmatic task, the relation between the two has seemed sometimes to be reversed, as theology has come to recognize the depth of the great gulf fixed between its tradition and contemporary modes of thought and language.

This bipolarity of the theological dialogue, as a dialogue with tradition and a dialogue with other disciplines, has made its presence felt within each of the conventional fields of theological study and within their treatment of each of the conventional topics of theological exposition. Nevertheless, there are certain fields of theology and certain topics in theology upon which the new situation of the theological dialogue has had an especially powerful impact. Similarly, there are certain cognate disciplines upon which theologians have drawn not only for the reformulation of traditional doctrines but also for the creation and adaptation of new concepts in theological discourse. The essays collected in this volume are intended to illustrate these several aspects of the theological dialogue in the twentieth century.

In many ways the one issue on which most of these aspects converge is the issue of *Revelation*, as the article on this topic suggests. A chapter on revelation had, of course, been a stock item in systematic theology long before the twentieth century. Both medieval Scholasticism and Protestant Orthodoxy had introduced their dogmatic systems with an analysis of the relation between revelation and reason and of the nature of revelation. But the presentation of the issue in twentieth-century theology has been markedly different. For one thing, it could no longer be taken for granted that the audience being addressed by the theologian had an *a priori* disposition to assert the uniqueness of Christianity and therefore to affirm the absoluteness of its claims to revelation. Such claims continue to be made in the twentieth century, and a result, though not perhaps an intent, of the work of Karl Barth has been to reinforce them. But a deepening relativism about any pretension to absolute truth, and especially about the supposed qualitative difference between one religion and all the others, has compelled theologians to adopt a more modest stance in speaking about Christian revelation. The nature and content of revelation has also come to be described in different terms. The usual way of stating the difference is to declare that revelation is not to be understood propositionally, as the communication of arcane truths, but personally or existentially, as an encounter with, and an involvement in, that which is Holy and Ultimate. This redefinition is shaped both by a new appropriation of the biblical message and by the insights of other disciplines, such as depth psychology, existential philosophy, and the history of non-Christian religions.

Many of these same factors are visible in the article on *Christology*, but with a special colouring because of the subject. As a study of the long article on *Jesus Christ* in Volume I of this set will show, the very possibility of a christology in anything resembling the traditional form had been rendered fundamentally questionable by the application of historical–critical methods to the data of the gospels. Even a 'life of Jesus', which had served as a substitute for christology for many theologians in the nineteenth century, no longer seemed possible, for it would require a disentanglement of authentic biographical information from the witness of the primitive Christian community—an impossible task. But in the present article it becomes clear that when history became a theological category in its own right, this did not automatically eliminate the issues with which christology has to deal; it provided new resources for coping with those issues, even as it added special difficulties to the assignment. The christology that emerged from this dialogue with history repelled some critics because it seemed excessively naturalistic; others found it still far too deeply caught in the private world of the Church. In a more profound sense, however, both the article on *Jesus Christ* in Volume I and the article on *Christology* here in Volume II demonstrate the true nature of theological dialogue; for while the problems with which they deal have been basically altered by a dialogue with history, these problems in turn raise the question with which even a professedly secular theory of history is obliged to come to terms: How was it possible for Jesus Christ to happen in the history of this world?

Theology has usually asked a quite different question: Why was it necessary for Jesus Christ to happen in the history of this world? And it has answered the question by its doctrine of the nature and destiny of man, the lineaments of which are sketched in the articles on *Sin and Guilt* and *Grace*. But if the problem of history and of historicity has created difficulties for traditional christology, it has proved disastrous for traditional anthropology. Whatever may be the facts of history about the Second Adam, the First Adam has disappeared from history, and with him whatever there was in the Augustinian theory of original sin that depended on the literal accuracy of the story of Adam and Eve and of their fall into sin. The evolutionary hypothesis, which undercut the assertion that men were sinful because they were all descended from a single human couple, went on to undercut the promise of salvation as well; for sin was taken to be a stage in the development of man which would eventually be put behind him, as previous stages had been. To meet this challenge, the Christian doctrine of grace also had to be rethought and the Reformation attack upon a mechanical or quasi-magical view of grace had to be carried to its conclusion. So it is that the issues of theology have been revised as a result of the dialogue with other disciplines, a dialogue which has raised new problems but also discovered new resources.

Among these other disciplines, philosophy is still the favourite *Gesprächspartner* of theology, as it has always been. But the period in the history of thought usually labelled 'the Enlightenment' is the time when philosophy, though long assured that it had the right to proceed according to its own canons, finally and irrevocably declared its autonomy, and specifically its independence from theology. This declaration of autonomy took place at a time when philosophical speculation was dominated, at least in the Protestant lands, by one or another school of idealistic thought. Therefore many of the most important and influential efforts by Protestant theology to adjust to the realities of the new philosophy have in fact been directed at a *rapprochement* with the idealism of the eighteenth and nineteenth centuries. In the German Protestant theology from whose *ambience* these articles come, this preoccupation with the problematics of idealism was responsible for the assumption—quite unwarranted, as subsequent history was to prove—that philosophers were in fact interested in such issues as the nature of *Geist*, which had for so long been the stock-in-trade of the philosophical descendants of Kant and Hegel, both of whom had, after all, been exposed to some species of Lutheran theology. The article on *Philosophy* is strongly influenced by this idealistic atmosphere, and there are only hints in it that if theology is to carry on a dialogue with philosophy, it may have to be with a less 'believing philosophy'. The article on *The Philosophy of Religion*, on the other hand, written by a man who was to become an influential historian of religion, seems much more prepared to cope with the philosophical implications of an essentially empirical description of the world religions, with all their practices and beliefs. Even here, to be sure, idealism is not far away, but the commitment of the article is clearly more open than is its basic orientation.

In part the openness of the new orientation is due to a deeper appreciation of the role of religious experience. The article on *The Psychology of Religion* seeks to come to terms with the new insights into religious experience that had become a central element of the theological discussion of the latter part of the nineteenth century. The contrast it draws between two methods of study in the psychology of religion is an effort to place this study in the context of the theological tradition, at least since the Reformation. With the recognition, so brilliantly documented by Schleiermacher, that dogmatic theology is derivative from religious experience even when it refuses to acknowledge that it is, a way had been found to take account also of non-Christian religious experience, especially when, as we shall see, it overlapped with the psychology of Christian piety. One problem that was closely related both to these issues and to the preceding was that discussed in the article on *Certainty*; for religious commitment obviously demanded some certainty about the reliability of that to which one was committed, but theological, historical, philosophical, and psychological reflection just as obviously demanded an honest recognition that subjective certainty was no guarantee of the objective validity of one's beliefs. 'Psychologism' is too facile a term for the recognition that any theology, regardless of its orthodoxy, must acknowledge its roots in religious experience and must therefore find some way of conceding at least tentative validity to forms of religious experience alien to itself.

Implicit in much of what we have already said is the recognition of the role which the history of religions has begun to play in theology during the twentieth century. The processes by which it acquired that role are not easy to discern within the general history of culture. Everything from the founding of the Theosophical Society by Madame Blavatsky in 1875 and the subsequent World Parliament of Religions to the phenomenal increase in world travel by both military and civilian personnel after World War II has received credit for a decisive shift in religious attitudes, viz., that more Western Christians than ever before have discovered the reality of Eastern religions for themselves and have had to relate their own Christian commitments to this reality. For theological scholarship this discovery meant an end, probably forever, to any theory about the uniqueness of Christian revelation based upon a comparison of the best within Christianity with the worst within paganism. It also meant, however, a dawning recognition of the unmistakable similarities between the biblical religion of both the Old and the New Testament and the forms that have characterized not only the religious traditions surrounding Judaism and Christianity, such as the Canaanite or the Gnostic, but also quite exotic traditions with which Western religions had not had direct contact until the rise of modern missions. An entire new vocabulary arose, together with a new framework within which the older vocabulary had to be rethought.

Perhaps the most traumatic illustration of the new vocabulary is the domestication within Christian theological discourse of the problem with which the article on *Myth and Mythology* is concerned. Myths had traditionally been something with which the non-biblical religions had been obliged to concern themselves, while Jewish and Christian theology had been able to claim a special historicity for their message. Now it began to dawn on the apologists for Judaism and Christianity that the structure of their very claims for historicity, as set forth in their liturgies and creeds, had mythological over-tones which could not be excised in any simple way, and that therefore 'myth' was, if anything, more of a problem· for them than it had been for their 'mythicizing' opponents. The problem was even more acute when Christians and Jews had to deal with phenomena which they shared with other traditions; among these phenomena, none was more inevitable or more troubling than the presence within Jewish and Christian history of the experiences described in the article on *Mysticism*. Even the attempt by one of the authors of that article—who, ironically, was to achieve an international reputation for his discovery of 'myth' in the New Testament—to deny the presence of authentic mysticism in the Gospel of John does not detract from the insistent demand that Christian theology acknowledge the decisive role of mystical experience and of mystical theology in its own historical development. Yet any such acknowledgement must be accompanied by the recognition that the parallels between Christian and non-Christian mysticism are not purely formal in character. The effort to discover the 'essence' of a religious tradition despite and beyond its historical forms has persisted even amid a deeper consciousness of its parallels with other traditions; therefore the article on *Religious Principle* seeks to go beyond 'historical facts' to some sort of abiding value and meaning that does not deny the distinctiveness of Christianity, even as it abstracts from the dogmas and practices of the Church to identify a more nearly universal content.

Those who helped to set the new theological dialogue into motion include the great, the near-great, and the not-so-great among twentieth-century German Protestant theologians:

24

Aner, Karl, b. 1879 (*Sin and Guilt, Grace*), lecturer in church history at Halle.

Arseniev, Nikolay Sergeevich, b. 1888 (*Mysticism*), professor at Saratov, Königsberg, Warsaw, and St. Vladimir, New York.

Baeck, Leo, 1873–1956 (*Revelation, Sin and Guilt, Mysticism*), lecturer at the Hochschule für die Wissenschaft des Judentums in Berlin, then a prisoner in Theresienstadt, finally in London.

Balla, Emil, 1885–1956 (*Grace*), instructor of Old Testament in Kiel and Marburg, professor in Münster and Leipzig.

Bauke, Hermann, 1886–1928 (*Christology*), instructor and then professor and pastor at Halle.

Bertholet, Alfred, 1868–1951 (*Sin and Guilt*), professor of Old Testament at Basel, Tübingen, Göttingen, and Berlin.

Bornkamm, Heinrich, b. 1901 (*Mysticism*), instructor in church history at Tübingen, professor at Giessen and Heidelberg.

Bultmann, Rudolf, b. 1884 (*Revelation, Myth and Mythology, Mysticism*), professor of New Testament at Breslau, Giessen, and Marburg.

Brunner, Emil, 1889–1966 (*Grace*), professor of systematic and practical theology at Zürich.

Clemen, Carl, 1865–1940 (*Grace*), lecturer at Halle, professor at Bonn.

Dibelius, Martin, 1883–1947 (*Christology*), professor at Berlin and Heidelberg.

Dörries, Hermann, b. 1895 (*Mysticism*), professor at Tübingen, Halle, and Göttingen.

Gunkel, Hermann, 1862–1932 (*Sin and Guilt, Myth and Mythology*), professor of Old Testament at Berlin, Giessen, and Halle.

Heim, Karl, 1874–1958 (*Certainty*), lecturer at Halle, professor at Münster and Tübingen.

Heimsoeth, Heinz, b. 1886 (*Philosophy*), professor of

philosophy at Königsberg and Cologne.

Leeuw, Gerardus van der, 1890–1950 (*Revelation, Philosophy*), teacher at Doetinchem, professor of history of religion, theology, and Egyptian philology at Groningen.

Leisegang, Hans, 1890–1951 (*Mysticism*), professor at Leipzig and Jena.

Lipsius, F. R., b. 1873 (*Philosophy*), lecturer in systematic theology at Jena, in philosophy at Leipzig, professor at Leipzig.

Mundle, Wilhelm, b. 1892 (*Grace*), lecturer and professor of New Testament at Marburg, pastor in Düsseldorf and Hamborn.

Piper, Otto, b. 1891 (*Sin and Guilt*), professor at Göttingen, Münster, and Princeton Theological Seminary.

Rühle, Oskar, b. 1901 co-editor of *Die Religion in Geschichte und Gegenwart*.

Schmidt, Friedrich Wilhelm, 1893–1945 (*Revelation*), professor at Halle and Münster.

Schmidt, Hans, 1877–1953 (*Revelation*), professor of Old Testament at Tübingen, Giessen, and Halle.

Schmitz, Otto, 1883–1957 (*Sin and Guilt*), lecturer in New Testament at Berlin, director of the seminary at Basel, professor at Münster.

Steinmann, Theophil, b. 1869 (*Mysticism*), lecturer in systematic theology at Gnadenfrei and Herrnhut.

Tillich, Paul, 1886–1965 (*Revelation, Philosophy, Myth and Mythology*), lecturer at Berlin, professor at Marburg, Dresden, Leipzig, Frankfurt, Union Theological Seminary in New York, Harvard, and Chicago.

Troeltsch, Ernst, 1865–1923 (*Religious Principle*), lecturer at Göttingen, professor of systematic theology at Bonn, professor of systematic theology and of philosophy at Heidelberg, professor of philosophy at Berlin.

Wach, Joachim, 1898–1955 (*The Philosophy of Religion*), professor at Leipzig, Brown, and The University of Chicago.

Wehrung, Georg, b. 1880 (*Christology*), professor of systematic theology at Strasbourg, Münster, Halle, and Tübingen.

Weinel, Heinrich, 1874–1936 (*Mysticism*), lecturer at Berlin and Bonn, professor of New Testament and of systematic theology at Jena.

Wobbermin, Georg, 1896–1943 (*The Psychology of Religion*), lecturer in systematic theology at Berlin, professor at Breslau, Heidelberg, Göttingen, and Berlin.

J. P.

I

Revelation

I REVELATION IN COMPARATIVE RELIGION

1. The Scientific Study of Religion and Revelation

Because of the explicitly paradoxical character of the concept of revelation (*cf.* below V*a*. 3), the decision as to what is in fact revelation lies outside the sphere of the scientific study of religion. The latter can only describe the outward religious phenomenon with the religious experience which accompanies it; it cannot deal with revelation. But if it is to do justice to the full richness of religious experience, *it must concede the validity of the experience of revelation in its full force*. That is, it must not rationalize this experience. The actual experience of revelation is that of the unveiling of what in principle cannot be unveiled, the self-manifestation of what no ear has heard and no eye seen. Thus in the first place we must exclude from the concept those phenomena to which we apply the expression revelation only by analogy. Any sudden insight, even in the realm of art and science, can come to us as an 'illumination', as a 'revelation'; but the way in which it was concealed is not that of what is revealed. Similarly, we must disregard what is called occultism; for if the occult is imparted to us, this means no more than the enrichment of our knowledge, and not a knowledge beyond all reason. Nor is it of any value to relate revelation to a religious *a priori* idea or a fundamental religious concept (as in natural religion), for such ideas may well give an adequate account of a religious tendency of the human soul, but not of the 'wholly other' which is manifested in revelation. The distinction between a *general* revelation, accessible to everyone, and a *special* revelation, only given to the followers of a particular faith (*cf.* V*a.* 7; V*b.* *1*), is even less valid. For revelation is intended to be experienced as such and is only accessible to those who share the same experience. Thus to speak of a *general* revelation in nature or history can only mean that nature and history appear to the great mass of humanity as peculiarly apt vehicles of revelation, since they have already been a source of real revelation to many people. Revelation as a purely personal experience can never be subject to any criteria of what is universally knowable or universally understandable. The scientific study of religion must therefore accept as revelation whatever claims to be so. It can only distinguish between a *genuine* and a *false* experience of revelation, separating what is derivative and imitative from what is original and real. It can only do this by constantly keeping in mind the nature of revelation as ultimate, unknowable meaning, which nevertheless makes itself known or, in religious terms, as an act of God.

2. *The Experience of Revelation through Visions and Objects*

The first form in which the experience of revelation takes place in the history of religion is that of objects and visions. A thing, a place, or a particular time is 'holy' as a result of its relationship to revelation. For *primitive man* there is revealed in some object a power which he knows that he does not understand, even though he makes use of it to obtain his ends. Dynamism, or the religion of *mana*, depends upon the experience of revelation in a characteristic way. In no theoretical sense, but purely empirically, the extraordinary 'powerfulness' of some object leads to the conclusion that it has *mana*, that a power lives in it which is beyond human understanding. The object then becomes taboo. If it reveals the power with which it is filled in a permanent fashion, it may also become a fetish. At this level of primitive religion, nothing is yet given theoretical expression; the experience of revelation takes place, but if it is not repeated it has no further consequences. A chief—who in this context is more an object than a person—possesses power, that is, there is revealed in him an extraordinary fullness of the 'holy'; but when he is weakened by age, he has obviously lost his power.

Semi-civilized cultures come closer to turning the experience of revelation into a *system of revelation*. Someone experiences an illumination under a particular tree; from then on, the tree is regarded as holy, and pilgrimages are made to it in order to receive an oracle; one can rely on the revelation still being present at a place once guaranteed as holy. People also begin to be astonished at a revelation; that is, there is now a conviction that the great majority of objects are not vehicles of revelation (primitive man is always ready to regard them as such) and the undeniable exceptions to this rule are regarded as miracles. In association with this, the objects which are regarded as vehicles of revelation become increasingly remote, distant, and immaterial. The solid fetishes are replaced by the fleeting figures of dreams, of illuminations, and visions. The young Indian, on coming to maturity, withdraws into a lonely place and, after preparing himself by continual fasting, comes to know in a dream-like vision his *nagual*, which is a kind of protective spirit intimately associated with his life, usually conceived of in the form of an animal. Everyone knows how often dreams appear as the instrument of revelation in the history of religion. A classical example of a vision is that of Moses and the burning bush, which becomes a vehicle of revelation. In all these cases, the rise of a theoretical view of revelation emphasizes its exceptional character. It can also lead to an attempt to *regulate* revelation, as we have already seen from the example of the oracle. This occurs particularly in the cult. At particular times the God reveals himself to his worshippers, either through miracles and signs (such as healings) or in a sacrament. He is called upon (epiclesis) and appears (epiphany). 'An angel of the Lord went down at certain seasons into the pool, and troubled the water' (John 5. 4). The revelation can also be linked to a particular place: if anyone lay down to sleep in the temple of Asclepius at Epidaurus, the god came to him in a dream (incubation).

3. The Experience of Revelation in the Form of Words

However, depending upon the degree to which the view of the divine as a power gives way to a more personal conception, revelation through objects becomes less prominent, being replaced by revelation through words. But it must be noted at once that even at the point of its highest intensity (*cf.* below) verbal revelation can never dispense entirely with objects: even in the spiritual and personal outlook of Christianity, there is still an element remaining which is not entirely absorbed by the word, and which leads to the doctrine of the sacraments. Words assume a speaker, that is a person, and a will. Consequently, revelation through words is associated not with the visual processes, but with the *intellectual* and *moral*; it only concerns the auditory processes in so far as it is an *inner voice*. Even the ancient Egyptians called conscience a 'voice of God'. Naturally, there are many transitional forms, in which the inner apprehension of the voice of God is associated with some external perception, and even with an external vision: in the account of Exodus 24 the whole emphasis of the revelation is on its intellectual and moral content; nevertheless, Moses and Aaron 'see the Lord' (*cf.* II, 2 below). But what is most important is neither the vision nor the message which is revealed, but the ineffable and numinous element. However, because words are used here, a certain degree of rationalization is unavoidable, and it is naturally greater than in the case of the revelation through objects. It begins to be possible to talk of the *content* of revelation. It was often forgotten that the content of revelation could never be anything but God himself; for everything else is not of its nature concealed. Thus what was merely the vehicle of revelation, such as doctrine and the law, came to be regarded as the true content of revelation. It was only in this way that the great systems of revelation arose. The ethical and ritual material that existed in society was proclaimed in a new sense as revelation. Nevertheless, this never happened without a true experience of revelation such as that of Moses, Mohammed, and Zoroaster, which enriched what they had received from tradition and inspired it with new energy, and even a completely new spirit. For revelation through words is only received in a personal dialogue with the overpowering will of God. Consequently, *mediators* of revelation, who appear as prophets and who proclaim the word of God, become very important. Such persons exist in every possible religion and sect. On the basis of their experience they found what is at least in part a new doctrine, a new law, and a new spirit. It is this spirit, not in so far as it is a cultural innovation, but because it seems to be numinous in content, which gives others the impression that it comes from 'elsewhere', and sometimes leads to further similar revelations. It is in this way that religious communities and new religions come into being. Ultimately they go back to the inspiration of men of God. An inspiration of this sort was received by the religious leaders mentioned above, and also by Buddha, by Jesus Christ, and in a derivative fashion by such persons as

Paul, as well as numerous founders of sects and religious movements (e.g. the Mormons, theosophy, anthroposophy). In the religion of the Old Testament, these mediators are overshadowed by the revelation given by God in the history of his people (*cf.* II, 3, 4 below).

The ultimate development of the concept of revelation takes place when words come to be regarded as inadequate, too rational or too material to be vehicles of revelation. Then the word becomes the *logos, while the mediator of revelation becomes the revelation itself.* Not only his message, but his whole life and personality become the revelation. Buddha opposed the placing of his person on a higher level than his teaching. In Islam, too, in a conception due to the polemic against Christianity, the word is regarded as at most an attribute of God; it contains no intrinsic power of its own. But the fundamental principle and premiss of *Christianity* is the incarnation of the *logos* in Jesus: 'The word becomes flesh' (*cf.* IV below) and, as a consequence of this, Christian dogmatic theology relates every revelation of God to Christ, even the creation and the whole of history (*cf.* V*b.* below). In the light of the concept of revelation described above this means that various modes of revelation, contradicting the absolute character of revelation, are avoided: at the moment of the incarnation heaven comes down to earth; everything else is comprehended within this revelation.

GERARDUS VAN DER LEEUW

II REVELATION IN THE OLD TESTAMENT

Like every other living religion, that of the Old Testament is convinced that God, who is not perceptible to the senses, sometimes comes out of his concealment, and 'reveals' himself (Hebrew: *gillāh*).

1. Revelation in Nature

There are echoes of the conception of pre-Israelite religion that the deity revealed himself in nature: 'When you hear the sound of marching in the tops of the balsam trees . . . then the Lord has gone out before you' (2 Sam. 5.24). Thunder is regarded as the voice of Yahweh (e.g. Pss. 18.13; 29.3), and the earthquake as the shaking of the ground beneath his feet (e.g. Habb. 3.6). In general, however, the phenomena of nature are no longer regarded as living expressions of God, but either as phenomena accompanying his presence (e.g. the different elements drawn from the image of a volcano in the Sinai stories); or else they bear witness to his power as creator, or proclaim 'his glory' (e.g. the stars: Ps. 19.1; Isa. 40.22). In this sense it is possible to say that the whole creation is regarded as a revelation of God (Ps. 114; Gen. 1). There is a very clear conviction of the inadequacy of even the most powerful manifestations of nature to reveal God in the experience of Elijah at Horeb (1 Kings 19.9 ff.): the storm, the earthquake, and the fire precede God; but they are not God himself; he is not even in them.

2. The Vision of God

Another view, equally ancient, is that some favoured persons are granted a bodily vision of God. For example, this is assumed in the sagas of Genesis. Elsewhere, this conception can be linked with the *cult*: one goes into the temple, as the expression has it, in order 'to see God'. It appears that at many sanctuaries this implied a vision in a dream (*cf.* for example Gen. 28.11 ff.; 1 Sam. 3). But the tradition of our texts clearly rejects this belief, by turning the expression 'to see God' into 'to appear before God' (Ps. 42.2; *cf.* 11.7; 17.15). But the extent to which this idea had taken hold of peculiarly Israelite religion is shown by the terror with which the appearance

35

of the godhead is greeted, where this is described, and especially by Exod. 33.22, where even Moses is not allowed to do more than look at God from afar. The vision of God also forms part of the experience of the Old Testament *prophets* (*cf.* Vol I, *Prophets* II). This experience, in fact, is normally referred to by the word *ḥazah*, 'to see'. It refers here to a perception given in ecstasy. In this ecstasy, he to whom the revelation has been accorded lies 'falling down, but having his eyes uncovered' (Num. 24.4).

3. *The Word of Yahweh*

But besides this, at an early period, and increasingly as time went on, the true content of what was perceived in the moment of revelation came to be thought of as the word of Yahweh. 'The Lord of hosts has sworn in my *hearing*' says Isaiah (Isa. 5.9). According to Jeremiah, a prophet is not someone who can say of himself: 'I have had a dream', but someone who has 'stood in the council of the Lord', so that he is able to 'proclaim his words' (Jer. 23.18, 22; *cf.* also Num. 12.6-8). The commonest introduction to the description of a revelation is: 'Thus *says* Yahweh'. In such an experience, he who receives the revelation in the Old Testament hears the words of God, as those of a quite specific person. Anyone who has once heard this voice is able to recognize it again immediately (1 Sam. 3.2). This emphasis on *verbal revelation* is particularly appropriate to Israelite religion, on account of its feeling of remoteness from God; a word can be heard even from a distance. But it is explicable above all by the close connection between Israelite religion and fundamental ethical experience. An ethical commandment, in fact, is only conceivable as a word of command. The result of this is that, as time went on, the concept of revelation in the Old Testament came to belong less and less to the sphere of sense perception.

Every powerful impulse of the will in conformity with God was regarded as based upon revelation. Not merely the moment of ecstasy, but the whole life of a prophet, seemed to be filled by revelation.

4. *Revelation in History*

In addition to this direct self-manifestation of the god-head, there was also an indirect revelation, which could be perceived in an extraordinary, meaningful, and morally determined course of events, both in *personal life*, and equally in *the life of the people as a whole*. That a man and woman who are destined for each other should find each other (Gen. 24.21), that a way of escape is suddenly found from a desperate danger—at the very moment, moreover, of passing by a sanctuary (2 Sam. 15.32), that someone is saved from a sickness or from ambush (Pss. 103.4; 118.13), or that evildoers should suddenly die (Ps. 73.17)—in all such personal guidance the activity of the living God is seen, and not merely his activity, but his nature, his loving kindness and faithfulness, his righteousness and holiness (Ps. 98.2; Jer. 33.16). The prophets in particular opened man's eyes to see *the history* of the nation or even of the world in this way, and to regard it as the product of their guilt and the intervention of God to punish, and of repentance and forgiveness.

5. *Revelation in Eschatology*

The observation of the activity of the living God in history, and of his 'counsel', naturally directed attention to its ultimate goal. The longing for a full and unrestricted knowledge of God, not satisfied by any cultic experience or moment of ecstasy, also looked forward to the *future*. Thus Old Testament literature, and that of the prophets in particular, was preoccupied very early by the conception of a 'day of Yahweh', the real content of which would be the complete revelation of the godhead and the end and conclusion of all things (*cf.* Vol. I, *Eschatology* II, 2).

6. The Value Given to Revelation in the Old Testament

However strong the emphasis in the Old Testament on the hearing of the word as a means of revelation, it is a long way from regarding this word as *unchangeable* or *infallible*. For example, Isaiah emphasizes (Isa. 28.23 ff.), in the image of the farmer who does one piece of work at one time and something else later, the sovereign right of God to change his will, and therefore also his word. The words of the prophets, explicitly derived from revelation, quite frequently contradict one another. Even in Deuteronomy, in which for the first time in the history of Israelite religion a book appears as a means of revelation, we occasionally find explanatory marginal notes to traditional words of God, which sometimes come very close to polemic (Deut. 7.9 f.; *cf.* Deut. 5.9 ff.). This *freedom within the Old Testament* must be taken into account, when one is considering the permanent value which even today is still placed upon the revelation given in the Old Testament; it is human thoughts which have here provided the form of revelation, and as such are conditioned and limited by the time in which they were uttered and the person who uttered them. Nevertheless, there are certain of the loftiest passages of the Old Testament in which these ideas and perceptions possess a clarity of which the author who speaks to us was not even aware himself, a profundity and force that transcends time, and is of such a nature that we are 'inwardly certain' that they come from God and are of eternal value.

HANS SCHMIDT

III REVELATION IN JUDAISM

In post-biblical Judaism the idea of revelation was expressed in two ways: as the *direct manifestation of God* to men, and as the imparting of revelation contained in the *holy scriptures*; both aspects were invariably associated with the idea of the Jewish people as the people of revelation.

1. Implicit in the idea of a biblical canon is the view that it defines both the beginning and the end of revelation, and thus the last of the biblical prophets is represented as the last person to receive revelation. On the other hand, the Bible is not truly concluded; it is continued by oral teaching (the *Mishna*) and many of those responsible for such teaching were regarded as having been inspired by the Holy Spirit, so becoming vehicles of revelation. Even in the Middle Ages religious and legal interpretations and decisions were regarded as imparted from heaven. In particular, the idea of the *shechinah*, the constant indwelling of God in the community of the *tōrāh*, maintained the idea of the *permanence of revelation*. A large part of mystical experience (*cf. Mysticism* III, 1 p. 365 below) goes back to this certainty. The attempt to unite a philosophical theory of knowledge with supernaturalism, and so to reconcile the universalist view of revelation with the particular and exclusive nature of the experience of the prophets was made by the rationalist Jewish philosophy of the Middle Ages, and especially by Maimonides. On the one hand, revelation was equated with 'natural' illumination, in which the human mind receives the influx of truth and attains to fellowship with God; while on the other hand, the unique nature of the revelation which Moses received directly from God is maintained. The irrational nature of revelation was decisively emphasized by *Jehuda ha-Levi*. According to

him, it is dependent upon a charisma, a 'divine faculty', and brought about entirely by God; consequently, he stresses the distinctive nature of the Jewish people, the capacity to receive revelation, imparted by God to his people alone. The view held in the nineteenth century continued in essence to follow these two views; the rationalist view was represented, for example, by A. Geiger, and von Cohen, who gave a profound interpretation of the concept of creation and of the correlation between God and man, while the irrationalist view was maintained by Steinheim and S. R. Hirsch.

2. The other form of belief in revelation is that of belief in *the character of the Bible as revelation (tōrāh min hashshāmaim)*, and in the constant access to revelation which the Bible guarantees. This belief had already been given solemn expression in the priestly liturgy of the second temple (*Tamid* V, 1), and it became the foundation of religious teaching (*Sanhedrin* X, 1 and *Siphre* on Num. 15.31). As a result, the Bible came to be regarded as *the* book, the only book for man. This belief determined the outlook of the whole subsequent period to such an extent that all commentaries which set out to present the fullness of revelation were based on the Bible, while philosophical and mystical writings, and also, for the most part, religious poetry, through the use of a style which was a mosaic of biblical material, attempted to be no more than an interpretation of the Bible; and even ecstatic experiences drew their intrinsic inspiration from this book. The profound study and experience of the Bible was a participation in revelation; 'Give us a part in thy *tōrāh*', says an ancient prayer. 'The gift of the *tōrāh*' (*mattan tōrāh*) is an expression used for revelation. In this sense, the feast of Pentecost became the feast of revelation, and the messianic period came to be thought of as both the time of a general and direct revelation (according to Joel 3.1 f.), and also that of the possession

of this gift by everyone (according to Isa. 54.13). Accordingly, as early as the Talmudic period, the day of the revelation on Sinai was closely linked with the creation of the world, and the historical event of revelation was given a cosmic significance. Here the *tōrāh* became the meaning and aim of creation, and was regarded as pre-existent; it was the *logos*, the principle, (*rēshīth*), through which God created the world (*cf.* the similar conception with regard to Christ, 1 Cor. 8.6; Heb. 1.2; Col. 1.15 f.; Rev. 3.14); it was the power that overcomes chaos and brings the world into being. Thus participation in revelation was a participation in the very heart of the universe. These ideas later became less prominent. The idea of the revealed book became associated with the historical idea of the election of Israel.

LEO BAECK

IV REVELATION IN THE NEW TESTAMENT

1. A Formal Definition of the Concept

In *traditional usage* revelation means in the first instance the miraculous imparting of supernatural knowledge (concerning the being of God, heavenly mysteries, the future, etc.). This sense occurs in the Old Testament, and also on occasions in the New Testament (Matt. 16.17; 1 Pet. 1.12; Gal. 2.2; 2 Cor. 12.1,7). Thus the author of the Apocalypse of John calls his book a revelation (1.1), and in worship individual Christians recounted the miraculous knowledge they had received as revelation (1 Cor. 14.6,26,30). But this is not the dominant usage in the New Testament; in particular the knowledge of God's existence and nature is not derived from revelation in the New Testament, as is obvious from the fact that theology is not considered to have the task of dealing with the relationship between revelation and natural and rational knowledge. Rather, in the New Testament, revelation is regarded in the first instance as *an event* brought about by God, through which he brings into effect on earth and for men what was previously only a reality in his plan and resolution (which may also be thought of as pre-existent in heaven).

Fundamentally, it is *God himself* who becomes visible in revelation, just as Jesus, in his Farewell Discourses, can describe it as the goal of his revelation that he had manifested God (John 17.6,26). But God is not revealed in the sense that he thereby becomes accessible to contemplation and inquiry, but in the sense that through the event which reveals him he carries out his work upon man, places him in a new situation and demands something from him. When God 'makes known' and 'manifests' something, he is carrying something out among men and demanding something from them (Rom. 3.25 f.; 9.17,22; Phil. 1.28). Two things result from this. First, it is possible *for God to remain concealed in the revelation*, particularly to someone who resists the action and the revealed will of God. Thus the heathen completely fail to see that God's anger is being 'revealed' among them (Rom. 1.18 ff.); while even in the gospel the revelation of God is concealed from unbelievers (2 Cor. 4.3 f.); and whereas for believers the gospel is a power for salvation (Rom. 1.16 f.; 1 Cor. 1.24), for unbelievers it is a stumbling block and folly (1 Cor. 1.22 f.). The preaching which 'reveals the knowledge of God' leads some to death and others to life (2 Cor. 2.14-16). Thus revelation is both *judgement and salvation*. Secondly, since as a result of this event man is placed in a new situation, and can understand this in faith, revelation is also the basis of *knowledge*, man's knowledge of himself in his relationship to God. But such knowledge is only genuine if its basis lies in 'being known' by God (1 Cor. 8.2 f; 13.12; Gal. 4.9; Phil. 3.8-11), that is, if it is based on faith, on obedient submission to the act of God. Consequently, in 1 Cor. Paul protests against the kind of 'wisdom' which shows by its lack of love that it is no true knowledge of God. And for the same reason, John says that the unbelief of the Jews shows that they knew nothing of God.

2. *The Content of Revelation*

The content of revelation can never be anything other than salvation (or judgement), simply because it is the revelation of God; but since the gracious God is also one who imposes a demand, his law, which contains salvation and judgement, can naturally also be regarded as revelation (Rom. 2.20). On the other hand, the New Testament never speaks of God's revelation in nature and history in the sense of asserting that the existence or the providence of God can be deduced from it. Jesus refers to birds and flowers (Matt. 6.25-30) not because God is revealed in them but because a man who already knows God can learn something from these creatures. And when 1 Cor. 10.1-13 refers to the history of Israel in the desert, this is not in order to derive the existence of God from the observation of history, but because it is uttering a threat of a revelation of judgement such as took place on that occasion. Nevertheless, the New Testament does make use of the Greek idea of a revelation present in the (created) world (Acts 14.16 f.; 17.26-28), while John 1.3 f. also says that God's 'word', through which the world was created, was the 'light' of this world from the beginning. But the assumption here, as is clearly shown by Rom. 1.18-23, is that God's revelation in the new world also implies his demand, and that to recognize it means to obey it. The statement in Rom. 2.14 f., that the heathen, even though they lack God's revelation in the law, know his will in their conscience, belongs to this context.

The usage most characteristic of the New Testament

proceeds from the premiss that revelation signifies *salvation*. Since the present, transitory world was regarded as an evil world under the rule of the devil, it was usual to speak principally, as Judaism already did, of the future revelation of God (or of the Messiah, the Son of Man), which would bring this world to an end and inaugurate salvation or judgement (Luke 17.30; 1 Cor. 1.7; 3.13; Rom. 8.18 f.; 1 Pet. 1.5; 5.1, etc.). Thus, while in its basic significance revelation had always been an *eschatological* concept, in so far as in revelation God brought the being and activity of man to an end, revelation was now understood in an emphatically eschatological sense as an event which brings this world to its ultimate end (*cf.* Vol I, *Eschatology* III). Consequently, the content of revelation can be described as everything which is expected from eschatological salvation: light (1 John 1.2), God's gift of righteousness (Rom. 1.17; 3.21), the destruction of sin (1 John 3.5,8), and freedom (Rom. 8.18 f.).

3. *The Distinctive Christian Sense of Revelation*

None of this, however, differs in any sense from the Jewish idea of revelation. Nor is such a distinction made in the words of Jesus, in which, moreover, the concept of revelation scarcely occurs. In so far as Jesus looks forward to the coming kingdom of God, he shares the Jewish concept of revelation (*cf.* also Luke 17.30). Only two sayings attributed to him speak expressly of revelation: Matt. 11.25=Luke 10.21 (perhaps derived from a Jewish work) and Matt. 11.27=Luke 10.22 (hellenistic in origin). It is not clear what is supposed to be the object of revelation in the first saying; in the second, it is the knowledge of God and his Son. The intention in both sayings is to emphasize that God (and his works) is not accessible to human knowledge and inquiry, and that revelation is something miraculous.

Revelation

The characteristically *Christian* idea of revelation arose with the belief of the Church that eschatological salvation did not belong exclusively to the future, but already existed in the *present time*, and that God had already carried out the decisive *act of salvation* by the sending and by the death and resurrection of Jesus Christ (*cf. Christology* I p. 62 below). This idea is developed in the New Testament with varying degrees of clarity, and is carried to its most logical conclusion in John, for whom the judgement had been completed with the coming of Jesus (3.17-19; 9.39; 12.31, 47 f.); but it is also found in Paul, for whom the sending of the Son signified the 'fullness of time' (Gal. 4.4), and for whom the righteousness of God was already present (Rom. 1.16 f.; 3.21; 5.1, etc.) and the 'life of Jesus' had already been manifested in our bodies (2 Cor. 4.10 f.). Consequently, the *gospel, the word as it is preached,* in which the saving act of God is continued, and so forms part of it, can now also be described as revelation (Rom. 1.17; 2 Cor. 2.14-16; 4.1-6; Col. 1.25 f.; 2 Tim. 1.9 f.), as also can faith, which bears the word (Gal. 3.23), and love (1 John 4.9 f.). And it is now possible to speak of the revelation of Christ as something no longer exclusively in the future (1 Cor. 1.7), but as something that has already taken place (1 John 3.5,8; 1 Pet. 1.20; 1 Tim. 3.16; Heb. 9.26). Thus for John it was the earthly Jesus himself, the incarnate Son, who is the revelation, and who is so as the 'word', that is by 'revealing' through his word the Father, and himself as the Son sent by the Father; in the same way, the revelation has been continued in the Church through the Paraclete, that is, in the word proclaimed in the Church.

Paul and John emphasize strongly that this activity of God and the faith which responds to it in obedience provide the basis of *knowledge*. This is in accord with the fact that it is the word which reveals (*cf.* 2 Cor. 4.1-6, and the frequent association of faith and knowledge in John, e.g. 8.31 f.). This knowledge can be nourished and developed; but it cannot be isolated from faith, and is therefore regarded as being bestowed by the Spirit or by God (e.g. 1 Cor. 2.6-16; Phil. 3.15).

Thus the idea of revelation in the New Testament contains not only the idea that the salvation of man depends upon revelation as the miraculous work of God, and on this alone, so that without it man would remain subject to death, but also the idea that the decisive revelation has already taken place in the sending of Jesus Christ, and is present at all times in the word and in faith.

RUDOLF BULTMANN

Va REVELATION AND THE PHILOSOPHY OF RELIGION

1. The Origins of the Concept of Revelation

The concept of *revelation* comes from two sources. The first source is that of *oriental and Jewish* apocalyptic. Here revelation is the unveiling of the divine plan for the world, especially with regard to the coming catastrophe of the end of the world (*cf.* Vol. I, *Eschatology* II). Revelation is conveyed by a seer, who is accorded a glance into the transcendental mysteries, and who receives the revelation in a visionary condition. The second source is the need of late *Greek* philosophy for a truth that was independent of the uncertainty of philosophical discussion. Here, revelation is a correlative of scepticism—the last tragic utterance of the attempt of Greek philosophy to obtain knowledge by its own resources alone. The later schools (Neo-Pythagoreans; Neo-Platonism) derived their doctrine from revelations which had either been imparted to the founder of their philosophical school, or had been taken over by their founders from ancient oriental sources of revelation. In both cases, the normal content of the revelations is the unveiling of hidden events, or the disclosing of the secrets of reality; they correspond to the Semitic and Greek ideas of truth. In *Christian* thought, both elements are united and enriched by a third: revelation has been revealed in the life of a particular person (*cf.* IV, 3 above). The revelation of the divine plan for the world in Jesus is at the same time a fulfilment; and in this fulfilment is given the truth which the Greeks sought in vain. It is the second point which was dominant in patristic theology, and led to a supernaturalist and intellectualizing understanding of revelation. This is expressed in particular in the distinction between natural and supernatural revelation, which goes back as far as Paul, was applied by the Fathers, dominated the distinction between reason and revelation in scholasticism, and was of decisive importance in the eighteenth century in the theological debate between rationalism and supernaturalism. Since the time of Schleiermacher theological and philosophical study has turned against this distinction, which has no basis in fact, but must be seen as resulting from the conflict between the Greek concept of nature and the religious tradition of the East. Consequently, a completely new basis for the concept of revelation has become necessary.

2. *The Concept of Revelation in the Philosophy of Religion and in Theology*

The question whether revelation is a concept of theology or of the philosophy of religion serves no purpose except in so far as it poses the concrete question, whether revelation is a *religious category* or a *unique event* transcending every religious category. However, this alternative, put forward by 'dialectical theology' and answered by it in the sense of the second alternative, is falsely posed. The unique and universal claim implicit in revelation and assumed by theology does not exclude other similar claims to a unique revelation raised elsewhere, but affirms them. The rejection or partial recognition of such claims (as was done, for example, by the theology of the early Church with regard to Judaism or even to paganism) assumes that all that is being accepted or denied exists on the same level, and thus makes possible the use of the concept of revelation as a single category. The idea of a *universal revelation* does not exclude that of a *general revelation* but implies it. And the reverse is also true: the concept of revelation shares the nature of all fields of intellectual activity, not by abstraction from them, but as a synthesis of them all. As a religious category, revelation is not the general idea which is left after the abstraction of the concrete elements of all revelation, but is the expression, summed up in conceptual form, of the *concrete revelation* which is actually perceived, and which is the sole basis on which the person who receives revelation can tell what is to be regarded as revelation. The idea of general revelation does not exclude that of a universal revelation (that of dependence upon a particular revelation), but assumes it. Thus the treatment of the concept of revelation must always see it at one and the same time as both unique and an inclusive category, as universal and general, or—to use scientific and systematic terminology to describe these two different points of view—as belonging to theology and to the philosophy of religion.

3. *The Source of Revelation*

Only what is *hidden* can be revealed. Now everything that exists is hidden in some respect. But what is hidden is disclosed to the cognitive consciousness in practical and theoretical inquiry. It is only relatively hidden.

There are some things that exist, and some aspects of what exists, which are always concealed from our knowledge. These things remain hidden, because they do not enter the realm of the cognitive consciousness in such a way that they can be disclosed to it. They are continually hidden, but they are hidden only in a relative sense, relative, that is, to the cognitive consciousness. The self-manifestation of what exists in this way—and since everything that exists is related to everything else that exists, of existent being in general—is not revelation. Revelation is the communication of what is hidden, and does not cease to be hidden as a result of being communicated, that is, it is the communication of what is absolutely hidden. What is *essentially hidden* can only emerge from its concealment in an act of revelation, so that it is that for which there exists no way or device to break down its concealment. Everything that exists is on principle accessible to the cognitive consciousness; but when what is *on principle inaccessible* is manifested to the consciousness, this takes place in the act of revelation. But the terms 'on principle inaccessible' or 'absolutely concealed' refer to the ultimate object of the religious act, the *Absolute*. Thus the source of revelation is the Absolute in its attribute of absolute concealment. This defines a respect in which revelation is a category of the philosophy of religion. Revelation is the way in which the object of the religious act becomes an object of consciousness. Revelation is the way in which the absolute and transcendent becomes an object of knowledge.

4. *The Content of Revelation*

If what is absolutely concealed is revealed, it can only be revealed as what remains hidden even though it be revealed. The content of revelation can only be something which does not remove its quality of concealment, but actually reveals it; yet it must reveal this quality in a positive sense, and so point to a true content of revelation. Thus the content of revelation can only be the self-manifestation of the absolute and transcendent as such. There are three consequences of this. The first is that there can be *only one* true and ultimately valid content of revelation. The content of each individual revelation expresses a particular aspect, representative of this one content. In the strict sense of the word, there are no 'revelations', but only the revelation of what alone can be revealed, the absolutely hidden. The second consequence is that *revelation is not communication* concerning a being, even concerning a transcendental being, which can be accepted as a communication concerning something which remains untouched by the fact of this communication. Rather, revelation is the self-giving of the absolutely hidden, which by the very fact of its self-giving emerges from its concealment. Revelation is not a communication concerning the existence, attributes or actions of some existent being, but the self-realization in being of the absolutely hidden, the apprehension of existent being by what apprehends absolutely. Revelation is a *realization*, not a communication. Thirdly, in the content of revelation the absolutely hidden is revealed *absolutely*. Revelation is not a partial or obscure manifestation. Revelation does not take place in the darkness; it is the self-giving, as absolutely revealed, of what at the same time remains absolutely hidden. It was in order to assure that revelation was absolute in this sense, that the early Church defended the 'divinity of Christ' (*cf. Christology* II, pp. 90 ff. below).

5. *The Character of Revelation*

There is a dispute about the nature of revelation between the supernaturalist and the rationalist views. The supernaturalist view thinks of the process of revelation, either inward or outward, as a miraculous supernatural intervention in the natural order of existent beings. The natural order is broken by revelation; the natural laws of the life of nature and of the soul are to some extent, and on some occasions, abrogated. On the other hand, the rationalist view understands revelation as the unveiling of the transcendent in the natural course of events, that is, within and through the laws of nature. Both views must be rejected. The supernaturalist view makes the Absolute one object above and parallel to the natural order of existent beings, its existence being attested by its negative effects upon the natural order. The rationalist view loses sight of transcendence in the immanent process of events, and so deprives it of the character of absolute concealment, which it is the intention of supernaturalism to maintain, although its means are inadequate. Revelation is neither the consummation nor the destruction of the natural, but its convulsion and reorientation. Its convulsion expresses the negative element with which supernaturalism is concerned; the natural balance of nature is not maintained. Its *reorientation* is the positive complement of this: the natural orientation of existent beings, which is turned away from the absolute and transcendent, is reversed, and turned towards it. But all this takes place without what is natural as such being abolished. Thus revelation takes place through natural things and processes. These become vehicles of revelation in that they manifest the convulsion and reversal through which the absolutely hidden realizes and reveals itself. Thus they do not become vehicles of revelation through what they are themselves, by their own mode of being, but by the fact that something is manifested through them which is not outside them but within them and also always opposed to them. They are made vehicles of revelation by being endowed with *transcendental significance*, but not with transcendental being. Since revelation is not of the nature of an object, but depends upon a mutual relationship which consists of being apprehended and of apprehending, it is always both objective and subjective. It does not exist, except it exists for someone. The self-realization and revelation of what is absolutely hidden is always a self-realization for someone. It is not one process parallel to or higher than other processes, but is a process marked by a distinctive quality which is always and necessarily a quality perceptible to an observer. Revelation only exists in the context of a specific revelation, in the unity of 'manifestation' and 'inspiration'.

6. The Norm of Revelation

If revelation is to be applied as a category of the philosophy of religion, it is necessary to name the concrete norm from which the category is derived, and with the help of which it can be used to criticize false claims to revelation. This concrete norm is derived from the Christian *proclamation of the cross of Christ as an act of revelation* (IV, 3 above; V*b.*, 3 below). The content of this norm is as follows. Every revelation in which the bearer of revelation claims that he himself and his revelation are absolute is a demonic revelation; the principle of the demonic is the exaltation of a finite existent to the level of the absolute, to the rank of what is absolutely hidden. A revelation is perfect, in so far as it subjects every element of its concrete realization to the convulsion and reversal of orientation which is associated with *true revelation*. A revelation is perfect when there is nothing absolute in it except the absolutely hidden itself, which is revealed in it (the honour of God in the Calvinist sense). These considerations provide a standard for judging the *history of religion*, a standard which at the same time must be applied to the religion from which it is taken and on which the judgement is based. For even perfect revelation is liable to become demonic, and its existential history, the 'history of the Church', is nothing other than a continual struggle of revelation against the tendency to the demonic which is essentially overcome in revelation. Consequently, the Christian Church, and in particular the Protestant Church, places the cross at the centre of its devotion and theology. For perfect revelation is the revelation of the cross, even over and above the bearers of revelation and the community in which the revelation is carried on. The absolutely hidden can only become the absolutely revealed by repeatedly convulsing and reorientating the whole corpus of revelation, in so far as it is a human possession.

7. The History of Revelation and the History of Religion

The distinction between natural and supernatural revelation has been broken down; every revelation is *supernatural*, in so far as it is the manifestation of the absolute and transcendent, and every revelation takes place in the *natural* order of existent beings, which it convulses and reorientates, but does not destroy. Instead of this distinction, another must be made: that between historical and unhistorical revelation. When any revelation takes place, it takes place *in history*; for only in history, either of an individual or of a group, can the absolutely hidden be revealed to that individual or to that group. But a revelation does not become historical by the mere fact that it takes place in history. It only becomes historical when it is *realized as history* itself, that is, when it appears not in the form of individual and unrelated revelations at various points in history, but when revelation itself appears as history, when the absolutely hidden reveals itself by being realized to existent being in a history of revelation. Thus *unhistorical* revelation is not natural revelation, but as such is 'supernatural', that is, real revelation that does not take the form of a coherent history of revelation.

This raises the question of the relationship of such a history of revelation to the history of religion in general. There are two opposed attitudes to the problem of the history of revelation and the history of religion. One is the idealist view advanced by Hegel and liberal theology, which simply identifies the history of revelation with the history of religion; and since the history of religion is an element of history in general, the history of revelation becomes history in general. The opposing view, advanced by Kierkegaard, and by dialectical theology, sees the history of revelation as a divine act, exclusively opposed to the history of religion as the work of man. Both views are inadequate. The identification of the history of revelation and history in general forgets in the first place that revelation is the convulsion and reorientation of all human potentialities, and even of human history; again, it forgets that revelation only occurs in the context of a specific revelation, so that it is therefore impossible to speak of a revelation in the proper sense, except as a revelation to whoever proclaims it. But it is equally impossible to dispute the existence of revelation where one cannot proclaim it oneself, and to make one's own revelation not merely the norm but the 'existential pattern' of all revelation. That there is revelation somewhere can neither be asserted nor denied in general terms, for it is possible to speak of revelation on a firm basis only in the context of a specific revelation. This in no sense means that the context of revelation extends no further than one's 'own' religion. This cannot be so, because each individual religion does not form a monochrome pattern, but always contains an almost unlimited profusion of different elements. Even perfect revelation, which is fundamentally free from the demonic, always contains demonic elements in so far as it is actual religion. And on the other hand, revelations which are fundamentally demonic contain numerous elements of the struggle against the demonic, in which perfect revelation can rediscover itself. This means that there are always possibilities of extending the context of revelation in concrete terms; but it is not possible to identify the history of revelation and history in general.

8. Revelation and Reason

The problem of revelation and reason can mean two things. *In the first place*, it can imply the question whether *reason* can *know* of itself what is given in revelation. All thinking inspired by rationalism agrees that it can; supernaturalism denies it. In *The Education of the Human Race* Lessing replied that revelation accelerated the process of the education of mankind, but gave nothing that was not in itself hidden from reason. This question, too, loses its meaning once it is realized that revelation is the manifestation of the absolutely hidden in the natural order of being, so that it can never be regarded as the act of an existent being. Rather, it is the convulsion and reorientation of every act of being, and so also of reason as the unity of those acts which give meaning to being. It does not deny reason, nor oppose, nor destroy it—an idea which is impossible, because the destruction of reason would remove the one point at which it is possible for the revelation to take place. But revelation does not leave reason untouched, with its original equilibrium and its natural orientation, but convulses and reorientates it. The question of reason and revelation can have a *second meaning*: how far is it possible to give a rational justification and description of the content of revelation? The answer must be that the justification of the content of any revelation, that is, of any utterance concerning the absolutely hidden, on the basis of insights into the realm of what is relatively hidden, that is, on the basis of knowledge of the world, contradicts what it means to be the absolutely hidden. But it is possible for the content of the revelations received by the convulsed and re-orientated reason to form a meaningful and coherent picture, in which they *support and justify each other*. In such a process, the means used to provide this representation must display their rationality by being appropriate to the 'matter'. That is, laws and categories must not be applied which are taken from an approach to being, the structure of which is completely alien to the structure of the content of revelation (e.g. that of the mathematical and physical representation of the world). Thus in every sense the opposition between revelation and reason is question-able. It must be replaced by the opposition between the convulsed and the unconvulsed reason, and that be-tween adequate and inadequate rational categories in the understanding of revelation.

PAUL TILLICH

V*b* CHRISTIAN REVELATION AND DOGMATIC THEOLOGY

1. Revelation as a Basic Concept of all Genuine Religion

Wherever we encounter *genuine religion* it appeals to revelation as the only process by which the way in which man can have dealings with God is made known; for the divine is the realm of the mysterious, completely con-cealed from profane knowledge, but manifesting itself nevertheless through this knowledge in a miraculous way (*cf.* I; V*a*. 5 above). Thus the concepts of mystery, miracle, and revelation are correlative, and in genuine religion express the fact that the 'object' of religious experience, the numinous, is on principle concealed, and provides access to itself either through its own spontaneous will, or not at all. Religious experience as a whole (as Schleiermacher already realized) stands and falls with these correlative concepts and the ideas they imply. Where they are inadequate, we have to do at best with illegitimate offshoots of true religion.

2. The Revelation of the 'Real' God

Although this phenomenological insight is fundamental and necessary, it does no more than describe the formal psychological structure of revelation. A more important point, on a different level, and fundamentally critical in nature, is that of the substance and content of revelation itself. When an inquiry into this is undertaken, it must at once concentrate on the more specific question of the substance and content of a particular revelation. For we cannot overlook the fact that not every revelation is related to others as a complementary alternative, or at least as a different grade of revelation; for there are revelations which put forward a claim to be exclusively opposed to other 'revelations', asserting that they are in fact demonic concealments of the 'true' God. Examples of this are the struggle of the prophets (*cf.* Vol. I, *Prophets*) against Israelite popular religion, with its syncretism, or Luther's dispute with Catholicism. This means that not every mystery in what is indubitably genuine religion appears to a critical view of religion as the real and *ultimate* mystery. Nor is every revelation *real* revelation, even though it asserts that it is; that is, it does not necessarily tell of a reality which no eye has seen and no ear heard, and the heart of man has not perceived.

Thus the theological question inevitably arises of the criteria of *real revelation of the true God*. Of course these criteria are all to be sought in the direction which we have already discussed, that is, they apply in all seriousness the phenomenological insight mentioned above. Revelation in the strict sense only exists where it deals with a real mystery, which, because it is ultimate, cannot be approached by man's 'own reason or power' (Luther), but which likewise is not, once it has been revealed, 'transparent' in such a way that it can become an instrument of theurgic action, or of a cultic and sacral or mystical and meditative technique. Revelation consequently only exists where it brings into force the *servum arbitrium* of the Reformers, that is, the consciousness that men never for a single moment have *God*, or any dealings with him, at their 'disposal', and that God is only God in so far as he remains here and now the 'Lord', the power over everything which in being revealed remains a mystery, or rather first becomes a mystery thereby. But this also means that the question of the criteria of genuine revelation itself assumes a specific attitude, just as surely as all thought on the subject is a consideration based on existence in the sight of God. For revelation is only meaningful when it finds *faith*, or more precisely arouses faith, which is the recognition of the truth encountered in revelation, and submission to it at a given point in time. Thus it is the actualization of revelation itself. Since without faith revelation is meaningless, and is not really revelation at all, then only faith can be the means of apprehending revelation and of recognizing its criteria of truth. In other terms, revelation in the strict sense is only that which arouses and provides the basis of genuine *faith*, which signifies God's coming to power, and therefore the coming into being of a new kind of existence.

Thus we can speak seriously of a revelation of God when we encounter a reality which subjects us totally to itself, by creating in us an attitude of unreserved trust. This must be a reality which reveals to us that the concrete difficulties of our temporal existence, such as sin (*cf. Sin and Guilt* p. 199 below) and death, are ultimately impossible for us to overcome, while at the same time it redeems us from them, consequently placing us in a completely new form of existence, within which we are saved from the disintegration of our natural being and from the impotence and failure of our moral struggle. Thus the revelation of the living God comes to us as a creative and life-giving power, qualitatively opposed to the impotence of our natural existence—it is the omnipotence of pure creative and inexhaustible goodness, which compels us to display boundless trust. In this 'wholly other', pure and selflessly self-giving goodness, which is a judgement on the hopelessness of our unlimited self-seeking, and a salvation from it, there is a real revelation of the *ultimate mystery*, wholly underived, supra-rational and comprehensible as the truth only in so far as it constantly reveals itself anew and makes itself visible to us, though by revealing itself it becomes at the same time more and more incomprehensible. In this 'wholly other' of pure goodness there is also revealed the *unique* reality of the majesty which simply makes us dependent upon itself and consequently becomes *Lord*, in an existential sense, over our soul, the Lord in whom alone we have real trust. For the only possible attitude before the reality which we can call God is that of total dependence. But a pure consciousness of utter dependence is only possible where it is the sign of free and convinced obedience. The faith created by the power of pure goodness is a union of both these elements. Any other form of dependence is a natural one, and takes the form of a determinist subjection to fate, or of an unavoidable force, and is moreover not absolute, in that it provokes our natural desire for life to resist it.

Thus the revelation of God is the overwhelming impression made upon our self-consciousness by an infinitely good and pure trust in a personal will which first makes this trust possible. More precisely, it is firstly the self-manifestation of God directly present to our being, and yet not unmediated. Secondly, it appears in 'history' rather than in the sphere of personal existence, that is, it is unique in space and time, and yet it is an historical revelation only in so far as it is accessible to us at the present. Thirdly, it is a fact independent of our subjective attitude, and yet it is only revelation in so far as it is a reality which is effected in the overcoming of our own souls. Finally, it submits us to itself in blind obedience, and yet it is not an externally imposed heteronomous authority. These more precise definitions avoid the principal errors of the traditionalist (super-naturalist), rationalist and mystical theories of revelation and show that they diminish the full content of revelation.

3. The Reality of this Revelation in the Jesus Christ of Faith

Such an understanding of the criteria of true revelation points us towards the *person of Jesus Christ* (*cf.* IV above; *Christology* III p. 144 below) as the sole fact which creates and provides a basis for true faith. And this is true in the more precise sense that these criteria do not provide the primary standard against which this personal and individual will is to be measured. Rather, it is in this person that the standard of true revelation is to be found (*cf.* V*a*. 6 above). Of course it is impossible for Christian faith to forget that 'in many and various ways God spoke of old to our fathers' (Heb. 1.1). But this does not prevent Christian faith from considering that the true *self*-revelation of God is to be seen only in this person, and that it is an eschatological self-imparting of God 'in these last days'. For it is only in Christ that the Christian faith encounters here and now the one will, the one truly 'other', which is the ultimate mystery of creative and uncreated goodness, which rules over history and provides the basis of a pure trust. This is the sole reality *respectu nostri* (Luther), which is able to take to itself the deepest need and distress of our being, for it is this person alone which, as the perfect instrument of the divine will, is the 'reflection of the fatherly heart of God' (Luther), and therefore brings us face to face with the claim of *God*, forgives our sins and demands of us an infinite submission and devotion. That God himself is close to us in Christ *alone*, but that he is truly *close* to us in Christ—this is the faith of the Christian Church, and it finds its most appointed expression in the fact that this Church (in the sense of the 'Church' as understood by primitive Christianity and the Reformation) is itself an object of faith.

FRIEDRICH WILHELM SCHMIDT

2

Christology

I THE CHRISTOLOGY
OF PRIMITIVE CHRISTIANITY

If by christology is understood a fully elaborated doctrine
of the person and work of Jesus Christ within the framework of a theological and philosophical view of the world,
then a christology was only gradually built up in the
course of the development of early Christianity. But if by
christology is meant certain statements concerning the
significance of Christ and the meaning of the events of his
life, then Christian faith, even the faith of the very earliest
Christianity, is unthinkable without a christology.
Christology in the first sense naturally always depends
on the philosophical speculation of a particular period;
but even the second sort of christology cannot do without
the borrowing of concepts and titles, and assumes certain
views about the relationship between God and the world,
and between time and the end of the world. With this
fact in mind, the main problem of primitive Christian
christology which modern study tries to answer is the
following: how did the knowledge of the historical
figure of Jesus change so quickly into faith in the heavenly
Son of God? It is known that the world in which
Christianity arose was acquainted with redeemer
figures with divine attributes: the Jews looked forward
to the Messiah or the Son of Man; the pagans of the
hellenistic world believed in gods sent down to the earth
to give revelations, while the religions of the East
(Mesopotamia, Iran) shared a belief in a divine emissary.

Thus a christology, the expression of an inner adherence to Jesus and the gospel, was bound to have arisen almost at once by the immediate association of the figure of Jesus with these conceptions, or by assimilation to them in the course of time. Scholars are to a large extent agreed on this. What is in dispute is how great a part is played in this christology by the person of Jesus and the events of his life (*cf.* 1*b*. below). There is also some dispute as to the extent to which the part played by these contemporary conceptions, either those which Christians had already inherited, or those which they adopted under the influence of new experiences, is to be assigned to Jewish or to hellenistic sources. Finally, there is the question of the time at which different conceptions were adopted by Christianity. The genuine epistles of the Apostle Paul (Eph., 1 and 2 Timothy and Titus are regarded as spurious here) form the only fixed point of reference for the early period; the only method of inquiry we possess into the views held by Christians before and at the same time as Paul is by working back from later sources.

1. The Primitive Church

a. TITLES AND CONCEPTIONS. We have to look back to an earlier period in this way, when in texts from the last third of the first century, e.g. in the synoptic gospels and the Acts of the Apostles, we find titles of Jesus which are evidence of a different and simpler christology than that held by the author of the writing in question. This is particularly true of the title *Son of Man*. If this title, which actually appears in the gospels as a solemn title applied by Jesus to himself, originally signifies the man from heaven who comes with the clouds, then to call Jesus the Son of Man implies the expectation of his glorious 'coming' from heaven, his parousia. But this assumes that he already is in heaven (Luke 22.69; Acts 7.56) at the right hand of God, and therefore, that his death does not mean his defeat, but was followed by his resurrection and exaltation to be with God. Thus the application of the title Son of Man to Jesus gives the true interpretation of his suffering: the Son of Man had to be 'delivered' into the hands of men (Mark 9.31; 10.33; 14.41; Luke 24.7; 1 Cor. 11.23). The necessity of this is expressed by saying that the suffering of the Son of Man 'is written' (Mark 9.12), and this statement was then taken up into the christological proof based on the Old Testament. Since the expression Son of Man (or 'man') already played a fixed part in Jewish apocalyptic, its use in Christianity would bring about the possibility of links with groups who thought in eschatological or cosmic terms (the end of the world, the pre-existence of the Son of Man). The figure of the Son of Man was already linked with that of the *Messiah* in Judaism (*Enoch* 37-71). This latter concept was changed in consequence—and the full effect of this change was first seen within primitive Christianity. For the Messiah is no longer the man of the tribe of David, who will ascend the throne to set up an eternal and blessed kingdom, if he is to come as the Son of Man in the clouds of heaven; and a description like that of the message of the angels in Luke 1.32 f. gives the impression of being very early, and does not seem to correspond to the historical destiny of Jesus. Mark 12. 35-37 could even be regarded as an objection against the traditional picture of the Messiah: no stress should be laid on his descent from David. Under the influence of the historical life of Jesus the earliest Christians came to regard the suffering of the Messiah as the way to his glory (Luke 24.26; Acts 3.18 ff.) and considered that what made him Messiah was his entry into glory and his return. Some perhaps considered that he only became Messiah at the resurrection (Acts 2.36; 3.13; in appearance at least there is an element here of 'adoptionist' christology, *cf.* below). It is very doubtful if any idea of a suffering Messiah which may have been present in Judaism played any part in this; no allusion to any such thing is made in Christian writings.

In spite of the few references, the title *servant of God* must be regarded as a title of Jesus which goes back a considerable way. It is used as a fixed formula in very early accounts (Acts 4.30; *Didache* 9.10; I *Clement* 59), and seems also to have been used as a formula by Christians in the healing of sickness. According to Acts 3.13 and Matt. 12.18, and to judge by the Greek word which was used ($\pi\alpha\hat{\imath}s$ not $\delta o\hat{\upsilon}\lambda os$), this title refers to the well-known figure of the suffering servant of Yahweh from Isa. 42 ff., and is not a general title in the way in which it is used of David in Luke 1.69. Thus the emphasis is not in the first place on subordination, but on being chosen by God and being destined to suffer; the true dignity of him whom God sends is visible in this destiny. Thus the title may originally have contained an interpretation of the riddle of the cross in the same way as 'Son of Man'.

Later it was felt to be an objection that the title 'Servant' gave too low a place to Jesus; consequently, the title was understood as 'Son of God' ($\pi\alpha\hat{\imath}s$ can also mean 'child'); there is no doubt that this is what has taken place in the prayer of Polycarp in the *Martyrdom of Polycarp* 20.2 (here the word $\mu o\nu o\gamma\epsilon\nu\acute{\eta}s$, 'only-begotten', qualifies $\pi\alpha\hat{\imath}s$). But the difficulty it caused seems to have brought about the decline and disappearance of this ambiguous title. It is probable that the essential significance of the title *Son of God* was originally the idea of election. For the Son of God is a title given to the king in the ancient East, and is connected with the myths concerning the divine origin of the king. But when, as in Ps. 2.7, the same is assumed of the king of Israel, though not said in so many words, a mythological basis is **not** possible, and a kind of adoption is signified: 'You are my son, today I have begotten you', which means, 'From this day on you will be my son'. This psalm was probably interpreted in a messianic sense in Judaism, and then given a christological significance in Christianity. In this case, too, it is probable that the moment at which the sonship began was originally regarded as that of the resurrection: this would then be a purely 'adoptionist' christology, in which Jesus was still a man upon earth, but became God's son at his resurrection. Later, his *baptism* was regarded as the moment when he began to be Son of God; the best evidence of this is the oldest form of the story of his baptism, which the tradition preserved outside the gospels which we possess, and which has only come down to us in the Western text of Luke 3.22; in it, the voice from heaven to Jesus at his baptism utters the words of Ps. 2.7, including 'today'. But even the canonical form of the story of his baptism, in which the voice says: 'Thou art my beloved Son; with thee I am well-pleased', contains the idea of a divine choosing, rather than that of a supernatural birth or a similarity of nature to God. Therefore it too expressed an 'adoptionist' conception, especially since the expression 'You are my son' in oriental legal usage signifies the acceptance of someone as a son ('You shall be my son'). And in any case, 'Son of God' in the earliest Christian texts is simply an alternative term for Messiah, and this view is not affected by the fact that 'Son of God' does not occur in the literature of the Old Testament as the title of the Messiah, and as far as we know was not current in this sense in Jewish literature.

Apart from these titles, certain phenomena of the life of the primitive Church can be used as sources for the very earliest christology: healings were carried out *in the name of Jesus*; the evidence for this is not only the stories of healings in Acts, but also the text of the prayer in

Acts 4.30, 'signs and wonders are performed through the name of thy holy servant Jesus'. Similarly, at the earliest period baptisms were carried out in the name of Jesus (see Vol. I, *Baptism* I) and the sacred meal (see Vol. I, *The Eucharist* I) was celebrated in expectation of the coming of the Son of Man. All these phenomena are evidence of the christology of their time, in so far as the disciples and believers in Jesus did not think of their master as someone who was dead and gone but knew that by his resurrection he was exalted to be with God, and were aware that his power was effectively present among them as a pledge of their reunion with him in the future. This certainty of the coming of the kingdom linked the divine intervention which had brought salvation in the past with the fulfilment of salvation in the future; the present time took on the character of an intermediate period, and what they had previously experienced in the life of Jesus was interpreted in the light of the future. This explains why even those who had eaten and drunk with Jesus could think of him in the terms of this simple christology.

b. THEIR ORIGINS IN THE HISTORICAL LIFE OF JESUS. We can no longer avoid the question, however, of the *moment of time* at which such christological views came to be held by the disciples of Jesus. The answer to this question depends on that given to another: How far did *Jesus himself* accept the title of *Messiah* (*cf.* Vol. I, *Jesus Christ*)? If one holds the view that the disciples of Jesus could not have ignored for any length of time the question of whether or not he was the Messiah, and that at least the journey of Jesus to Jerusalem gave a personal focus to the messianic movement, then this will imply that Jesus himself claimed to be Messiah and that the disciples acknowledged him as such. The consequence of this would be that the disciples would already have thought of his person in terms of their messianic expectations even when he was still alive; we do not know what form these expectations took, but we must not necessarily suppose that they were limited to a national monarchy. We would be able to say more if we knew to what extent Jesus anticipated an unsuccessful outcome to his visit to Jerusalem. If he had done so, then he himself would have linked together the idea of being Messiah and that of *suffering*, in the same way as the saying concerning the ransom for many, Mark 10.45, which as it stands is certainly stylized and Christian in form. A possible basis for this within the framework of Jewish thought can be found in Isa. 53 and 4 Macc. 6.29; 17.22. But we naturally do not know to what extent in fact he made this association of ideas; it can have made no significant impression upon the disciples, for they were surprised at the suffering and death of Jesus. We only mention these uncertainties, in order to show that the seeds of christological thought may possibly be present in the life of Jesus. We should also add to their number the very distinctive relationship of the disciples to their master, which, on the basis of analogies to be found in the history of religion, we cannot compare with that of disciples to their teacher in the Western sense, but which we must regard as the fearful veneration of awestruck adherents for the saint who lived in their midst, but who in his innermost nature remained alien to them.

The true origin of all christology is to be found in the events after the death of Jesus. The conviction that Jesus had *risen from the dead* was based, according to the oldest tradition (1 Cor. 15.3 ff.; Mark 14.28; John 21; the Gospel of Peter), not on the discovery of the empty grave, concerning which Paul remains silent, but upon the appearances of the master who was believed to be dead to his disciples. They concluded from these appearances that Jesus had not remained dead, but had been taken into the glory of God. This meant that the preach-

ing of Jesus was right, that the kingdom of God was on its
way and that the final phase of time, with the promised
resurrection of the dead, had already begun with the
resurrection of Jesus. His resurrection was not therefore
an event which would have found no place in the
disciples' picture of the world but, in terms of their view
of the world, was the 'right' consequence of what they
had experienced. What was strange and full of promise
beyond all experience was the recognition that in spite
of the apparent defeat of Jesus, his gospel of the kingdom
had now been confirmed by God. It is only now that they
felt confident that they fully understood the meaning
of what Jesus had done, and the significance of his
person and his destiny. Thus *faith in the resurrection* is the
beginning of all christology. For the first decisive change
in the relationship of the disciples to their master was
that the idea of the revelation of the kingdom of God,
which was beginning to dawn on them, turned into a certainty, which summed up all that had happened to them
and all they were looking forward to, the interpretation
they put on the past and their hope for the future.

2. Hellenistic Christianity before Paul

a. THE VENERATION OF JESUS AS 'THE LORD'. The second
change in this relationship consisted of a partial shift
in the main point of emphasis from the future to the
present; the Church which looked forward with certainty
to salvation became a Church which *possessed* salvation;
the Son of Man, whose coming on the clouds of heaven
was awaited, came to be regarded, without any weakening of this expectation, as present in the Church, ruling
over it, and venerated in its worship. This relationship
was expressed in particular through one title given to
Jesus: this is the title *Lord*, in Greek κύριος, which in
the Greek-speaking churches soon became the most
common title for Jesus. In the religions of the neigh-

bouring countries it had possessed for a long time a special significance as a divine title. In *Egypt* the word 'Lord' seems largely to have been used with the divine rule over the world in mind. When the Egyptian translators of the Old Testament into Greek used the title κύριος instead of the divine name Yahweh, they could point to the Jewish practice of pronouncing Yahweh as *adonai* (Lord) out of cultic considerations. But in these passages, the translators did not transcribe the word *adonai*, as they frequently did elsewhere, but replaced it by κύριος. Thus they evidently regarded the connotation of this title as significant; this means that they too principally had in mind the divine rule over the world, and Philo's explanation of the name κύριος (*De Plantatione 86*) confirms this. By contrast, in *Syria* the divine 'Lord' was the god whose 'slave' one was; thus this title is very closely related to the idea of service, that is, of the worship which gathers together the 'slaves' of the god before their 'Lord'. When the Christian Church worshipped their 'Lord', the immediate significance of the title obviously is not that of his rule over the world, but is related to the cultic service they are offering him. But when Christians went on to refer the passages of the Greek Old Testament which speak of the Κύριος to their 'Lord', the cosmic meaning is associated with the cultic. And an important extension of christology to the whole universe takes place. On the other hand, the use of the title 'Lord' in *emperor worship* seems to be related to the Egyptian practice. The use of the title for the reigning prince is in any case a useful analogy to the Christian practice rather than its cause; in both cases an historical person is exalted to become God through the use of this title (although not through this alone); but it was only when Christians became aware of this parallel that they consciously contrasted their use of the title with that of the worship of the emperor.

One may ask whether this veneration of Jesus as the 'Lord' was connected with any kind of *mysticism* before the time of Paul (compare *Mysticism* IV p. 370 below). Paul uses the expression 'in the Lord', e.g. Rom. 16, where 'to be in the Lord' means simply 'to be a Christian', as a kind of fixed formula, which almost implies that the formula was already current in this sense before his time. It would then mean that everyone who took part in Christian worship was in consequence a member of the mystical body of Christ, and therefore 'in the Lord'. A kind of cultic mysticism is also suggested by the idea that baptism (*cf*. Vol. I, *Baptism* I) means being buried and raised from the dead with Christ, an idea which in Rom. 6.3,4 Paul evidently assumes to be familiar to the Church in Rome, which was not known to him personally. Here the burial of Jesus is interpreted as a kind of 'aetiological myth', describing the cause (αἰτία) of the sacred action as an historical incident carried out by God, so that those who take part in the cult, in the same way as in the mysteries, mystically experience what has happened to the god. One ought to remember how widespread the myth of the dying and rising God was in the regions where Christianity was first preached. And just as Christians had earlier used the titles Son of Man and servant of God to interpret the riddle of the cross, so they now used this myth, understanding the passion and death of their Lord as the progress of a god through a mythical action; perhaps the interval of three days ('raised from the dead after three days', or 'on the third day') has its origin in this myth. That he who suffered was himself accorded divine honours may also be shown by the hymns to the *lamb* incorporated into Revelation, which must have been composed at a very early period, since in part they have been formed from Jewish texts. It is possible that the expression 'lamb' itself is a title for the Messiah (*Testament of Joseph* 19.8) associated with Isa. 53. Such a connection (but *cf.* 1*b*. above) could provide an insight into the meaning of the suffering of Jesus. In fact the phrase 'died for our sins in accordance with the scriptures' was already traditional for Paul (1 Cor. 15.3); thus this insight was not one first made by Paul.

b. THE ORIGIN OF THE CULT OF CHRIST. Thus apart from ideas peculiar to Paul, we can trace various concepts, not always entirely consistent with one another, which expressed the importance of Christ as one who is present here and now: the cultic veneration of the 'Lord' and also, in certain circles, of the 'lamb', the celebration of his suffering and his resurrection as events in the career of a god, in baptism and naturally also in the Eucharist, and the cultic mysticism of being 'in the Lord'. According to the ideas described above (1), Christ was not expected in his full divine glory until the end of time; the conceptions mentioned here present him as the Lord of the Church, venerated as God, at the present time. The meaning of the confession of faith: 'Jesus is Lord' (1 Cor. 12.3; Rom. 10.9; Phil. 2.11) is that in the name of Jesus, who is the 'name above all names', that is, 'Lord', all knees shall bow (including the spiritual world), and that this claim to the title of Lord exists even in the present.

The question arises, when this new form of relationship to Christ, this association of christology with the present, first came into being. Individual features of the whole picture can be traced back without difficulty to the primitive Church as it existed in Palestine (the 'lamb', the idea that the death of Christ was on account of men's sins; *cf.* 1*b*. above); for the interpretation of his death and resurrection along the lines of the mysteries (*cf.* 2*a*. above) a pagan environment has naturally to be assumed. The most hotly disputed question is *the dating of the title 'Lord'*, not in its use to address Jesus, but as **a** solemn title. An examination of the texts shows that the use of this title for Christ first becomes frequent in the Greek-speaking churches. In the accounts of the synoptic gospels it appears only gradually; in Mark, it is absent in this more solemn sense (except in 11.3; but there it is questionable whether the title has any religious significance), but in John, and especially in Luke, it is found in numerous cases, and also in the *Nazarene Gospel* and in the *Gospel of Peter*. Further, it is only in Greek-speaking areas that the title 'Messiah' began to give way to that of 'Lord'. Messiah was translated into Greek (χριστός), but when it was carried over from Greek into Latin it was merely transcribed as *Christus*, and not translated; this means that in the course of time the title 'Christ' had come to be regarded simply as a proper name, and was replaced by κύριος as a title. Thus it seems that the great significance of the solemn title 'Lord' was first given to it in the hellenistic Christian churches before the time of Paul (e.g. Antioch and Damascus). Of course it is not certain whether it was they which invented it. The use of the expression 'Christ the Lord' in the nativity story, Luke 2.11, seems to imply that it was derived from Palestine, unless in this case the original meant 'the anointed of the Lord'; the same origin is suggested by the Aramaic formula 'Marana tha', 'Our Lord, come!', which is found in 1 Cor. 16.22, and *Didache* 10.6, and which refers to the end of time, and calls upon Jesus as Lord (*cf.* also Rev. 22.20). But we do not know the origin of this formula. We can certainly conclude from it that *prayer to Jesus* goes back to the earliest period, and even to Christians who spoke Aramaic. Support for this is provided by the fact that Paul can describe Christians as those who 'call on the name of our Lord Jesus Christ' (1 Cor. 1.2), in what appears to be a formal and therefore presumably long-established turn of phrase at the beginning of his letter.

The Son of Man awaited from heaven, and the Lord of the Church who is with God, can be named and called upon in prayer (2 Cor. 1.20?) without doing any damage to monotheism or obscuring the memory of the earthly life of Jesus. However uncertain this historical construction may be in detail, the impression is obtained that *very fundamental developments of christology had already taken place before the time of Paul*, but that they are not all to be ascribed in consequence to the primitive Church of Jerusalem, since hellenistic Christianity played an important part in this process.

3. Paul

The letters of the Apostle Paul largely assume the basic christological ideas described above; but one can see from them the way in which Paul carried forward the development of christology. This is true both of the theology of Christ, and of devotion to Christ; the question of the relationship between these two entities is one of the most hotly disputed problems in the present-day study of christology. Both the theology of Christ and devotion to Christ in Paul have their origin in the *conversion of Paul* before Damascus. For the fruit of this vision of Christ was not in the first place a theoretical conviction, as it were in christological terms, but before all else a total reversal of all Paul's standards of judgement, which he describes in Phil. 3.4-11: the persecuted Christians were right. Thus God had made himself known to him who was crucified on Golgotha and to his despised adherents, whom Paul would certainly have reckoned among the sinful lower orders (*am haarez*). The most impossible paradox has become a reality (*cf. 3a.* below). But Paul was also conscious that from this moment on his life was subject to the world from which the revelation had come. Consequently he can compare his conversion to the creation of the light at the beginning of the world

(2 Cor. 4.6), and can describe it by saying that the Son of God was revealed in him (Gal. 1.16). For him the difference between this new form of existence and earthly life is a profound experience joyfully affirmed; the result is a life lived under the tensions of dualism (*cf.* 3*b*. below). Finally, the conversion of Paul made possible his acceptance into the Christian Church of Damascus. There he was able to make his own the experience of worship and faith of the church in Damascus, and unite it with his personal experiences (*cf.* 3*c*. below).

a. THE CHRIST MYTH. For Paul, the beginning of all Christian theology, and therefore of christology, lies in the acceptance of the great paradoxes, that the Christians form the true Israel and that Jesus is the Messiah, for Jesus had appeared to him as 'Lord' in heavenly glory. Paul, who had been brought up to believe in God who is just, and was schooled in Jewish theology, had immediately to go on to ask how God could let his own people fall into error, and how he could bring his own Son to the cross. This starting point can be traced in all the decisive theological expositions in Paul's works (Rom. 3; 7; 9; 10; Gal. 3; 2, Cor. 5.14 ff.), for the purpose of all his fundamental theological ideas is that of developing a theodicy. Thus the christology of Paul is *a theodicy of the life of Christ*. Paul always has in mind the exalted Christ who had appeared to him, and who was worshipped by the Church. The task of christology for him was to explain what the exalted Lord had undergone before his exaltation. He was always the Son of God, and had only taken on a human existence on earth as the Son of David for a certain period (Rom. 1.3). The pre-existence of the Son of God, which, as we have shown, can probably be accepted as the belief of Christians before Paul, from their use of titles such as that of Son of Man, is a firm assumption in Paul's christology; probably he already accepted it along with his Jewish belief in the Messiah, if in that belief the Messiah was already regarded as a heavenly man, or as the original pattern of man (*cf.* below). In any case, the possibility of an adoptionist christology (*cf.* 1*a.* above) became very much less from the time of Paul on, being replaced by the 'pneumatic' or spiritual view, which assumes a pre-existence in heaven. In this view, the career of Christ begins in heaven, continues in the world, and concludes again in heaven. Such a conception is in its form, though not necessarily in its content, to be regarded as a *myth*, even though it may not be possible to prove that an alien mythical framework was being employed. The decisive events in this myth are the incarnation and the resurrection or exaltation; the form in which it was manifested on earth, the stories of the virgin birth and the empty grave, are not mentioned and were presumably still unknown to Paul. One can see that the driving impulse is not the portrayal of miraculous events, but the *concern of faith for theodicy*: the central concern is the paradox of the events that Christ underwent (the incarnation) and their final conclusion (the resurrection). This paradox had formed a stumbling block to Paul the Jew; now it could become the object of his constant and repeated consideration. The idea that Christ had left the world in which he belongs, in order to enter our world, and that in consequence he had lifted us up into his world, occurs in various forms: the two separate spheres of existence are characterized and distinguished by the antitheses riches—poverty, 2 Cor. 8.9, sin—righteousness, 2 Cor. 5.20, Son of God—born of woman, Gal. 4.4. (*cf.* also the form of God—the form of a servant, Phil. 2.6 f.). The *incarnation* is due to God's love and the grace of Christ; it is a proof of the humility of Christ ('He did not count equality with God a thing to be grasped', Phil. 2.6, that is, he did not make full use of his status, but emptied himself of it.). The opponents of

Christ are not men, but demonic powers: sin (Rom. 8.2) and the 'rulers of this age' (1 Cor. 2.8). A close examination of the latter passage shows that the Apostle was familiar with a detailed portrayal of the incarnation. The spirits who rule the present age brought the Lord to the cross without recognizing him; thus his humanity was a kind of disguise; he had 'emptied himself' of his divine form (Phil. 2.6 f.).

This is the presentation of the incarnation which we meet again in the apocryphal Christian writings, in the *Ascension of Isaiah* and in the *Epistola apostolorum*, as well as in gnostic texts; it is possible that the same kind of account had been given in Judaism of the wisdom of God, and in syncretistic pagan religions of all kinds of bearers of revelation. The present state of our knowledge of the subject suggests that behind it lies the Iranian myth of the *first man* who sets the soul free (*cf.* the 'last Adam' in 1 Cor. 15.45); we have no direct tradition of this myth, but can only reconstruct it from later Manichaean and Mandaean texts, some of which were only produced in the final period of this form of religion. The value to Paul of this mythical framework for the events undergone by Christ is obvious: they explain for him the inconceivable fact that the Son of God was led to the gallows by his own people. In this setting, Christ's death on the *cross* is the lowest stage of his humiliation (Phil. 2.8). But this death also possesses a special significance, expressed by Paul in the words of a traditional confession of faith, 'for our sins' (1 Cor. 15.3). This is set out in numerous different images: God's rule over the world, which has been significantly disturbed by human sin and which cannot permit this sin to be overlooked, is restored once again by this act of Christ; he is the Adam in a new humanity (Rom. 5.12 ff.; 1 Cor. 15.45 ff.). In this view of the world, room is found for the paradoxical grace of God towards sinners through the belief that Christ has destroyed every claim of sin, and atoned for all the guilt of men. Consequently, the *resurrection and exaltation* of Christ signify the beginning of a new age in the history of the world, in which, according to the belief particularly maintained by the Pharisees, the resurrection of the dead is to take place; thus Christ is the 'first-born' or the 'first fruits' of the dead, Col. 1.18; 1 Cor. 15.20.

In the mythical descriptions we have been discussing, the redeemer ascends to heaven in glory and is recognized with dismay by the hostile spirits; Paul too speaks in similar contexts of a great victory over the spiritual powers (Col. 2.15). What Christ has attained by his exaltation is described in Rom. 1.4 by the words 'Son of God in power', and in Phil. 2.9 ff. by the title 'Lord', and by the idea that he is worshipped by men and by the spirit world. For Paul, this vision of Christ's cosmic status led without difficulty to the *cosmological* significance of Christ. The unity in creation and redemption of the bringer of divine revelation was taken for granted in the Jewish background to his thought. And here again we encounter a view derived from the Iranian myth, in which the First Man is the redeemer, and redemption takes the form of a cosmic event. This myth, the progress of which we can follow in the so-called Hermetic literature, influenced in Judaism the doctrine of the personified wisdom of God (Prov. 8.22-31; Wisdom 7.22 ff.; *Enoch* 42), and also the way in which the Son of Man was represented (*Enoch* 48); in Philo the same position was occupied by the *Logos*, or, in association with certain ideas of Greek philosophy (*cf.* Plutarch's conception of the world as the Son of God), the 'ideal world', which provided the pattern on which the world is created. Since this ideal world was thought of almost in personal terms, and was associated with the Logos, it was an easy step to connect it with man made in the image of

God (Gen. 1.27). Like Philo, but without his philosophical assumptions, Paul began by interpreting Gen.
1.27 as referring to a *heavenly Adam* (whom he identified
with Christ) created in the image of God (1 Cor. 15.45;
11.7), and so came to attach a special importance to
the idea of the *'image of God'* (2 Cor. 4.4; Col. 1.15).
For this expression had evidently already become a
technical term for the cosmological mediator of God,
be it the world itself, or the Logos, or the wisdom of God.
But in the religious devotion of the period, 'the image of
God' also meant the visible revelation of the invisible
God, God *epiphanes*, revealed; this is how King Ptolemy
V of Egypt is described, in the language of the royal cult,
on the Rosetta Stone. And finally, it could also be said of
the Christian that he was an image of Christ (2 Cor. 3.18;
cf. also Col. 3.10 and the series of God-Christ-man-
woman in 1 Cor. 11.3), which makes a living connection
with devotion to Christ.

b. DEVOTION TO CHRIST. Paul's devotion to Christ has to
be understood, like the Christ myth, from his experience
of the paradox of the events undergone by Christ. The
duality in this paradox—the humility of Christ crucified
and the glory of his exaltation—also characterizes the
existence of Christians: poor, despised, weak, and sinful
according to the 'flesh', but rich, glorified, imbued with
miraculous powers and justified according to the 'spirit'
or 'in Christ'. And this very paradox is joyfully affirmed;
the enthusiastic pathos with which Paul describes it
in whole series of antitheses (1 Cor. 4.11-13; 2 Cor.
4.7-12; 6.8-10) or in sharp epigrammatic form (1 Cor.
15.9 f.; 2 Cor. 12.9 f.) shows what power he drew from
this division between the world and Christ, flesh and
spirit. The formula 'in Christ', 'in the Lord', which
probably referred in the first place to the cultic community (*cf.* 2*a.* above), was individualized and became
independent of the cult: the whole life of a Christian is

the life of one who is identified with Christ, and the love of Christ (2 Cor. 5.14) and 'the affection of Christ' (Phil. 1.8) and similar expressions do not refer to the historical Jesus, but to the exalted Christ, now united with the believer. For even Christ himself is no longer to be regarded in his historical and existential life, but as the Lord who is present now, and to whom the Christian is united; this is the meaning of the much discussed passage 2 Cor. 5.16. But the sphere in which this union takes place is designated by Paul, who uses a word which was already current, and extends its meaning, as the 'Spirit', (1 Cor. 6.17). Thus Spirit and Christ can be used as alternatives (Rom. 8. 9-11), and the transformation of man which takes place in the contemplation of Christ can be traced back to the Spirit; this is true even if the expression 'the Lord is the Spirit' (2 Cor. 3.17) is not, as many suppose, a general statement concerning Christ, but an interpretation of the story of Moses which is referred to in the immediately preceding passage.

The question arises, how far it is proper to speak of all this in terms of *Christ-mysticism* (*cf. Mysticism* IV. p. 371 below). In favour of this usage one may refer in the first place to the terminology. Paul uses the formula 'in Christ' in many places in the full mystical sense, and at least hints at the corresponding formula 'Christ in us' (Gal. 1.16; Rom. 8.10; 2 Cor. 13.3; Col. 3.11); and the equivalence of active and passive language, so characteristic of mysticism, is found in the use of the word 'know' (1 Cor. 8.2 f.; 13.12; Gal. 4.9) and 'apprehend' (Phil. 3.12; R.S.V.: 'make my own'). Secondly, the images of birth and marriage point to mysticism, as does that of the putting on of Christ, and above all, the conceptions of light, vision, and knowledge (*gnosis*) which do not in fact merely remain images: Paul's conversion set up in him a condition which consisted of the vision of the glory in the face of Christ, or of the 'knowledge' of Christ in the mystical sense and the transformation into 'glory' which is brought about by this (Gal. 1.16; 2 Cor. 3.18; 4.6; Phil. 3.10 f.). The exaltation to which one who is 'spiritual' (not every Christian) can attain in this way is shown by the passage 1 Cor. 2.6-16; and the contrasting figure, in truth a surprising manifestation in Christianity, of the natural ('psychic') man, the man who lacks the grace of the Spirit of God, is also present. Thirdly, the mysticism of suffering is a particular example of the mystical union with Christ: everything that Paul suffers as an apostle is a reproduction of the suffering of Christ (Col. 1.24; 2 Cor. 4.10; Gal. 6.17). This evidence would suggest that Paul's devotion to Christ could be associated with hellenistic mysticism; but there are objections which prevent us from describing Paul simply as a mystic. First of all, his gospel of faith and the justification of the sinner rests on the consciousness of the distance between man and God (Christ), not on the unity. And again, he teaches that all Christians are involved in the great forward progress of the history of salvation, which is being objectively fulfilled, and which leads from the history of Israel to the decisive turning point in world history in the life of Christ, to the existence of the Church and the events at the end of time; and in this movement there is no place for the mystic's repose in God. Thus Paul can also regard the mystical unity as something which is still under way, still striving for consummation (Phil. 3.11; 1 Cor. 13.12). We do not know how or when the devotion of Paul took on this mystic note; there is every likelihood that this had already taken place in his Jewish period.

c. THE FORMATION OF THE FEATURES OF CHRISTOLOGY COMMON TO ALL CHRISTIANITY. There is a certain unity between 3*a.* and 3*b.*, apart from the fact that they are associated in the person of Paul, in that both his christology proper (3*a.*) and his devotion to Christ (3*b.*) have certain connections with the linguistic usages and the faith of Greek-speaking Christianity. The eschatology which was common to almost all Christians—the coming down of Christ from heaven, the resurrection of the dead, the meeting of Christ by Christians, and the messianic kingdom of Christ, lasting until he hands over his rule to God (1 Thess. 4.16 f.; 1 Cor. 15.23-28)—completes the Christ-myth but, as we have shown, also contains the final consummation of what the mystic is striving for. Paul sees the effect of the Spirit not only, like many Christians (e.g. in Corinth), in ecstatic experience, but also in its ethical manifestations; but in christology proper the word which has been entrusted to all signifies the pledge of the glory that was to come and also describes the nature of the mystical union with Christ. The Church has an eschatological significance, in so far as it conveys the promise that its members will be citizens of the kindgom that is to come: but it also possesses a mystical significance, in so far as it is the 'body' of which Christ is the 'head'; whatever the origin of these expressions may be, they express the relationship by means of which the blessings of the Lord are bestowed upon the worshipping congregation. We can observe as well the way in which Paul takes up and develops the christological conceptions which have come down to him. He is able to associate his mysticism with the sacraments, but as can be seen from a comparison of Rom. 6.6 in relation to 6.4, he does not associate it exclusively with the sacraments. The expression *'faith in Jesus Christ'* (this is the correct translation of Gal. 2.16, not the faith or faithfulness of Jesus) is particularly noteworthy in this respect. In Paul, faith is directed towards the paradoxical will of God, which in Christ, however, is concealed as his grace, and which justifies the sinner; the word 'faith' in its true Pauline sense (in contrast to 'works') does not, therefore, require any closer definition, and it consequently appears that the expression 'faith in Jesus Christ' was not coined by Paul. But it was he who gave it the specific content which 'faith' has for him: the affirmation of the paradox which is displayed both in the life and death of Christ and in the history of the people of Israel, and so ultimately in the bestowal of God's grace on the sinner (and in the conversion of Paul).

This paradox also characterizes the interest which Paul has in the historical and earthly life of Jesus. The unimaginable events of his humiliation and suffering are guarantees of salvation; the 'form of a servant' and the 'poverty' (Phil. 2.7; 2 Cor. 8.9) are not manifested by the stall, the crib and Jesus's lack of all possessions, but by the fact that the Son of God came down into the realm of sin, into the flesh. And to have Jesus Christ publicly portrayed as crucified before one's eyes (Gal. 3.1) means to know not about Gethsemane and Golgotha, but about the new 'righteousness' by which the world is ruled, and through which sinners (and the heathen) have access to salvation. A religious awe prevents Paul from simply identifying the historical Jesus with a man; he uses the word ὁμοίωμα: in the 'likeness' or 'form' (Rom. 8.3; Phil. 2.7) of the flesh (or of man). But the evidence we possess does not show him calling Christ 'God' (or, if Rom. 9.5 does in fact refer to Christ, only in a cultic formula which has been reapplied to him) in spite of the fact that he prays to him (2 Cor. 12.8). Here again, one recognizes how, in spite of the non-Christian origin of many ideas in the christology of Paul, the decisive experience of the paradox of Christianity is still dominant; for what was decisive in his conversion was not the vision of the heavenly Lord, but the recognition that this Lord was the condemned and crucified Jesus who had been persecuted by Paul, the image of human shame and heavenly glory in one!

4. Gnosticism

The outlines of the *further development* of early christology can already be seen in Paul, even though not every process in this development is visible in his works. In Paul, the fact of Jesus's earthly life was taken into the Christ myth, though not all its details were given full value (*cf. 3c.* above); even before Paul's time, a sacramental practice that was similar to that of the mysteries had come to be associated with the myth, without overshadowing the essential nature of the Christian gospel. Both these processes were so natural in that period and environment, that they were able to become the essential features of Christianity. This is what happened in the christology of *gnosticism* (*cf.* II, 2b. below). The dualism of flesh and spirit in Paul becomes a radical cosmic dualism, which cannot tolerate the idea that God should become flesh, and consequently allows the story of the passion to be watered down into docetism.

5. Christology in the Church after Paul

a. THE MESSIANIC SECRET, THE VIRGIN BIRTH, THE DESCENT INTO HELL. The greater part of Christendom, which adhered firmly to the tradition concerning Jesus, found it necessary to interpret the details of the life of Jesus in a christological sense, and so to link together the myth and the history in a quite different way from Paul, with his rejection of 'knowledge according to the flesh' (2 Cor. 5.16; R.S.V.: 'regard from a human point of view'). There is already a distinctive christology in Mark; it is, however, only expressed by the framework, the ordering, and the occasional interpretation of the traditional material; consequently, we do not learn whether he regarded Jesus's baptism in an 'adoptionist' sense as his institution as the Son of God, with the idea that Jesus came to his baptism as a mere man, or whether the miracle of the baptism signified

for him, like the transfiguration, the manifestation or
'epiphany' of the Son of God. But there is a christology
implied in the theory of the *messianic secret*: according
to this view, Jesus kept secret the fact that he was the
Messiah, and forbade both the demons and his disciples to speak of it (*cf.* Vol I, *Jesus Christ*). This theory
is meant to explain how the people could crucify their
Messiah; thus it represents an earthly parallel to the
mythical theme of his concealment (*cf.* 3a. above).

Matthew and Luke already contain the story of the
virgin birth; in Matt. 1.18-25 it is assumed, while in
Luke 1.26-38 it is described in a delicate and reticent
way. Here we are introduced to an idea which underwent a long development in the history of religion; its
first stages are found in the stories of the divine begetting
of Egyptian and other rulers, and its ultimate form is the
concept in Philo, that God can only have dealings with
the soul (and only dealt with Sarah, as the Bible records),
after he has restored it to the state of virginity (*De
cherubim* 48-52), and the idea in Paul that Isaac was
born according to the Spirit, not according to the flesh
(Gal. 4.23,29). Thus the miracle of revelation is portrayed by the introduction into history of a mythical
theme already extant in Judaism. There is a tension
nevertheless between this theme and the tradition of
Joseph as the father of Jesus, which is preserved by
Matthew and Luke in the genealogy of Jesus, and also
in Luke 2 in the story of the nativity.

There is a similar tension in the case of the *descent into
Hell*, which, originally a mythical theme, is presented
in 1 Pet. 3.19; 4.6 (Rom. 10.7; Eph. 4.9?) as the mission
of Christ among the dead; it is mentioned in the *Gospel
of Peter*; in Matt. 27.53, it is barely hinted at out of context. The same is true of the *resurrection*: instead of the
account of Christ's appearance, with which Paul was
acquainted (1 Cor. 15.5; *cf.* 1b., 3a. above), Mark's

gospel has the story of the empty tomb; the resurrection itself is first described in the Gospel of Peter and is touched on, in an incomplete account which distorts the passage in which it is placed, in Matt. 28.2,3.

b. THE GOSPEL OF JOHN. The myth and the history are not drawn into a single coherent picture until the *Gospel of John*. Here a tradition consisting of material of very different origin and value is so illuminated that a true christology is clearly visible. The decisive factor is a change of emphasis. The coming of Christ as Messiah is not imminent, it has already taken place; the earthly life of Jesus has begun the great revelation of God, which is continued in the Church; Jesus is called the Son of Man, because he has come from heaven (3.13); his appearance is a judgement upon the world, and brings life to those who are his own (3.18 f.; 5.24); the events at the end of time merely bring about the final consummation (5.28). Thus the earthly life of Jesus is already regarded as the great revelation of all the powers which properly belong to the future (7.38 f.), and which in consequence are not promised until the Farewell Discourse, Ch. 14-16. Thus the acts of Jesus which the tradition records are revelations of the exalted Christ: the water of life, the bread of life, light to the blind, life for the dead, and above all, the revelation of the invisible God (17.3); this is what Jesus brings. The substance of salvation is described in expressions which are borrowed from the syncretism of that period: in the Hermetic writings 'light' and 'life' signify the world above; contemporary philosophy describes the kingdom of the Spirit as 'truth'; 'the way' is an expression of the gnostics; and we have already mentioned (*3b.* above) the idea of the appropriation of salvation through a vision (of life, John 3.36; of glory, 1.14, 11.40; of Jesus, 14.9). Jesus does not bring or bestow these as gifts, he embodies them: 'I am' the light, etc. Without him they cannot be obtained. Consequently, christology becomes the central issue of the whole book: in Jesus—and not in the earthly Jesus, but in the exalted Christ who imparts himself in the Spirit, 16.7—Christians possess God. His words and deeds are actions of God, conveyed through him as though through a mere receptacle (5.19-30, etc.). Consequently, it is possible to express the identity of nature of Jesus with God, as for example when he is described by the word 'God' (20.28; *cf.* also 1.1).

The word 'love', used of God and the 'Son', also has more than its purely moral significance: it refers to the way in which God imparts himself to Jesus. In the use of this word, as of the mystic expression 'in me', 'in you' (*cf.* 3*b.* above), a distinctive characteristic of the gospel of John can be seen: the relationship of believers to Jesus is equivalent to the relationship of Jesus to God. Such an equivalence must, strictly speaking, have been alien to the experience of Christianity; here again, therefore, one must suspect the influence of the Iranian myth (*cf.* 3*a.* above) of the First Man, in which the redeemed are most closely associated with the redeemer, and the redeemer himself is redeemed. Even John describes how Jesus brings about the sanctification by God of those who are his own and sends them into the world and glorifies them, as he himself is sanctified, sent into the world and glorified (17.1,5, 16 ff., 22,24; 10.36). The mysticism of John finally leads to the statement that the faithful enter into a direct relationship with God (14.23; 16.27); this idea is on exactly the same lines. And when the title actually given to God in the discourses of Jesus is 'he who sent me', one is inevitably reminded of the figure of the divine redeemer sent by God in the myth. The conviction that Jesus was sent by God is decisive for John; besides the title 'Son of Man' he can use various titles, some of which occur elsewhere: 'Lamb of God' (*cf.* 2*a.*), 'Lord' (*cf.* 2*a.*), 'Messiah' (*cf.* 1*a.*), 'the Holy One of God' (only found elsewhere in Mark 1.24), 'Son' (without qualification, *cf.* 5*c.* below), 'Saviour' (*cf.* 5*c.*). When he speaks of the *Logos* in 1.1-18, he assumes the whole cosmological association of the myth (in which the figure who brings revelation is the mediator in the creation of the universe), already known to us from Paul (*cf.* 3*a.* above); but he does not use this expression in a cosmic sense like Philo, or to expound the history of salvation, like the early Christian Apologists (*cf.* II below), but simply employs this current expression to introduce Jesus as God's instrument in the world. The phrase 'the Logos became flesh', no doubt deliberately meant to scandalize, is intended to link together the myth and the history: the basis of the universe becomes an historical person. In the story as John tells it the mythical background is maintained: Jesus acts as a supernatural person, emotionally unmoved, protected from any influence or danger from men, the master of his own destiny. Consequently no man perceives who he is or understands him; the misunderstandings with which his words and actions are met display their divine character; but they also show how it was possible for this world to fail to recognize the revelation of God, and to bring the bearer of that revelation to the cross; and therefore they form an equivalent in historical terms to the mythical theme of concealment (*cf.* 3*a.* above).

c. IMAGES AND TITLES OF CHRIST IN OTHER PRIMITIVE CHRISTIAN WRITINGS. The christology found in the remaining early Christian texts is very varied and unsystematic. The most unified and comprehensively thought-out picture is that in the Epistle to the Hebrews, where Christ is the *High Priest* sent from heaven (8.2 'not man'), who through his own blood enters into the heavenly sanctuary—an interpretation which provides a parallel to Philo's doctrine of the Logos even in its mode of expression. No place is found for the resurrection, but use is made of details of the life of Jesus contained in the tradition or assumed (2.18; 4.15; 5.7; 13.12). Then there is the impressive figure of the *heavenly Son of Man* of Rev. 1.12-18, seen in a vision, and resembling a cultic image; and in the same book there is also the portrayal of the *divine child* assailed by the dragon, which can only be explained on the basis of a non-Christian myth (12.1-6), and the vision, based on earlier Jewish material, of the *messianic horseman* (19.11-16) who goes out to judgement, and bears the names '*Faithful and True*', '*The Logos of God*' (as an honorific title without any philosophical basis) and '*King of kings and Lord of lords*'. This latter title is also found in 1 Tim. 6.15, and is evidence of the adaptation to Christ of the language of the hellenistic cult of the divine ruler (Titus 2.13: grace bringing salvation, the appearance of glory, goodness, and loving kindness=φιλανθρωπία) which is typical of 1 and 2 Tim. and Titus as a whole. Here as in Luke 2.11; John 4.42; 1 John 4.14 ('Saviour of the world'), Acts 5.31; 13.23; Phil. 3.20 and 2 Pet. he is given the title '*Saviour*' (σωτήρ). In most passages this does not mean the bringer of life, as in the mysteries, but, as in the cult of the divine ruler, the 'revealed' (ἐπιφανής) God, who brings with him a new era full of blessing (*cf.* Titus 2.13). Here also, as in Ignatius of Antioch (*cf.* II, 1d. below), Christ is now described as *God* in the full meaning of the word, in the sense of the religion of revelation of the Gospel of John, so that Ignatius can even speak of the blood of God and the suffering of God (*To the Ephesians* 1.1; *To the Romans* 6.3). He links with this a mysticism orientated towards the Church, such as is already found in the Epistle to the Ephesians, as elsewhere in the New Testament: Christ is the head of the body, who is to fill the whole world; the *ecclesia* is of a cosmic extent. Other passages which record the christology of primitive

Christianity contain nothing new in so far as they refer to Christ in traditional expressions which often seem to form part of a confession of faith (Eph. 4.5; I Tim. 2.5: 'mediator'; I Pet. 1.19 f.: 'lamb'; *2 Clement* 1.1: *'judge of the living and the dead*) or have only an incidental christological significance which is not worked out in full. But the christology of primitive Christianity constantly bears witness to the tension between myth and history. This is not only the theme of the development of the christological doctrine at a later period, but is an enduring and inevitable problem; for Christianity acknowledges both the supernatural and timeless nature of its revelation, and the historical nature, subject to time, of its realization in the world.

MARTIN DIBELIUS

II THE HISTORY OF CHRISTOLOGICAL DOCTRINE

1. The Beginning and the Early Development of the Christological Problem

a. Christology and the related doctrine of the Trinity form the nucleus of the development of Church doctrine. From the very beginning christology manifests the consciousness of the Christian religion that it is both an historical as well as a supra-historical entity; that this dual character displays both the profound tension and the unique possibility of a real relationship between God and man; and that in it lies the distinctiveness and superiority of Christianity. It was similarly clear from the first that this duality, the expression of the greatness and superiority of Christianity, would also be the occasion of constant unrest and difficulty, a source of innumerable changes and errors, and the reason for an imperfection which would last until the final and eternal perfection. To understand the development and history of christology from its very beginning, it is first necessary to realize that the ancient world, the historical environment in which Christianity arose, for the most part did not possess the concepts with which we work today, neither that of historicity, nor those by which we distinguish what is metaphysical, spiritual, or material. They were never aware of them in the form, definition, and clarity with which they are employed today. In the course of the development of doctrine, each crisis in the understanding of these concepts eventually brought with it a crisis in christology. This is how we distinguish the principal periods in the historical development of doctrine and theology, and also the points at which an established position remains fixed in history in a rudimentary form. But from the very first the underlying problem has always been the same, and if we are to understand the history of christology we must always recognize this problem behind every attempt to solve it, even when the forms taken by these attempts, as for example in the fully developed doctrine of the two natures in Greek christology, no longer seem adequate to us today.

b. For various reasons there can never be a final and scientific solution to the problem of the historical *origin of the Church's christology*. The first reason is because the sources we possess for the earliest period are very far from adequate. This inadequacy, furthermore, is not merely accidental, but can be observed in the embryonic stages of every great historical phenomenon. The ultimate origins of a movement that takes place in the minds of men can invariably be explained only by working back from later evidence (*cf*. I, Introduction, above); and in this process an objective general judgement on the nature of the whole phenomenon is always involved. Of course neither primitive Christianity nor the Church of the early centuries recognized the *basic theological problem* of christology as such, and there are no christological statements in the dogmatic sense to be found in the older sources. But the theme of this basic problem was certainly already present, even within the gospel itself (*cf.* I, 1*b*. above). It is not of course possible to begin by identifying with certainty each individual theme according to its origin, and then to go on to give an historical description of the whole doctrine both in its historical dependence on other religions of the period when it came into being, and in its own distinctive nature and content. On the other hand, it must be affirmed that the development of the Church's christological doctrine as a whole is a clear sign that from the very beginning some kind of organic unity did exist, even though all its details cannot be known.

c. The most certain link between primitive Christianity and the developing christology of the Church is the *Jewish heritage,* the understanding of Jesus Christ as the Messiah handed down from the primitive Church (*cf.* I, 1,5). Justin Martyr asserts this fundamental title of Christ in answer to Trypho the Jew (*Dialogue* 48). It is true that soon afterwards the title of Messiah for Christ disappeared as such from the Church's dogma, because, for a Church that had become entirely Gentile, it was no longer meaningful or useful. But its essential implication remained, and has been maintained in the christology of all denominations up to the present day, that is, the idea of the messianic or eschatological return of Christ to judge the world and to bring into being the kingdom of God (*cf.* Vol I, *Eschatology* III; IV). The great stumbling block which the first coming of Christ in the flesh, to be despised and humiliated, represented for the Jews, was overcome, in the minds of the primitive Church and of the generations that followed, by this concept drawn from the Jewish faith itself. The idea of the messianic judge and ruler of the world, who is to come, is the first christological concept which we can see establishing itself and spreading from the beginning. It is a pre-Christian idea, but even with the primitive Church it had already undergone a decisive change in its content. The proof of this is the fact that the name that enshrined it, the title received from Judaism, disappeared when it was no longer of use.

A much more difficult problem is presented by the development which can be seen to result from the assimilation of the Church's christology with the *heathen* religious concepts of its contemporary environment, the process that is called *syncretism*. Here the study of the history of religion in the last few decades has made a large number of discoveries, but has also advanced numerous premature conclusions and false theories. It is probable at least that as a result of the intensive international trade and exchange of ideas which had drawn humanity closer together since the time of Alexander the Great, the most various kinds of cult had developed something like a common pattern, and that at least a number of individual ideas, conceptions, cultic practices and rites were being adopted and exchanged from one cult to another. It is certain that Christianity was from the very beginning unable to avoid the influence of this state of affairs (*cf.* Vol III, *Christianity* II, 2*a*.). In this respect, a most important influence seems to be that of its great rival, the Roman emperor cult. Almost all the titles which are applied to Christ can also be found in other contemporary cults, such as those of Saviour (σωτήρ), Lord (κύριος), Son of God, God, etc. Even what are known as his acts of salvation (*cf.* I, 3*a*. above), such as his death and resurrection, can be observed elsewhere, as can the sacred acts of initiation and admission to membership (*cf.* Vol. I, *Baptism* I), cultic meals (*cf.* Vol. I. *The Eucharist* I), etc., which were equally important at this early period for the Christian Church. This raised two fundamental questions. First, how far do these religious themes represent ideas which are universal and spring up spontaneously in each cult, which seems to be true in particular of the title 'Lord' for the deity (*cf.* I, 2*a.* above); and consequently, what is the significance and effect of the adoption of heathen titles and conceptions? The title σωτήρ, Saviour, may in fact be derived from the emperor cult or elsewhere, but it is nevertheless the case that within Christianity, as every stage in its later development clearly shows, it takes on a new and entirely different content. And this leads to the second and more important of these two problems. Almost all cults have their own myths; Christianity also possesses its myths. But from the very beginning (*cf. 1a.* above) this myth is utterly distinct from all other cultic myths, in that it is an *historical* myth, a true historical event occurring to an historical personality, and is presented as such, even though the concept of what is historical is not understood in such a scientific sense as it is today. The struggle for existence of the growing Church with gnosticism in the second century is totally incomprehensible if this point is not understood.

Much more important than the influence exercised on the Church at its early stages by the heathen religious environment, was that of late Greek *philosophy*. As it grew in size and importance, Christianity could not isolate itself from this body of thought, nor ought it to have done, unless it intended to remain a barbarian religion, and as such to disappear. Thus towards the end of the second century it came to terms with these Greek ideas in order to work out its christology. But even in the christology of the Apologists and the Alexandrian school, where this union took place, one can clearly see a linking together of philosophical ideas and conceptions handed down from primitive Christianity. We have already spoken of a tradition which goes back behind the

Apologists, which is purely religious in its purpose, and unphilosophical, and which contains nothing more than ideas derived from the historical gospel, a tradition which was continued and finally consolidated in the Antiochene theology (*cf.* 3*c.* above). There is, however, another tradition within Christianity, older than the Apologists, the direct successors of which are the Apologists themselves and the Alexandrine theology. This was the *cosmological* problem, the relationship between God and the world, or between God and man, which in its origins was purely a metaphysical problem, but gradually took on a religious aspect as well. Here a religious atmosphere reigns which is quite different from that of the reconciliation of the sinner with God, derived from Judaism. There is nevertheless a real religious concern, which is that of the relationship of the omnipotent God, altogether above this world, with man, imprisoned in the material world. In order to deal with this problem, hellenistic metaphysics, which had a genuine religious concern, adopted from the Platonic heritage the λόγοι, the original archetypes of things, and from the speculation of the Stoics, the idea of the powers which pervade the world; this process is similar to that which took place in late Judaism when the cosmological problem became a pressing one. We cannot tell whether or to what extent there was a direct and material influence on christology, with its ideas of the mediator and the Logos, before the time of the Apologists (*cf.* I, 3*a.*; 5*b.*, *c.* above). All that can be said is that the general formal relationships were already present, and that the Apologists and the Alexandrines were able to make use of them and elaborate their content.

d. Since from the beginning, even in the gospel itself, Jesus Christ was accorded a special status and dignity as an historical person which raised him above the human sphere (*cf.* Vol. I, *Jesus Christ*, and I, 1*b.* above), an association and a tension between the actual historical person and his supra-historical divinity was present from the first, and forms the basis of the Church's christology. Both the primitive Church and the generation of the *Apostolic Fathers* which followed possessed numerous different ways of expressing this state of affairs, all of which were quite unsystematic and existed side by side without any attempt being made to make them compatible with one another. They agree in this, that they express their fundamental theme by giving the historical human figure of Jesus the title God, or more frequently that of the Son of God. The general outlook of the ancient world, which did not use the title 'God' in so closely defined a sense as we do today, affected this process in the formal sense, as did also the cultic and philosophical conceptions of hellenism. In spite of this, it is clear from the way the Apostolic Fathers maintain and continue the ideas of primitive Christianity, that the use of the title 'Son of God', and the fact that they 'think of Christ as of God', that is, as the judge of the world (2 *Clement* 1.1), is not a usage taken from the mystery cults, nor does it have a cosmological sense; rather, it is related to the understanding of Jesus Christ as the historical and divine redeemer from sin and guilt.

The attempt has been made to reduce the unsystematic variety of christological ideas found in this early period to some order, and at least to distinguish certain basic patterns. Although every typological pattern advanced by one scholar is disputed by others, yet each of the types that have been distinguished correctly expresses one theme or element of this development of christology; in particular, the development which Loofs called the 'theology of Asia Minor' (the title 'theology of Asia Minor' and the geographical limitation which it implies have in fact more recently been abandoned) emphasizes the way in which the earliest christology, following the gospels of John and Paul, is concerned with the *history of salvation* (*cf.* I, 3, 5*b*. above). Their *naïve modalism*, that is, the unqualified identification of Christ with the Father in order to exalt his saving work, and in association with this, the limitation of the title of Son of God to Christ after his incarnation, with a firm grip on the idea of an historical redeemer, are all present (*cf.* I, 5*c*. above). But the other types which have been named (e.g. by A. von Harnack) possess considerable value, as well as certain limits, notably those of *adoptionist* and *pneumatic* christology. Both conceptions can be traced back into the New Testament; neither can be understood apart from the direct influence on their content of metaphysical religious ideas. In the case of adoptionist christology, the picture is of the historical man Jesus, destined by God to be the redeemer of men, who is accepted and adopted by God to share completely in his divinity, after the act of redemption has been ratified and consummated. In the pneumatic christology, there is a heavenly and spiritual being which descends for a time from the divine sphere and takes on flesh, in order to carry out the work of redemption. There is no question that this latter conception is present in the New Testament, without any cosmological overtones. The task of future study will be to see whether other patterns of ideas can be distinguished, perhaps even superseding those already established; these types will continue to be of importance as guiding principles for study. In general, however, it must be insisted that at this early period there is no threat to monotheism, and this is not only true of the first, adoptionist christology. Neither the christological conceptions we have mentioned, nor the triadic formulae which existed from the very beginning, represented any threats to monotheism, largely because no reflection on them had yet taken place. It was not until the period which followed that a threat to monotheism, and the whole complex of new and related problems in christology and in the doctrine of the Trinity, were recognized and dealt with, notably in disputes with the heathen.

2. The Triumph of the Logos Christology and the Triumph of the Physical Doctrine of Redemption

a. From the obscurity and the numerous unsolved and insoluble questions of the early period, we emerge into the period in which the history of doctrine properly begins, and which can be handled by historical methods and with at least relative certainty. The period begins with the writers who are called the *Apologists*. Here again, there are many historical questions which remain unanswered. But we are now able to distinguish a definite pattern of thought and a clear line of development, which continues into the future, and we also observe the narrowing down of christological concepts and ideas, which in essence prevailed up to the time of the Reformation, and in fact to a considerable extent is still of decisive importance today. But we can tell that for a long time a quite different complex of thoughts and themes maintained its existence in parallel to this line of development. These other themes are attested not only by the opponents of this christology who are known to us, but also by the popular devotion of the Church, which is less well known, but which we are able to deduce from a good deal of available evidence (as for example from the opponent of Christianity, Celsus). The decisive action of the Apologists in the history of doctrine was their conscious application to Christ of the concept of the *Logos*, taken from hellenistic philosophy, and their association of it with the title of Son of God. This has been seen not only as the creation of a one-sided and limited christology, but even as a perversion of christology, in accordance with the theory of the decay of the Church in the course

of its history (*cf.* Vol. III, *Christianity* II, 3*b*.). Yet even
if this view must be accepted as in the main correct, it
must not be forgotten that the Apologists were formally
influenced by the development that preceded them, and
that they could call upon John 1 as a scriptural proof.
They understood the Logos, as also the Son of God, as a
heavenly and divine being, clearly distinct from the
Father, his 'first creation', who had come into being by
a distinction from God, not a separation (Tatian). He
was a distinct substance—and a distinct person, even
though the modern concept of personality cannot be
applied in this context—a second God beside the first
(Justin). As such, he had come into the world in Jesus,
taken on flesh in order to carry out the work of redemption, and afterwards returned to his fellowship with the
Father. Any closer examination of the problems, and
any attempt to solve them, was lacking. But it is clear at
once that the religious philosophies of the decline of the
ancient world, both the rationalism of the Stoics and the
teaching of the successors of Platonism, were obtaining a
dominant position in theology and therefore in christology. Thus, while the historical person of the redeemer
was asserted, this assertion created a problem which was
not merely incomprehensible in these terms, but quite
unanswerable, and as a result receded in practice more
and more into the background. And finally, the physical
and cosmological doctrine of redemption tended to
replace the work of salvation to which the New Testament bears witness, at least in the theoretical picture of
dogmatic theology. That God was in Christ and reconciled the world to himself was still maintained, simply
because it was in the scriptures; but in the Church's
christological doctrine it no longer had a place. The
concept of the Logos brought with it from its origin this
cosmological and physical character; the Logos appeared
as a substance distinct from God, important as a reality

and essence in itself, independent of its actions. Once the concept of the Logos had been introduced, the Logos as such became the central concern, an independent pre-existent and post-existent being; the idea, so important in the philosophy of history and religion, of the λόγος σπερματικός, the Logos at work as a hidden seed in previous history, as Justin described it, arose as a result of this situation. The consequence was that the idea of the incarnation, essential to any christology, fell completely into the background, or at least lost its essential importance and, in particular, was not incorporated into the whole theological structure.

b. The task left uncompleted by the Apologists was at once taken up by two theologians who can be regarded as a link between the Apologists and the Church's new doctrinal theology, and as both the last and most important of the Apologists and the first of the Church's dogmatic theologians, *Irenaeus* and *Tertullian*. They were particularly concerned to resist the errors of *gnosticism* and *docetism*. Neither of them diverted the Church from the path followed by the Apologists, nor were they able to provide solutions strictly dogmatic in form. Their achievement was to give an effective refutation of gnosticism, with its docetic christology, by establishing *the incarnation* as the centre of the doctrine of the Logos. Irenaeus did this principally in his important theology of recapitulation, which excluded forever any purely mystical view of the redemption. Tertullian, with his philosophical background, as well as his own personal and strictly moralist attitude, which must not be overlooked, was able to create formulae which in fact concealed an even greater number of difficulties and problems, but advanced the development in the sense that they made it impossible ever again to forget that the *saving act* of the Logos was a true *historical* event, thus finally defeating gnosticism. But Harnack has constantly and rightly emphasized that, in studying early Catholic theology, one must remember that its attitude to gnosticism was not merely one of negative opposition. The theology of Irenaeus cannot be understood without reference to the school of Valentinus and Marcion. By his stress on the reality of the incarnation, Irenaeus emphasized as powerfully as his opponents the work of *redemption*; to this extent he represents an advance upon the Apologists. But *physical* categories are affirmed along the lines introduced by gnosticism, and Christ's work of atonement falls entirely into the background (in practice it was to some degree preserved in the moralistic penitential system). In the doctrine of Irenaeus, as in the formulae of Tertullian, there is a clear premonition of the later doctrine of the two natures. It is a remarkable fact that Tertullian, a western and ultimately unphilosophical thinker, provided the formulae which became of decisive importance for the main development of christology in the East in the fourth century (*cf.* 3 below). Tertullian recognized in the one person of Christ two substances, though how he regarded their relationship to each other, and the way in which he supposed that these two substances, existing side by side, were able to carry out the task of the deification of man, remains obscure. Thus the first theological expression of the Logos christology contained the seeds of all later disputes.

c. The Logos christology made wide claims, was introduced by profound thinkers, and was made acceptable by its ability both to provide an answer to the most important question of the relationship of Christ to God, and to serve as a useful weapon in the struggle against the gnostic heresy. Nevertheless, its pluralism and consequent polytheism were bound to give rise to objections based on the exclusively monotheist character of Christianity. And the period at which the Logos christology had still been completely unknown was not so easily forgotten. Those who resisted the Logos christology in the Church are known in the history of doctrine as the *Monarchians*, because they laid the principal emphasis on the *monarchia*, the unique rule of God. They regarded themselves, by contrast with the newer theologians, as champions of the traditional theology, with relative justification at least. Two forms of monarchianism can be clearly distinguished. They are characterized on the one hand by their relationship to the 'adoptionist' and the 'pneumatic' christologies mentioned above (*cf. 1d.*). Secondly, they re-occur in one form or another throughout the history of christology, right down to Luther, Schleiermacher, and Albrecht Ritschl, etc., so that one is bound to say that they express certain requirements in christological doctrine which will constantly make themselves felt, even though no certain historical connection can be traced; in particular, there is no need to look for such a connection between these types of christology before the time of the Apologists, and the first Monarchians properly so called. In fact one can perhaps say that the opposition between monarchianism and the Logos christology represents one expression of the intrinsic tension found in the christological problem as a whole. These two groups are known as dynamistic or adoptionist monarchianism, and modalist monarchianism.

Adoptionism attempts to defend the monarchy of God as it were from below. That is, it portrays Christ as a man imbued with a special power (δύναμις) of God, sent by God in a miraculous way to carry out the work of salvation, and raised up by God after its completion to divine status. Theodotus, the leather-worker from Byzantium, can be regarded as the founder of this group; like the leaders of all theological schools of this period he travelled to the capital, Rome, and there gathered adherents, among whom Theodotus the money-changer and some others are known to us. The Bishop of Rome, Victor I (189–198), recognized the danger and excommunicated the Dynamists, consequently making it impossible for them to spread their arguments, even though they succeeded in maintaining for a period a separate existence independent of the Church, especially after Artemon (ca. 230) adopted their views. In the second half of the third century their christology gained an important adherent in the East, in the shape of Paul of Samosata. For even though the connection, constantly asserted by the Church Fathers, between him and Artemon cannot be historically demonstrated, and although Paul of Samosata in fact presented his views in the form of a Logos doctrine, yet we must accept that he reveals a material connection with the first Dynamists, and therefore also with the traditions of the period before the Apologists, particularly with regard to the unphilosophical character of his Logos doctrine. We must note in particular that this whole school of thought, critical as it was of a 'high' christological doctrine, was as far from entertaining other critical ideas as was Arius at a later period. Neither the first Monarchians nor Paul of Samosata ever had the slightest doubt about the virgin birth or the bodily resurrection. When they are later described as having spoken of Jesus as a mere man (ψιλὸς ἄνθρωπος), this is certainly not to be understood in the modern sense.

The *Modalists* attempted to defend the monarchy of God as it were from above, by explaining that Christ was merely a form (*modus*) in which God appeared. It was the Father himself who in this form carried out the work of salvation, was born, suffered, and died; this explains the name which was later universally applied to them, *Patripassians*. Here again one must not overlook the identity of content of their doctrine with the so-called 'naïve' modalism of the period before the Apologists; the power of this doctrine is seen in the fact that it was able for a time to be officially accepted by the Church of Rome. We know that it was first propounded by Noetus of Smyrna, and after him was spread in the West by Epigonus, Praxeas, etc. In spite of the sharp opposition of Tertullian it was favoured by the Roman bishop Zephyrinus and also, at first, by Calixtus I. After about 215 it was expounded with particular force by Sabellius. In the course of time, however, the Logos christology, which was always able to bring forward an ancient and traditional proof in its defence in the shape of the prologue of the Gospel of John, had become too powerful. By means of a formula of agreement, Calixtus disassociated himself from his adherents and excommunicated them. This decided the fate of modalism, and the Logos christology was accepted by the whole Church in the West. This is shown in particular by the theology of Novatian (ca. 250), who in spite of archaic survivals and some reminiscences of monarchianism, essentially maintained the formulae of Tertullian, and consequently carried out an important service in preparing the ground for the struggles that were to follow.

d. The Logos christology was systematically expounded, and finally came to prevail, in the Alexandrine theology, through its great genius *Origen* (see Vol. III *Origen*). Ultimately, the triumph of this doctrine is due to his overwhelming intellectual influence. He incorporated it into the first true dogmatic system in such a way that it could no longer be isolated from it, even though the particular system of Origen itself collapsed, and gave birth from its ruins to the numerous problems of the period which followed. There are two basic themes in the christology of Origen; since he was not able to reconcile them with one another, they in fact sowed the seeds of its destruction, and explain why the christology of Origen could not prove wholly satisfactory in the later development of Greek dogma, even though it continued to provide its foundation. The first theme is the strictly monist conception of God, constructed in accordance with the traditions of Platonism, and which absolutely excluded any division or change within God, thus pre-figuring the ideas of Schleiermacher in an astonishing way. The effect of this theme in christology is the idea of the eternal generation of the Logos, by which Origen preserves the absolute oneness and unity of God. The second theme is that of the complete subordination of the Logos as an independent being, an οὐσία (substance) or ὑπόστασις (*persona*) in itself—the two latter concepts, clearly distinguished by Tertullian, are still wholly equivalent in Origen and are only distinguished in later Greek theology under pressure from the West. The second idea only contradicts the first in appearance; in itself, it is wholly in accordance with it. But because Origen was unable to avoid the necessary consequence of understanding the Logos as δεύτερος θεός, a second God, and could not overcome the apparent contradiction, his christology collapsed. Although these two themes were in essence entirely philosophical, yet on the basis of his biblicism Origen introduced a specifically Christian element, albeit a minor one, into his christology, in that he substituted for the earthly appearance of the Logos the pre-existent and pure soul of the man Jesus. But this concession was made void within the system of Origen, in that he reduced the incarnation to what is ultimately merely a symbol and an act of assistance for ordinary men, so that 'history evaporates' (Harnack). The perfect Christian, who is the true gnostic, has no need of incarnation; he receives the revelation directly in the Platonic, intellectual way through the Logos. Thus Origen maintains a theory of the incarnation which is monophysite in tone, in consequence of which his monist concept of God was bound to develop in a pluralist direction.

The thought of Origen dominated the rest of the third century and once again shows a remarkable similarity to Schleiermacher, in that Origenists were divided into a theological right and left wing. We might call the right wing those who placed the decisive emphasis on the first theme of his christology, the absolute unity of God, whereas the others emphasized the second theme, the subordination of the Logos. Thus in spite of the efforts of individual theologians, such as Methodius of Olympus, to modify the purely philosophical treatment of the christological problem by going back to the ideas of Irenaeus and by a renewed emphasis on the incarnation, in the hope of bringing about a unity of thought, the basis of the severe disputes of the period that followed, with its numerous conflicting opinions, had been laid. In the sharp conflicts which followed, one view of Origen's was pitted against another.

3. The Final Elaboration of the Dogma in the Struggles of the Fourth and Fifth Centuries

Under the rule of Constantine, immediately after the recognition of Christianity by the state, there began the profound dogmatic conflict in the Church, which even at the present day must be regarded as the stage in the history of the Church's doctrine when it was struggling κατ' ἐξοχήν, for the fundamental issues of a precise definition of the Christian concept of God and of the place of the person of Jesus Christ within this concept. The first important part of this struggle, that which is known as the Arian dispute, where the principal problem was the place of Christ, and later of the Holy Spirit, in the being of God, leading to the formation of the dogma of the Trinity, lasted from the beginning to the end of the fourth century. The second stage immediately follows this, and continues in essence up to the middle of the sixth century; the problem here was the more accurate portrayal of the person of Christ, and the relationship of divine and human nature in him. It cannot be denied that these profound disputes brought with them numerous most unpleasant and even very evil moments, particularly as they were carried on at a period when religion and politics were very closely involved with each other, nor that they aroused the most violent personal passions and brought about much hatred, falsehood and wickedness on the part of important churchmen, who to outward appearances were very devout. Thus, from one point of view this dispute forms one of the most painful memories of the whole history of doctrine. But this is not all. It seems that its poisonous effects took root in the Church in such a way that it was never able to be completely rid of them. It is as though it were the prototype of all doctrinal struggles in the Church, and the contentious spirit of those ancient theologians, most of whom— particularly the main spokesmen—were by no means particularly eminent people, never seems to have died out in the Church. On the other hand, the necessity of the struggle cannot be disputed. A clear confrontation between the concerns of faith and conceptions based on the contemporary structure of thought had to be attempted, and this had to take place on such a level that it could be understood not merely by a few eminent philosophers and theologians, but in some way by Christians as a whole. That the formulae which were finally evolved and established were in fact merely forms of words, which concealed in themselves at least as many new problems as had existed before, was something that no one at that period was capable of recognizing, since in any case this is an idea which most people can never appreciate. And in spite of all, the dogma which was in the process of being formed and established in the fourth and fifth centuries was able to fulfil its purpose in the historical task of the Church with decisive success. The impulse that led to this great dispute was the problem of setting Jesus Christ in a relationship to God which was clear in every respect and satisfied every contradictory demand. The Logos christology, which was now fully accepted everywhere, served as a generally recognized philosophical instrument in this process. As we have already said, the ultimate author of this struggle was Origen.

a. The date of the outbreak of the dispute, its immediate cause, and the course of its early stages are not certainly known. However, it seems probable that in the year 318 *Arius* was denounced in Alexandria for heretical pronouncements about Christ, by the Bishop Alexander, who subsequently excommunicated him in 320/321. The doctrine of Arius which was objected to was that God alone existed, uncreated and unbegotten, in perfect unity, whereas the Logos did not form part of his true being, but was the first creation of God in time; this was naturally even more true of the man Jesus Christ, who later in the course of history became united with the Logos. This seemed to him to be the only true guarantee of the unity, transcendence and absolute distinctiveness of God. Thus his dogmatic slogans were: 1. 'The Logos is different from and unlike the being of the Father in all things'; 2. 'The Son has a beginning, but God is without beginning'; 3. 'There was once when he was not, and he was not before he came into being.' These slogans clearly show his speculative interest, his dependence on Origen, and also the playing down of the concern with redemption by contrast with his speculative ideas. After his excommunication and deposition, Arius undertook a journey to the North, to Palestine, Syria and Asia Minor, in the course of which it became obvious that Alexander, who had acted so abruptly and autocratically, by no means represented the general opinion, but that a large number of bishops shared the opinion of Arius, especially the clever Συλλονκιανιστής (fellow-disciple of Lucian the martyr), the bishop Eusebius of Nicomedia. This gave Arius the strength and the courage to return to Alexandria and, in spite of the episcopal ban, to begin to preach again. The result was that the affair in Alexandria turned into a tumultuous struggle which eventually came to the hearing of the Emperor. The Emperor was fully aware that at a period of such spiritual confusion the Church could only be of value and significance to him in his general plans for the outward and inward reconstruction of the Roman Empire if it formed a truly unimpaired unity. First, therefore, he tried to deal with the matter by sending one of his court bishops, Hosius of Cordova, to Alexandria (324). But when this was not successful, the matter was brought before the first General Council at *Nicea* in 325. Under the pressure of the Emperor, who was present himself, and probably above all as a result of the political skill of Hosius, who belonged to the West, and here succeeded in carrying through a dogmatic decision of the West for the first time, the Council established the view of Alexander as dogmatically correct, and condemned Arius, although this result by no means accorded with the view of the majority of Eastern bishops at the Council. The Council accepted a confession of faith made by the bishop Eusebius of Caesarea, who tended to a position between the opposing extremes; but they added to it the crucial and anti-Arian phrases, and, as a conclusion, an explicit condemnation of Arius. It was the wish of the Emperor, and the view of the West, and especially the concept of the ὁμοούσιος (*una substantia*, of the same substance), an expression previously unknown in the East, and avoided by Athanasius himself, which brought about the unity of the Church by force, and obtained the victory of the Origenist right wing among those who adopted a mediating position, although there is no doubt that this view had previously been held only by a tiny minority.

The unity of the Church seemed to have been preserved, and the Church saved and established as a state Church. But it soon became obvious that the unity was only apparent. This was so in spite of the fact that *Athanasius*, who became the real spokesman of ecclesiastical orthodoxy and in fact played a decisive part in the formation of the Church's dogma, had now appeared on the scene. He had been present at Nicea as Alexander's deacon, but had not been a member of the Council. In 326 or 328 he succeeded Alexander. Now he intervened officially and actively in the dispute. Naturally, we have much more accurate information about his theology than about that of Arius. It is in fact based on the concern for redemption, though it must constantly be stressed that he has in mind the Greek idea of redemption, which can by no means be identified with that of Augustine, far less with that of Paul. In spite of this, there is no doubt that, by contrast with Arius, Athanasius continued a different line of Origenist thought, rejected speculations about a mythical demi-God, and maintained the two essential aspects of the unity of God and the person of the Logos. But even his formulae were inadequate, since formulae can never be adequate; this can be seen by the fact that they ignore the whole activity of the man Jesus, which continued to be ignored right up to the time of Luther. And this has been the case in all orthodox teaching, right up to the present day. Further, in his first treatise on the subject he did not make use of the word ὁμοούσιος (*homoousios*); he only gradually became acquainted with this concept. In spite of the intervention of this powerful champion, Nicene orthodoxy declined considerably in the years immediately following. Eusebius of Nicomedia, the clever leader of those who, while not sharing the views of Arius, nevertheless opposed the extreme Alexandrine theology, was able to renew his influence with the Emperor and convince him that the decision taken at Nicea by no means represented the unified view of the Church. Since of course Nicea was an Ecumenical Council, it was not possible simply to issue a command cancelling its decisions. But Eusebius adopted a no less effective method; he brought about the deposition of those who held the orthodox Nicene theology. Thus in 330 Eustathius was deposed, and in 336 Marcellus of Ancyra; and a series of local synods finally succeeded in deposing Athanasius. He went into exile into the West for the first time from 335 to 337. A synod in Jerusalem in 336 declared that the Arian view was the Church's doctrine, and rehabilitated Arius and his followers. This development was then interrupted by the death of Arius (336 in Constantinople) and the death of Constantine which followed shortly afterwards. At the end of this first phase of the struggle the situation had become extremely obscure and confused.

b. The development of the second phase of the Arian struggle, which might be termed a tug-of-war between different opinions, leading up to the establishment of the late Nicene orthodoxy, took place largely under the new Emperor in the East, Constantius, who during the whole period took part in what went on with considerable interest. He himself, it is true, was strongly inclined towards Arianism, and he had no time either for Athanasius or for the western formulae, especially since, as Emperor, he rightly saw in them an attempt by the Church to break away from its domination by the state, and an assertion of ecclesiastical independence and control. But it was only in the last years of his exclusive rule that he was able to impose his will through his court bishops. Yet it was clear from the start that this domination by the will of the Emperor could not last for long, even though the old orthodoxy would have to submit to a certain degree of compromise. The first great synod which took place under Constantius, the so-called Council of the Dedication at Antioch in 341, was entirely under the control of Eusebius of Nicomedia, who held a middle view, and introduced a new formula, which certainly made no concession to the Arian doctrine, but was aimed against a further development of the orthodox view, and reverted to a pre-Nicene conception, with a subordinationist Logos doctrine.

However, this first success on the part of the Emperor did not last for long. The West intervened, and with it the Emperor Constans, whose view followed the western pattern entirely, and in consequence was inclined to be friendly towards Athanasius. The great Imperial Council of Sardica in 343 (?) made it clear that Athanasius, and the West in particular, were powerful factors, and that as long as Constantius was not sole ruler, there was no question of getting the Church to agree on his opinion. The Council concluded with the withdrawal of the eastern bishops, and mutual excommunication. This was a public schism in the Empire and consequently in the Church. To do Constantius justice, it must be recorded that as a result of the imminent danger from the Persians, he did not cling intransigently to his own point of view but, in order to save the Empire, sought to make an approach to the West. The result of this attempt at reunion was a formula produced by a synod at Antioch in 344 which described the Son as ὅμοιος κατὰ πάντα τῷ πατρὶ ('In all things like the Father'), and which, since the Greek word ὅμοιος (*homoios*) meant a great deal more than the English word 'similar', represented a total concession to the West and to Athanasius. The Emperor also permitted the return of Athanasius from his second exile (339-346).

In the meantime, the hard-pressed situation in which the Emperor had found himself had once again been relieved. After the death of his brother Constans and the overthrow of the military revolution of Magnentius, it was no longer necessary for him to take the West into account, and he was now able to guide the course of the doctrinal dispute according to his own views and with the help of his court bishops. His first ecclesiastical enterprises were the two synods of Arles in 353 and Milan in 355, which pronounced against the ὁμοούσιος (*homoousios*) and sent all refractory and unrelenting western bishops into exile (Liberius of Rome, Lucifer of Cagliari, Eusebius of Vercelli, Hilary of Poitiers, and Hosius of Cordova himself). In order to escape a fresh exile in the West, Athanasius withdrew beforehand from Alexandria and went into the Egyptian desert; this was his third exile, from 356 to 362.

The years that followed are characterized by the so-called formulae of Sirmium; the imperial court was for the most part in residence in Sirmium during this period. Great energy was spent in working on formulae of unity, which it is true did not display an unrelieved and extreme Arianism, but were certainly intended to water down the view of the West and of Athanasius as much as possible. The word ὅμοιος (*homoios*) was constantly used, but was not applied to οὐσία (*ousia*), and consequently left wide scope to all opinions. Thus the second formula of Sirmium (327) simply described the Son as ὅμοιος τῷ πατρὶ (*homoios to patri*). But it satisfied neither side. The thoroughgoing and radical Arians were once again active, having found two new and energetic leaders in Aetius and Eunomius; their arguments led to the opposite extreme, and they described the Son as ἀνόμοιος (*anhomoios*), so that they and those who shared their views became known as the party of the Anhomoians. The other side found leaders in the

great Cappadocians, who were perhaps helped in bringing about a real advance by not being tainted by involvement in ecclesiastical politics to the same extent
as Athanasius. The Council of Ancyra which took place
under the spiritual leadership of Basil the Great (358),
once again used the formula ὅμοιος κατὰ τὴν οὐσίαν
('like in being'), which, for the party which had previously occupied an intermediate position between the
other two, was intended to form a bridge to *neo-Nicene
orthodoxy* in the form of homoousianism. The reputation of
this Council and the Cappadocians was so great that
the Emperor agreed with them in the third formula of
Sirmium in 358. This came very close to bringing about
its ultimate acceptance. The fourth formula of Sirmium
in 359 represented a new victory for the term ὅμοιος
(*homoios*) in its ordinary usage, in that it described the
Son as ὅμοιος κατὰ τὰς γραφὰς (*homoios kata tas graphas*
'like according to the scriptures'), that is, as the scripture
teaches, which in fact said everything and nothing.
After the two preparatory Councils of Arimanum and
Seleucia, those of Nicea and Constantinople meant once
again the official imposition of the Emperor's theology,
based on the term ὅμοιος (*homoios*). But this lasted only
for a short time. The death of Constantius brought an
end to this forced unity, and now the *rapprochement* of the
Homoousians and the former Homoiousians could go
ahead, and the result was the neo-Nicene orthodoxy.

The turning point at which this last phase begins was
the Council of Alexandria (362) at which Athanasius
was once again able to be present in person. From then on
the task of restoring unity made rapid progress in spite
of some interruptions. It was brought to a conclusion
by the *Council of Constantinople* in 381, under the
Emperor Theodosius the Great; it did not introduce any
new confession of faith, but simply renewed that of
Nicea, although it so altered the interpretation of it that

the Eastern bishops could now be satisfied with it. This neo-orthodox interpretation, which in essence was that held henceforth by the Church, rejected the extreme form of identity of substance, and replaced it by a unity of substance which implied a likeness of substance in the usual sense of homoousianism. Arianism was condemned for all time. This meant that its death warrant was signed, although it still remained dominant among the Germanic kingdoms for almost two centuries. Not until the conversion of the king of the Franks, Clovis, and the acceptance of the Catholic faith by the Visigothic Church, did it come completely to an end. In the final phase of the Arian struggle the doctrine of the Holy Spirit was fixed, so that the dogma of the Trinity attained its final form.

c. The object of dispute in the *second period* was the other problem which demanded a solution, that of the relationship of divinity and humanity in Christ. It was in fact raised by the Arian conflict, but not decided. The fourth century had already introduced several lines of thought that were to be of use in dealing with it. One can in fact speak of certain types of solution. One is that of the three great Cappadocians, Basil, Gregory Nazianzen, and Gregory of Nyssa, and the other is that of *Apollinaris* of Laodicea. By the energy with which he asserted the unity of Christ, admittedly by denying the presence of the most important part of his humanity, the νοῦς, the latter has had a powerful influence on the whole history of christology, and on the orthodox thought of the Church down to the present day, in spite of his official condemnation. The Cappadocians asserted the two natures of Christ in a much stronger form, and by the concepts of compenetration (περιχώρησις) and mixture (μίξις) sought to establish this view, without being able to make it really comprehensible. Their successors developed a third type, the *neo-Alexandrine theology*, which was put forward by Cyril of Alexandria and returned to Origenist ideas, and in which the crypto-monophysite character of Origen's christology is very obvious; the humanity of Christ remains incomplete. The final type among these mutually conflicting groups is the theology of the Antiochenes, in which a forceful appreciation of the human person of Jesus is a genuinely living force, as a result of their intense preoccupation with the Bible. But they themselves were not capable of presenting a unified doctrine which would make comprehensible the two natures which they asserted with such assurance, so that they were later reproached for teaching that there were two Sons, one pre-existent and one historical. In spite of this, they saved christology from relapsing into pure speculation, and it was due to them that the perfect human nature of Christ was affirmed once for all, at least in principle, by the formula of the Council of Chalcedon (451; *cf.* below).

A distinctive type of christological doctrine appeared during this period in the *West*, which, because of its use in reconciling opposing views, was of very great importance in the vital dogmatic decisions which followed. Tertullian's skill at producing satisfactory formulae underlay this development (*cf. 2b.* above). By the conception of both substances in a single person, the humanity of Christ was safely established, and with the help of Tertullian's background in Stoic philosophy, a reconciliation of ideas was achieved which at least as a formula proved to be a real step forward. They avoided both the danger of the confusion and therefore the changing of both natures, and also the deprivation of one—invariably the human nature—of its essential characteristics. The result of the Arian dispute had been to bring the West into closer communication with the East. It had meant that the West had become acquainted with the Logos christology in its Alexandrine, and especially its

Athanasian form, and had adopted these thoughts into its own formulae. This placed the West in a fortunate position of superiority with regard to the separate and conflicting groups of the East, especially with regard to Apollinarianism and to the Antiochenes. The heavy cost that of course had to be paid for this was that from then on the West also derived the person of Christ from the Logos. But with its skilfully composed formulae it was equipped to exercise a decisive influence on the definitions which were to be made.

The outbreak of the actual conflict was brought about by ecclesiastical politics and the desire for dominance of the bishops of the patriarchical sees. The first phase was conducted by the patriarch of Alexandria, Cyril, and ended with his victory over the patriarch of Constantinople, Nestorius. This ultimately monophysite christology triumphed over the radical dyophysitism of Nestorius; Mary was recognized as θεοτόκος, bearer of God. This first victory was made possible by the Bishop of Rome, Celestine, who also took the part of the patriarch of Alexandria for fear of the rivalry of Constantinople. But the victory of 431 was only a preliminary, and the Formulary of Reunion of Theodoret of Kyrrhos of 433 lasted only as long as Cyril was still there to interpret it in his own sense. The new phase, after Cyril's death, began when the theology of the old monk Eutyches developed the Alexandrine christology to its logical and radical conclusion, and made its monophysite character clear to everyone. Rome now altered course, and after the condemnation of the Council of 449, the so-called 'Robber Council' of Ephesus, obtained at the Council of *Chalcedon*, the fourth Ecumenical Council of 451, the deposition of the successor of Cyril, Dioscurus, and the acceptance of a formula which avoided the two extremes of Eutychianism and Nestorianism, and sought to present a middle way: this speaks of *one* Christ *in* two natures, according to Western theology, ἀσυγχύτως, ἀτρέπτως (without confusion and unchanged, against the view of Eutyches), ἀδιαιρέτως, ἀχωρίστως (undivided and inseparable, against the views of Nestorius), and according to the Alexandrine theology Mary was recognized as θεοτόκος. It is impossible to deny that there is a certain artificiality in the definition of Chalcedon, particularly as it included within itself the elements of the contradictory views which were held to be correct, and in addition introduced the clear Western distinction between person (ὑπόστασις) and nature (φύσις). But from the moment of its introduction it invited the possibility of different interpretations; the formula was not simple enough.

Thus the battle was renewed over its interpretation, particularly as the East saw it as still dyophysite, reviled it as the 'image with two faces', and continued to hold a monophysite view along the lines of Cyril. In what is called the *monophysite* dispute, an attempt was made to bring about a union on the basis of Cyril's ideas in the so-called *Henotikon* of the Emperor Zeno in 482. The consequence of this was a schism with Rome which lasted until 519. Even this formula was not successful in restoring the unity of the Eastern Church, and bringing an end to the monophysite separatist movements which presented so great a threat to the unity of the Empire. The resistance which was at once aroused by the definition of Chalcedon, which brought about schisms under various leaders, especially in Palestine and Egypt, continued, and finally resulted in the foundation of the separate monophysite Coptic, Syrian Jacobite, and Armenian national churches. The monophysites presented a continual threat to the unity of the Empire, until the territory they covered was lost in the seventh century before the advance of Islam. The policy of the Emperors that followed, and especially of Justinian, was a continual attempt to restore and maintain contact between the West on the one hand and, on the other hand, the radical monophysitism and the crypto-monophysite view of the rest of the East. The great difficulty of the task was shown by the theopaschite dispute (as to whether God is able to suffer) and the so-called dispute of the Three Chapters, which Justinian brought about by his edict in 543 against the person and writings of Theodore of Mopsuestia, the writings of Theodoret on behalf of Nestorius and the letter of Ibas of Edessa, and which was understood as an attack on the definition of Chalcedon. In the Ecumenical *Council of Constantinople* of 553, however, Justinian was able, on the basis of the new orthodoxy of Leontius of Byzantium, the most important theologian of the sixth century, to permit a definition to be made. It interpreted the definition of Chalcedon in accordance with ideas of Cyril, and resulted in the restraining of all Western and Antiochene ideas. This represented the culmination of christological dogma in the crypto-monophysite direction mentioned above.

What follows must be regarded as an aftermath, lacking any real importance, as exemplified by the affirmation of two wills in Christ at the Sixth Ecumenical Council at Constantinople (680), resulting from the *monothelite dispute*. Its definition was a simple consequence of the fact that the two natures of Christ were still asserted, but made no change to the virtual denial of his human individuality. The West, in fact, protested at first, but had finally to accede to the doctrinal wishes of the Emperor, especially since the important new churches which had recently been founded accepted the Council of 553, the Anglo-Saxons in 664, and the Franks in 792, 794, and 799; and since in the course of the Western adoptionist dispute, in which Elipandus of Toledo and Felix of Urgel were involved, the Church of the Franks condemned ideas which were derived from the older

Western traditions. The spirit of the Greek Church, and ultimately that of the Alexandrian theology, gradually achieved a doctrinal victory, in spite of the influence of the Western formulae, which had still not been forgotten, and in spite of the fact that it was the language of Tertullian and Augustine which underlay the specifically Western creeds, the Athanasian Creed and the confession of faith of the Lateran Council.

4. The Undisputed Acceptance of Christological Dogma in the East and the Medieval West

a. For the East, the established christological doctrine provided for the future an adequate expression of ecclesiastical life and piety. It was always properly understood only by a few theologians, and never by the Church as a whole, and this is true up to the present day. But it was genuinely derived from the spirit of the Greek Church, which was constantly, therefore, able to recognize itself in this doctrine, and time and again to draw strength from it, even though, or rather because, it had become an incomprehensible mystery to all its members. The $\mu\acute{a}\theta\eta\sigma\iota\varsigma$, the doctrine, that is the christological dogma itself, became as a result of the $\mu\upsilon\sigma\tau\alpha\gamma\omega\gamma\acute{\iota}\alpha$, the mysterious effect and influence of the cult, the very substance of salvation in the Greek sense. This *mystagogia* was brought about by everything in the mystery of the cult right down to the most primitive devices, the images. The historical person of Jesus Christ is absent, as also are the Pauline concepts of sin and grace. The sole aim of salvation is $\dot{\alpha}\theta\alpha\nu\alpha\sigma\acute{\iota}\alpha$ (immortality), to be obtained by deification through the God-man. Only in the most recent period does the way seem to have been prepared in the Russian Church, through the work of Dostoyevsky and others, for a return to Jesus Christ himself and so to his passion.

b. The Greek doctrine had always been an alien element

in the *West*, and remained so. But it had penetrated to the very heart of Western Christian thinking with such elemental force that it has not been possible to remove it up to the present time; and in the future it will never be abandoned by the Roman Church, nor completely forgotten even by the Protestant Churches. One of the reasons for this was the fact that, as we saw, the West played an important part in providing the formal structure of the dogma at the decisive period of its definition. Of even greater effect was the domination of the Greek genius over the whole intellectual world from the time of Alexander the Great until the final decline of the ancient world, an influence which is particularly clear in the thoroughly western thinker Augustine. Finally, however, it must be remembered that the Greek doctrine represents a series of questions and several attempts to answer them, and it is no accident that the first attempts took this form, but a necessary result of the nature of the whole problem. At any rate, there is in the West from the beginning an evident tension, increasing in the course of the centuries, between the doctrine and actual living devotion. Before and during the Middle Ages, these tensions were not sufficiently great to bring to the fore the christological problem as such. But they provide the reason why it was exclusively the West which was the site of the outward and inner development of the Church, and finally created a completely new christology.

Augustine, whose conception of salvation was based on Paul, gave full weight to the idea of redemption from sin, by contrast with the mere hope of ἀφθαρσία (*aphtharsia*, 'immortality' 'incorruption') and in consequence was able to preserve the basic theme of Christianity, and to restore the passion and cross of Jesus Christ to a decisive place in the work of redemption. In consequence, greater weight was laid, at least to some extent, on the human person of Jesus, as well as on the Logos in the mystical doctrine of deification. This remains true throughout the whole of the Middle Ages, during which the Augustinian tradition remained alive in spite of being overlaid and restricted from time to time. For this reason too, the mystical piety which arose in the West in the *Middle Ages* (*cf. Mysticism* V*b*. pp. 378 ff. below), and which continued in post-Reformation and modern Catholicism, was never a purely metaphysical and cosmological mysticism like that of the East, but has always maintained some contact at least with historical reality. This is evident from the paradoxical expression, 'Christ-mysticism'. This reaches its climax in Bernard of Clairvaux, with his 'passionate love of Jesus'. But in spite of the very distinctive forms taken by this movement, especially at the height of the medieval period, and in spite of the fact that scholasticism elaborated christological dogma in every direction, these were side issues which had no effect on the dogma as such, and certainly could not provoke a revision of it. In fact as time went on, devotion turned more and more away from Christ. He became more and more withdrawn; the oppressive conception of the judge of all the world made him more and more inaccessible to practical devotion. The Augustinian tradition was not strong enough to bridge the great gulf. Mary and the saints took his place in satisfying the longing for redemption; mariology replaced christology in the practical teaching and devotion of the Church, just as *mystagogia* had done in the East. And the cleavage between theology and ecclesiastical practice, which by its sacramentalism cut the laity off more and more from the direct knowledge of Christ, did not lead within the Catholic Church itself to the effective tension which was the cause of the new christological development.

5. The Christology of the Reformation and
of Orthodox Protestantism

a. Luther's Reformation brought with it a complete
recasting of the faith and devotion of Christianity, and
therefore also of doctrine, and in its turn of christology.
As is well known, it is a characteristic feature of the
Reformation that Luther did not begin by a rational
criticism of the ancient dogma, as did the parallel dogmatic movements of the end of the Middle Ages and the
beginning of the modern period. What he did was rather
to conceive the Christian faith completely anew in its
basis and nature, which resulted in a complete change of
structure and emphasis in dogmatic theology, without
the need for a detailed criticism at first. Instead of making religious and metaphysical speculations the centre of
faith, Luther, going back to the spirit of Paul, placed
the question of salvation at the heart of Christian
theology, thereby making it a separate and independent
entity, which inseparably linked *soteriology and christology.*
This meant that the *nature* of Christ was related to his
work once and for all. And since this work took place
within history, then Christ in his own person must
always be acknowledged in association with his work,
which is the divine work of salvation within history. There
can be no christological speculation in isolation from
this; all statements concerning Christ must follow
from this fact and be in accordance with it. 'This was the
picture the sophists painted of him, to show how he was
both man and God, counting his arms and legs, and
mixing his two natures together in a marvellous way;
this is only a sophist's knowledge of the Lord Christ,
for Christ was not called Christ because he had two
natures; for what effect has that on me? But he bears this
glorious and consoling title through the office and work
which he took upon himself, and this brought him the
title. That by nature he is man and God is to his credit,

but that he carried out his task besides, and poured out his love and became my saviour and redeemer, it is this that brings me consolation and benefit, for what I am concerned with is that he desires to set his people free from sin. In the first chapter of Matthew the Angel Gabriel tells us that he is to be called Jesus. Not because he is God and man, but because he is to carry out his office and enter into his work of helping us to escape from sin and death. This makes him a man, and for this reason we should also regard him as the head and Lord of Christianity and of all godliness '(Weimar ed. XVI pp. 217 f.). Compare Melanchthon's *Loci Communes* 1521 (ed. Plitt-Kolde, p. 63): '*Hoc est Christum cognoscere beneficia eius cognoscere, non quod isti* (the Fathers) *docent, eius naturas, modos incarnationis contueri*'.

This is the basis of the new christology. But it must be noted that in this christology the work and benefits of Christ are God's work of salvation, the work of God who reveals himself *in him* and not merely through him. It is an apparent deficiency in recent studies of Luther, so fruitful in other respects, that they do not perceive the central position of Christ and therefore of christology in Luther, but say that for Luther Christ is, to sum it up in a few words, merely the last and greatest of God's prophets. If this were true, not merely Luther's christology, but his whole work would ultimately be incomprehensible. But it can be seen from the basis of Luther's thought as we have described it how he was able to transform Christianity. Thus for him the *metaphysical* problems of Greek dogmatic theology present no immediate problem. The conception of divine and human nature disappears. In the work of salvation the Creator and the Redeemer, a divine and human person, is united in a way that can be described as dynamic (and not 'dynamistic'), by contrast to the static conception of Greek metaphysics. This view of Luther's has been described as his 'naïve modalism' (*cf.* v. 2 of his hymn *Ein' feste Burg*), and this is perhaps acceptable so long as one is clear that it is merely an analogy, since the ancient concept of the *modus* was not available to Luther in that form. In the further progress of the work and the theological task of the Reformation, Luther's christology also underwent a development. It was characterized by the doctrine of *ubiquity*, the presence of the body of Christ everywhere, which was worked out during the disputes over the Eucharist (*cf.* Vol. I, *The Eucharist* II, 4). This has been regarded as a defection from his original understanding. This, however, is only partly true. It is certainly the case that once the statements of Luther on the subject, which were occasionally almost grotesque, were taken in a materialistic sense and reduced to dogma as in the later orthodoxy, the doctrine became meaningless. But it does not follow that the utterances, in the sense in which he made them, are to be regarded merely as a manner of speaking. For underlying them is the deepest concern of faith, that of establishing a higher synthesis between the *finitum non capax infiniti* and the *finitum capax infiniti*, which must naturally be resolved in the latter sense. And therefore his christology begins to look like the doctrine of Cyril (*cf.* 3*c*. above) by contrast with the undoubtedly Nestorianizing view of Calvin (*cf.* 5*b*. below), though of course one must remember that categories from the early stages of the history of doctrine are at best only analogies to its later structure. It may be held in this context that Luther's doctrine developed in an adverse direction, and his genuinely naïve use of the technical terms of the Greek doctrine, and especially the doctrine of the two natures, may be quoted in support of this view. But as we have already said, one must remember that these terms represent certain necessities which held good for Luther as for anyone else, and also, in particular, that contemporary philosophy offered no concepts which would be of use to him in expounding his soteriological christology, the dynamism of his christology, so that he was restricted to these ancient means of expression. The philosophy of Kant was the first to provide terms in which the progressive development of a new systematic christology was possible. In the meantime, Lutheran orthodoxy, building on the scholastic framework of Luther's thought rather than its real content, brought about a renewal of the traditional 'high' christology, particularly in the doctrine of the *communicatio idiomatum*, the constant relationship joining the two natures (*cf.* 5*c.* below).

b. The independence of the Swiss Reformation from Luther in basic matters of faith was also demonstrated in christology. The basic principle of a complete reconstruction was accepted. But since other theological traditions from the Middle Ages, and especially from the new humanism, were present in the Swiss Reformation, the structure of its christology was different, and in fact more rational and simpler. This difference was the source of the severe disputes which later took place. *Zwingli*, and later also *Calvin*, did not understand the profound concern of Luther for the doctrine of the ubiquity of Christ. But this is why they failed to break away from the traditions of the Middle Ages. They remained bound by its rationalist categories, which displayed a combination of inner contradictions, but did not represent a real attempt to solve the problem. Thus Zwingli regarded the interchange of predicates between the divine and human natures as a rhetorical confusion of terms (the doctrine of *alloiosis*). In this view, as in the basic principle maintained by Calvin, the *finitum non capax infiniti*, and in what was later known as the *extra Calvinisticum*, according to which the Logos exists entirely outside the human nature, it is clear what is meant by the 'Nestorianism' of Reformed christology. This makes the doctrine of the states of humiliation and exaltation in itself superfluous, but it was later restored because it was traditional. Reformed christology also avoided the difficult christology of Lutheran orthodoxy, derived from the paradoxical statements of Luther himself, in that they would not have anything to do with what Calvin described as the *portenta*, the 'monstrosities' of Luther as such; but this meant that, since they refused to build upon any new foundation and could not call on the help of any new philosophy, they were unable to create a genuinely new christology. They succeeded only in juxtaposing various ancient formulae, and their tendency towards Nestorianism damaged their soteriology, as was rightly recognized by the Lutheran theologians in what was admittedly very often a malicious criticism.

c. In the second half of the sixteenth century and the beginning of the seventeenth century the work carried out on the Formula of Concord and the dispute between the theologians of Tübingen and Giessen, led to the formation of *orthodox Lutheran christology*, which it is true did not lead to a unified view, far less to any real progress. Instead, and in spite of the fact that the New Testament could not be altogether forgotten, it became more and more a parallel to the old christology which in no way improved upon it. The Swabian theologians, following Brenz, clung to the doctrine of the states of humility and exaltation. On the other hand Major, Crell, and Eber of Wittenberg rejected the doctrine of ubiquity. The mediating efforts of Chemnitz, who tried to combine with the doctrine of ubiquity drawn from eucharistic doctrine the historical person of Christ the Redeemer, described in terms of his double status, by making use of the doctrine of the kenosis (the self-emptying of Christ), led on to the Formula of Concord. But the latter simply placed the two theses side by side, and was unable to find any underlying agreement between them. And like the definition of Chalcedon, this formula simply gave rise to fresh disputes. The theologians of Helmstedt did not accept the Formula of Concord, but even those who did were not united. One group tried to impose the pronouncements of Chemnitz as the standard interpretation, against the Swabians. The dispute of the Giessen theologians with those of Tübingen (Mentzer, Hafenreffer) brought about a bitter conflict. The Giessen theologians tried to solve the problem by following Chemnitz in their doctrine of kenosis, and by distinguishing between the possession and use of the divine nature. They recognized that Christ possessed a divine nature, and that these attributes were as it were transferred to his manhood, besides his natural human attributes, but asserted that he renounced the use of his divine nature in his humanity when he was in the state of humiliation. The Tübingen theologians saw in this distinction a division which removed the unity of his person, and consequently defined his self-emptying merely as the concealment of the use of his divine nature. Neither of the opposing parties was able to give a completely logical exposition of its christological views. In order not to degrade the passion of Christ to the level of mere play-acting, the Tübingen theologians had to accept a real self-emptying at least in this case, which meant the abandonment of their basic thesis. The Giessen theologians were unable to overcome the dualism between the Logos and the humanity of Christ, and since they asserted that the Logos still possessed omnipotent power over the whole world during the period of humiliation, they were forced to posit the *extra Calvinisticum*, which as such was impossible for a Lutheran christology. But above all, the distinction between possession and use was itself an illogical feature which not even the Giessen theologians were ever able to apply consistently.

A decision made in the Electorate of Saxony in 1624 attempted to reconcile the two views. It condemned the 'docetism' of the Tübingen theologians, and rejected certain difficult propositions in the Giessen doctrine of kenosis, but in essence accepted the latter. This view therefore had the stronger position, but no solution was reached. The Tübingen theologians maintained their view up to the end of the seventeenth century, but were able to preserve it from the prevailing view of the time only by forbidding discussion. The orthodox theology of the seventeenth century was only able to develop existing ideas in the sense of the decision of 1624, and produced nothing new. The similarity to the situation at the end of the formative period of christological doctrine is obvious. The Catholic dogma was reaffirmed, and the main emphasis was given to the negations of the old doctrine, so that it was not possible to arrive at any genuinely new position. With some justification both Catholics and Protestants characterized the doctrine of the *communicatio idiomatum* as Eutychianism (*cf. 3c.* above). Nevertheless, the orthodox christology of the period, like the whole of orthodox dogmatic theology, must be regarded, by contrast with the repeated attempts made later to re-express its doctrines (*cf. 7b.* below), as a genuine and serious theological effort, but one which was unable to succeed because it still relied on the means provided by the philosophy of the ancient world.

6. *The Breakdown of Christology in the Eighteenth Century*

The roots of the *breakdown of orthodox christology* lie partly in the period before it was set up. For the rationalist tendencies in *humanism*, and also the excessive *spiritualism* of the Anabaptists, inevitably came into conflict with the doctrine of the Trinity and therefore also with christology. But since Zwingli and Calvin belonged to the humanist tradition in a quite different way from Luther and his followers, the seeds of decay can be seen everywhere from the start, even in Reformed christology, especially in the *extra Calvinisticum* and the rejection of *communicatio idiomatum* (*cf.* 5*b*.). A large number of those who opposed trinitarian and christological dogma from various points of view escaped the persecution of the Catholic and the Protestant Churches by taking refuge in Poland. Here Faustus Socini in the Racow catechism (1605) provided *anti-trinitarianism* with a confession of faith which rejected the doctrine of the two natures and the pre-existence of Christ, and subjected the whole dogma to a rationalist criticism. There was no question of a real refutation, far less a reconstruction of the doctrine. Even the heretics did not deny the Virgin Birth, the miracles of Jesus and his physical resurrection. It remains a mixture of the traditional supra-naturalism with rationalist and even biblicist elements. Luther's new faith in salvation had no influence at all in this direction. The general principles of the Arminians led them to deny the union of the two natures in the old doctrine; but they were not able to introduce anything new, or to bring about the breakdown of the dogma by denying that it is necessary to salvation.

The christological dogma was not ultimately refuted by ecclesiastical and theological study or conflicts, but after becoming incapable of sustaining itself in being, it was destroyed by the new world view of the Enlightenment, which went back to the Renaissance and humanism, and was related to ancient philosophy. The preparatory stage (represented by S. J. Baumgarten, Döderlein, and Reinhard) consisted of a cautious supranaturalism which, however, had already simply abandoned the traditional doctrine. The rationalism that followed pictured Jesus as a human being with extraordinary gifts and outstanding moral character, who was therefore to be revered as a religious hero, and who conveyed to mankind a natural religion and especially an ethical doctrine, which in itself, as it was purely natural, could have been found out without him. The intrinsic connection between Christ and the Christian religion was destroyed; faith in salvation and eschatology were replaced by a moralizing and eudaemonist theory of reward (Röhr, Wegscheider, etc.). Weak attempts to develop new lines of approach were made by Semler, Lessing, Jean Souverain, Herder, etc. That the christology of rationalism was not in fact without its effect, is shown by the fact that up to the present day it is the prevailing view among large numbers of Christian lay people.

7. Nineteenth-Century Attempts to Reconstruct Christology

a. Meanwhile, rationalism was not able to defeat the essential nature of Christianity. Even when it seemed outwardly to be at its highest peak, the forces of early idealism, especially in the activity of Hamann and Herder, were at work to overthrow it. Here it was the important concept of the growth and development of an original and intrinsic idea in any historical manifestation, and above all the new consciousness of the factual nature of history, by contrast with the rationalist constructions of human understanding, which shook the edifice of rationalism. Once it had reached its highest point, it was recognized that it offered no hope of progress. It was the task of Schleiermacher to restore the integral association between Christ and Christianity. And it is characteristic of him that he based his work firmly on the Reformation tradition. His christology proceeds from the basic doctrine of the Reformation, systematically worked out for the first time, of the necessary connection between the person and work of Christ, in the context of an ethical doctrine of redemption which dispensed with the doctrine of the two natures. In the Christian's experience of self-consciousness, and in the liberation of the consciousness from enslavement to the senses to share in the consciousness of God, he recognizes the redeeming work of Jesus, and therefore his person. This is, of course, a construction 'built up from below'. The Redeemer takes the believers into the sphere of influence of his own consciousness of God, and this can only be understood if this consciousness of God is itself perfect in him, if God himself is in him. This Schleiermacher expresses by the idea of Christ as the archetype rather than as a pattern for imitation (*cf.* III 2*a*. below). But this archetype is described as 'unfathomable perfection'. The human development of Jesus has to be understood both archetypally and historically. Further, Schleiermacher was the first to give a systematic justification for rejecting the association of the resurrection, ascension, and eschatological expectation of the second coming with the person and work of Christ, in the same way as he also disassociated the doctrine of the Trinity from the body of dogmatic theology properly so called.

Schleiermacher's christology at once became the centre of discussion. Violently opposed to the earlier points of view (supra-naturalism and rationalism), it was followed by many younger thinkers, in spite of the excessive and unjustified criticism of D. F. Strauss (*Glaubenslehre* II, 1841, p. 180 f.). who compared it to a worthless and flimsy modern structure contrasted with an old castle which was dilapidated but an abundant source of useful material. The influence of Schleiermacher's christology is explained by the fact that in the course of his development he himself took a constantly more positive attitude to individual details of the doctrine, and by orientating his doctrine on the Creeds and confessions of faith he reintroduced material from the traditional dogma, albeit in a much altered form. In this way he actually prepared the way for the false attempts to reaffirm the older dogmatic theology, which failed to understand the completely different basis of his thought.

b. There arose a kind of right wing among Schleiermacher's supporters, whose christology seemed extraordinarily close to that of the older orthodoxy. The *Restoration* which manifested itself everywhere at the beginning of the nineteenth century in revivalist movements, in romanticism, and in the fragments of orthodoxy salvaged from the period of rationalism, itself played a part in the renewal of the old doctrine, but soon turned energetically against Schleiermacher (Hengstenberg). For it at once became clear, particularly when an attempt was made to reconcile his view with the older doctrine, that his 'construction built up from below' was completely opposed to it, in spite of every attempt to bridge the gap; and it was also notably evident that Schleiermacher's view did not give due place to the basic Reformation concept of salvation, to the ideas of justification and atonement, nor to the historical person of Jesus. Thus those who themselves had been disciples of Schleiermacher reacted violently against him and returned to the older christology (K. J. Nitzsch, Twesten, Umbreit, Ullmann, Martensen, R. Rothe).

A new stimulus to christology was provided by *speculative and idealist* philosophy. Its assumptions were basically those of ancient Platonic idealism, and on this foundation it reaffirmed the ancient Logos doctrine in its cosmological form. In this way it prepared the way for the revival of the 'high' christology. It is true that one form of this philosophy was consistent in developing only the speculative aspect of this approach, making Christ the bearer of the idea of the unity of God and man, and consequently treating everything on the level of a metaphysical idea, in spite of taking into account at first the historical person of Jesus; this school saw christological dogma as a preparatory form of an idea which could adequately be attained by human thought (Schelling). The proper consequence of this view was a radical rejection of the older christology. On the other hand, from this point of view the older doctrine had to be recognized as being of value, because it contained, prefigured, and prepared the way for a most important understanding. Thus Hegel concluded that the conviction of the incarnation of God in a human being, Jesus Christ, was necessary for the non-speculative consciousness. The right wing among Hegel's followers took up this idea, asserting against the conclusions of D. F. Strauss that the essence of the idea included the absolute significance of its appearance as an individual phenomenon; and from this they deduced the necessity of a personal God-man (*cf.* Rosenkranz). In this way speculative philosophy came to provide the principal support for the renewal of ecclesiastical dogma.

It was not possible, however, for the matter to end here. It was recognized that the essentially cosmological approach of speculative philosophy made it unsuited to play a decisive part in the formation of christology. And in any case, the attempt merely to re-express and reaffirm the traditional doctrine (Philippi) remained isolated, since it was impossible merely to ignore the changes in the whole intellectual situation since the eighteenth century. Even the *new 'orthodox' theologians* had to look for a new method of approach. This they found in the doctrine of kenosis, set forth in different ways by such theologians as Liebner, Sartorius, Gottfried Thomasius, Gess, F. H. R. Frank, etc. The most thorough-going advocate of this doctrine was Gess. He went so far as to assert the complete self-emptying of the Logos, and a development of this consciousness during the human development of Jesus. This was not merely, in Biedermann's malicious words, a 'complete kenosis of understanding', but also a heresy more monstrous than even Arianism had dared to propound. It was a quite obvious tritheism, that is a form of polytheism; no one had previously gone so far as to speak of a development in God himself. But the degree of recognition obtained by this monstrous christology casts an illuminating light, in a way, on the situation that has lasted up to the present day. Because it was based on the 'high' christology which Luther, of course, had so energetically rejected, it was regarded by comparison with other attempts as 'orthodox' and acceptable.

c. The attempts in the nineteenth century to reaffirm christology and traditional theology as a whole, which for the most part must be regarded as thoroughly reactionary, had a powerful influence on the official teaching of the Church, as much as on the circles which gave rise to these attempts and supported them. Rationalism was completely demoted from its position in the Church. The attempts to set up a *liberal theology* (Biedermann, Lipsius, Pfleiderer), carrying on the traditions of the Enlightenment, as well as those of Schleiermacher and Hegel, had too little religious force to obtain wide acceptance. The name is ultimately true of the so-called *mediating theology* of H. Weiss and Beyschlag. But since the christology which had regained its hold over the official Church represented in essence merely a reaffirmation of the old doctrine which was in most respects very unsatisfactory (it was a 'high' christology which had not been thoroughly worked out in dogmatic terms, and contained a number of very unsubtle formulae), it has itself, like the movement of religious revival which forms an historical parallel to it, played a large part in opening up the wide gulf which for several generations has separated the official Church, and small groups of orthodox and pietistic laity, from the large majority of baptized Christians. The collapse of the Hegelian system and the rise of positivism and materialism in intellectual life and culture was soon, however, to take away all support and approval in leading intellectual circles for the reaffirmation of traditional christology, unless there was some impulse to maintain it for the sake of tradition, or for the non-religious or political motives.

The last third of the nineteenth century experienced the beginning of a completely new atmosphere. Behind this lay on the one hand the philosophy of Kant, which did not really become effective until now, and on the other side the ever-increasing preoccupation with history. The precursors of this approach were the Tübingen school of F. C. Baur, with their deep concern with the history of primitive Christianity and the development of doctrine, and also the Erlangen school (F. H. R. Frank, von Hofmann) with their close concern with the picture of Jesus presented by the New Testament. The first really new attempt at a christology on a Reformation basis was made by *Albrecht Ritschl*. His thought derived from the Tübingen school, and he was influenced by Kant and Schleiermacher, but the most important factor in his thought was his adoption of the true position implied by the basic Reformation idea of Luther; thus his christology was provided with a sound *theological* basis, while he also made use of the genuinely scientific philosophy of Kant in developing it. Thus he was able to lay the foundations of christology which, in spite of the sharp opposition it aroused among both conservative and liberal theologians, represented a genuine carrying forward of the suggestions made by Schleiermacher, and a new approach on the basis of Reformation thought. For while he firmly associated the Protestant understanding of salvation with the person of Christ, which is irreconcilable with the doctrine of the two natures in its metaphysical form, he related his whole doctrine to the revelation of God in the historical Christ. In the content of Jesus's calling he recognized his divinity, the full revelation of the love of God, which was able to be manifest in a truly human life as a demonstration of the merciful disposition of God towards men in the form of his grace and faithfulness. There was no room here for theories about the physical constitution of the God-man and the pre-existence of the Logos, since faith in salvation is only concerned with God who has revealed himself in the historical Christ. There is no doubt that for the first time a step had been taken in a new direction in christology, which can be seen from the fact that Ritschl's christology not only influenced his own direct followers but, in spite of the bitter charges of heresy which were made against him, is nowadays held to be entirely orthodox, although his name is not always mentioned in connection with it. It avoided both dangers of speculation and of rationalism. Thus the christology of Ritschl, in association with the study of the history of doctrine (as in the work of A. Harnack), which he strongly encouraged, has meant a great and positive step forward towards the replacement of the traditional dogma. Although it is frequently denied by scholars themselves, the most recent theological work on the subject often goes back to the ideas of Ritschl, through the influence of his great disciple and colleague, Wilhelm Herrmann. It must nevertheless be admitted that, however important the steps he took in this direction, he never exhausted the fullness and profundity of the fundamental Reformation insights of Luther, especially in the association of christology with the concept of God (*cf.* III, 2*b.* below) and consequently with justification and atonement.

These are the great tasks which still remain for a truly Protestant christology, capable of forming a nucleus of a dogmatic theology and of providing the basis for the discussion of all other theological questions, especially for such urgent present-day problems as that of the absolute truth of Christianity. If such a christology is ever to gain acceptance, it must be in the true spirit of the Protestant Church; that is, it must do justice to the full faith with all its consequences, and at the same time not be in conflict with the contemporary intellectual situation.

HERMANN BAUKE

III CHRISTOLOGICAL DOCTRINE

1. Methodology

We shall begin by considering methodology; at the same time we shall discuss christological statements in order according to the method they employ.

a. Just as *speculative* and *idealistic* christology (*cf.* II, 7*b*. above), in spite of their considerable value in general, have gradually ceased to be convincing, so also has the traditional *dogmatic and deductive* approach, which proceeded from the consideration of the attributes of God himself (*cf.* II, 3-5 above) and the pre-existence of Christ to his earthly life. In such a christology revelation must be regarded principally as the making known of eternal and divine relationships, that is, as a knowledge which goes back behind history and has a doctrinal authority. But we do not directly possess knowledge which goes behind history, but only the concrete historical phenomenon as it manifests itself in history. Any attempt to renew the speculative and deductive point of view will always break down on the gospel itself. Luther himself (*cf.* II, 5*a*. above) warned against speculation.

Equally inadequate is the *inductive* procedure which is

in a sense the opposite of the above, that is, the attempt to work out the significance of Jesus by a summary of all the historical effects he has brought about. Such a study, based on the *history of thought*, is perfectly justifiable; but even when it is brought to the level of a fine art through the use of a sophisticated understanding of religious psychology and the comparative history of religion, it cannot provide an adequate approach to the innermost being of Christ. In such a study, attention is first directed to what has effectively been attained in the course of history, and the description of Christ is based upon these attainments, on the tangible and known effects he has brought about. This assumes not only that these effects can in some sense be regarded as finished and complete, but also that the extent of these effects in fact depends on the person who gave rise to them and the extent of his personal activity. Now it is certainly possible to speak of the extent and limits of the person of Christ, when he is seen as an historical phenomenon restricted to what is possible within a given human life, but this extent and limitation is fixed by the form that life took, not its inner content. In any case, the gospel blames the limitations which restricted the historical success of Jesus's mission on those who refused to receive him: 'You refused to come to me.' And with this blame the gospel associates judgement. Thus faith can see effects which are outside the purview of the history of human thought; only faith is capable of judging rightly what are the limits of the effects of Jesus's life that have occurred in history. Faith does not consider that these limits are in any way opposed to the complete authority which Christ possesses over history and over this present age, any more than it regards the mere fact of the unlimited power and effect of Christ as in itself capable of proof. What is decisive for faith is not the greater or lesser effectiveness of Christ's mission, but its meaning. Historical effects are relative, because human life is relative; that is why they can deceive the eye which does not see beyond them. For this reason, the point of view adopted by Schleiermacher with regard to the whole of Christian life does not seem methodologically satisfactory. He himself emphasized that the power of Jesus's consciousness of God is always realized in human life as a whole. In this judgement, therefore, he already assumes faith in Christ.

The simple *historical and critical* study of the life of Jesus (*cf.* Vol. I, *Jesus Christ*) brings us no nearer our goal. The great esteem in which this method used to be held has been much affected by the present-day reaction against historicism, and rightly so. For it is bound up with insoluble questions of detail, beyond which it cannot go; these matters of detail affect the understanding of the whole and make it problematic. And our concern is with the central question and its significance for us. It is more and more widely recognized that the understanding of the central issue of christology demands assumptions which are not provided by the formal function of critical studies; that, for example, without the acceptance in faith of the overriding claim of Jesus it is not possible to obtain a thorough historical understanding of his claim or to judge his place in the history of religion. Historical criticism is a valuable tool; but its value depends upon how it is used, in what spirit and by whom.

The attempt to produce a more general *ethical* portrayal of Christ in isolation from the more limited vision of faith, in order to present an account of him which might be accessible to a wider circle, is in fact also impossible. Jesus himself would have rejected it, because his ethical ideal and his ethical powers are only to be understood as the expression and affirmation of his unity with God, not as the basis of that unity. We can only understand the ethical content of his work on the basis of his lofty task and of everything that was bestowed upon him. The truth of his ethical ideal cannot be perceived by someone who does not regard himself as united by him with God. In itself, the ethical thought of Jesus would be very great and significant, but enigmatic and difficult to understand and consequently subject to doubt. The ethical account of Jesus cannot be isolated from that given by faith, but must form part of it, as one aspect of it. Yet we must bear in mind that faith itself must have a clear picture of the ethical side of the work of Jesus.

b. From the point of view of *faith*, Christ has to be understood according to the meaning of his mission. Thus he demands a decision, a personal answer and attitude, obedience and total devotion. He demands all this for God, by demanding it for himself. Only this inner confrontation can open our eyes to him, to his work and to his person. We thereby attain to a knowledge which comes under the two categories of salvation and revelation, which cannot be separated from one another; so that we can say that it comes under the one category of the revelation of salvation, which gives us the choice between life and death and touches the very foundation of our existence. It is not a natural or impersonal form of knowledge, for it is not concerned with an impersonal relationship; it is a knowledge drawn from the situation of salvation in which we have been placed, a knowledge drawn from faith (*cf.* the saying of Melanchthon: *Christum cognoscere hoc est beneficia eius cognoscere*; *cf.* also II, 5*a*. above). No statement purporting to convey knowledge of Christ should be made which precedes faith or is isolated from it, for this would bring us back to dogmatism and intellectualism, which are both equally remote from the biblical gospel. Paradox alone is not enough; the leap into the dark of which faith consists is not a meaningless commitment to a paradox which the intellect finds attractive, but a turning to Christ and to the heavenly Father. The more wonderful his fellowship with God appears in the eyes of faith, the more deeply meaningful it appears. The sole decisive element is the position of Christ which sets up this fellowship with almighty God. In Christ, faith knows that it stands in a new absolute relationship to God, that of his child; this relationship is something complete, however little or however much its temporal effects may be limited. In this relationship the Mediator is not a source of division, but of union; he does not take away direct access to the Father and direct association with him, but brings them into being once for all. The true task of christology is to describe this; the greatest achievement of those who have taught the Christian faith has been to understand and recognize this problem. But all have failed to solve it, and fail even now.

The knowledge obtained in faith, however, cannot consist of a conclusion about Christ based on the inner experience of what he is carrying out, for it would be impossible to avoid a purely relative judgement in such a procedure. However large the subjective element of faith may be, it must by virtue of its origin be orientated towards Christ, on whom the absolute relationship of a child of God is based. The experience of faith is not worthless, and points towards Christ; but what is important is that it directly comprehends and so recognizes and accepts the claim and the authority of Christ, including what he carried out in his earthly life. Nor is the right approach that of working back from the glorified Christ. For faith, the glorified Christ is the Christ who struggled and suffered upon earth, and was crucified. The true task of christology is an *overall view*. The *historical* Jesus must at the same time be understood in his *supra-historical* significance, which is what Luther means in his solution drawn *ab humanitate* (*cf.* II, 5*a*. above).

Faith does not proceed from the man Jesus to his God, but sees Christ directly as defined by God, that is, in the light of God, and also in his relationship to God, seeing God in the light of Christ. Faith sees in Christ one who acts in the name and the power of God. In place of a construction based on logical deduction, or an inductive view from a consideration of all the historical phenomena, the *synthetic* view of faith enables us to look rightly at Christ and the meaning of his mission. Faith understands that, even when knowledge has been obtained, it remains faith. The way of gnosis, a knowledge alleged to go beyond faith, is rejected for the sake of faith itself. It is another matter to think out and work out in full the inner structure and basis of God's revelation in Christ, as far as this is possible, and in so far as it does not obscure concentration on the one thing which really matters, which is above all the concentration on the unity of the personal life of Christ, which is the foundation of faith.

The *person and work* of Christ form a single reality, and consequently point to and illuminate each other. The work of Christ assumes his personality; his personality is only consummated in his work. When it is described as bringing revelation, atonement, or redemption, both aspects are expressed in these terms. And by contrast to the intellectualism of traditional theology, faith also knows that its *knowledge is limited*. It remains content to understand the salvation brought in Christ, and Christ who brings salvation, and to let the way this is done remain a mystery known only to God. What we can know is the life of Jesus as it is turned towards us, in which God's approach to us is made effective; on the other hand, his life as it is turned towards God, his intimacy with the Father, and the life of prayer which gave him power to bring God close to us, remains a mystery. This is something unique, which maintains its inexhaustible originality even when it is possible to share in its fruits. Wherever it has been supposed possible to have a full and complete knowledge of the nature of Jesus Christ, it has always been too easy to give the impression of no longer needing to be concerned with him.

Finally, does the *relativity of the sources* not imply the relativity of Christ? If something can be the object of historical investigation, does it not itself become relative? It is true that an historical account or description is relative. But is this also true of the person they describe? The innermost essence of a person lies beyond the grasp of historical study, and indeed of any definite knowledge. Thus it is possible for the relativity of the historical source, with all its accidental features, to testify to the absolute nature, beyond this relativity, of the person it describes. A fragmentary source can be a true expression of faith in the supreme authority of Christ by contrast with everything human. The highest achievement of faith is to do equal justice to what is relatively human, and that in the picture of Christ which possesses the character of a transcendent revelation surpassing everything relative, in spite of all tensions between the two.

2. The Person of Christ

a. Statements concerning the person of Christ are not meant to explain it, but seek to understand and name the fundamental points of view from which an understanding can best be obtained. An important feature of the formula of Chalcedon (*cf.* II, 3*c.* above) was the determination with which the tension in the nature of Christ, its duality, was expressed in all its severity. Because it renounced all attempts to understand (as is shown by the negations) it did not carry out the service to faith which was required of it. It was not successful in making possible a picture of a truly personal life. In recent Protestant theology (*cf.* II, 7 above) great emphasis has been laid on the necessity of achieving an approach to the understanding of Christ which will cast light on his *personal* life. But there is always a danger that this may be done at the expense of the tension mentioned above. This is true of Schleiermacher's attempt to understand Jesus as the archetype, the fulfilment, the perfection, the fundamental act of human nature, the second Adam. He is an archetype in the sense that he manifests the immanent truth, the metaphysical profundity of human nature. But this does not explain why the archetype is not realized more frequently, at least under the influence of Jesus. If, instead, the Redeemer is regarded as *unique* and possessing an exclusive status, this is clearly because of the desire of the faith of the Church to exalt him, just as the presentation of him as an archetype results from a speculative view of the world. The complexity, but also the fascination of this christology, results from the failure to reconcile religious and philosophical interests. The religious evaluation of Christ appears artificial, and not an intrinsic part of the whole construction, because it is carried out with inadequate conceptual tools. By contrast, in Paul the idea of the second Adam (*cf.* I, 3 above) is by no means the principal element in his christology, but forms merely a subsidiary concept. In its place it is valuable, in that it draws attention to the importance of Jesus's obedience: he has shown the obedience which has been refused by the sons of Adam. Other similar explanations exist on the same lines, without following the particular theory of Schleiermacher. Since all difficulties are skirted, one becomes even more conscious of the absence of the tension caused by the duality in the picture of Jesus. This is true of the school which regards him as a religious *genius*, a view which is attractive to many because it appears to do justice to what is most distinctive in him, and at the same time to avoid a rigorous exclusiveness. The messianic consciousness of Jesus is regarded as the product of his contemporary environment. Behind it stands a religious genius with a profound and original vision of God, which contains its own truth and is self-verifying. We are right to hold the genius, and notably the religious genius, in high esteem; his mission comes from God the Creator, the Lord of history, and he can put it at the disposal of mankind either out of a desire for self-glorification or in a purely selfless way. We could regard Jesus as a religious genius if his nature could be seen purely from the strength and profundity of his consciousness of God, that is, in his personal religion, and even if the way he was moved and directed by God meant that he was in no way distinctive and was of the same nature as is common and fundamental to all mankind. His importance for us in this case would lie only in his understanding and the power of his inspiration, not in a special, underlying and continuous relationship with God. It is a different matter when we turn to the question of the basis of the defeat of sin and the setting up of a new fellowship with almighty God; here it is recognized that the certainty of this fellowship depends on a *decisive act of testimony to himself by God.* A genius can arouse enthusiasm like a hero or an ideal; but Christ brings us face to face with the inescapable reality of God, who simply demands man for himself. He brings us prostrate before the holiness of God, forces a choice upon us, and thereby makes life in the sight of God a heavy burden; but at the same time he resolves the choice, takes away the burden, and is the embodiment and assurance of the redeeming and holy love of God, and gives us access for ever to fellowship with him.

b. If we are looking for an approach to the understanding of Jesus from the reality of his historical life and work, we do best to go back to the personal and unique title of *messianic Son of God* (*cf.* I, 1*a.* above). In the first instance, this title contains a claim to a unique vocation granted to one person alone, and of exclusive character, a claim to be understood in oneself, and not in relation to other groups. This forms a stumbling block to reason, which thinks in classes and categories, and to the point of view of the philosophy of history. But anyone who has come to the conclusion that Christ is more than a religious genius must be ready to tolerate this stumbling block. Again, the title contains a claim to an essential and unique duality, beyond rational understanding and full of tension. It comes to us out of a concrete historical process, and refers to a particular historical figure; at the same time, however, it points beyond history, and links this single historical figure in a unique way with the life of God, and with his dealings with humanity; someone who is one man among others is isolated from the rest of humanity, and all salvation is traced back to him alone. The task of the understanding of faith is to do justice to this duality, both to the form of a servant and to the authority of the messianic Son of God, extending over all history. The power of God is revealed in human weakness. We possess the gospels, in order that we can bow down before reality as it is.

We have gone beyond the traditional doctrine of the Church in that we perceive the duality in the nature of Jesus Christ as a unified *personal life*. Any explanation we give of the person of Christ must be based on this fact. Thus we cannot accept the doctrine of the impersonality of Christ's human nature. The most human and most personal thing we know of is faith and prayer. Jesus practised a living faith and prayer. There is of course a mystery here; as the subject of this activity of faith, he is the object of our faith; this man exercises divine authority. His faith and his prayer are a sign that he constantly receives from God, and maintains a constant subordination to him. In everything he does, he seeks the guidance and help of the Father in prayer. Even in his mighty acts of salvation he relies entirely on the Father. He is aware that he has received miraculous powers from the Father only so far as it was necessary to carry out his messianic task. His miracles were given to him in order to arouse faith, which is why they are unacceptable to obstinate unbelief, and are denied to the crowd that is seeking for a sign. He humbly admits that he is not able himself to promise a place on his right hand and on his left hand in the Father's kingdom. His prayer of intercession for the wavering faith of Peter and for the Jews who rejected him gives honour to God alone. The intervention in history and the inauguration of the kingdom of God are acts of God alone; the task of Christ is the vital historical preparation in which the forces of the kingdom are visibly effective. This, it is true, is so decisive that Christ is constituted as the representative of God at the final judgement. The task of Christ is redemption at the final judgement, the bringing of salvation and the setting up of the kingly rule of God over men and the human conscience. He demands penance and repentance of men, and carries out his redemption through the word of forgiveness. It is true that he never spoke this mighty word without being certain that it was the will of God, a certainty given to him in prayer; that is, he spoke it only in the name of the Father. This was something quite without precedent, as his opponents rightly pointed out. For forgiveness of sins is the privilege of God. It would be possible to regard Christ, with his pronouncement of forgiveness, as still belonging to the category of the prophets. But in so far as he is distinguishable from the prophets as the Son of God, he possesses something more. He has not merely pronounced the forgiveness of sins, but his word of forgiveness has become powerful, in that in his own nature he embodies God's desire to forgive, because in his own person the holy grace of God is effectively brought to us. The unique and unprecedented thing is that his word pronounces what his person effectively brings about in historical circumstances; through his own person he leads the sinner into the death which is the way to life. In this, the deepest significance of his faith and prayer is concealed. It is his faith, in which he is so abandoned to the Father in prayer, that he can offer himself to men as a pure expression of the holy love of the Father, and can even submit to the misery and desolation of human life in order to deliver mankind from it. Wholly sanctified by the Father, he utters his word of forgiveness in such a way that it arouses faith and overcomes our consciousness of sin. Thus he leads us to the Father, by calling us to himself, and unites us directly with God by uniting us to himself.

As one who underwent the moral experience of an historical human life, as one who believed and prayed, Jesus was exposed to *temptations* (*cf.* Vol. I, *Jesus Christ*). There are stages in the moral life. At its higher stages, the temptations of the lower stages fall into the background. The inner struggle of Gethsemane was not the ordinary earthly fear of pain or death, but the messianic fear of one who understood that death is a judgement hanging over a sinful humanity. Thus Christ had to face messianic temptations, that is, temptations which lay beyond the moral limits of human life, which he who was designated as the Messiah had to resist and overcome alone, which were aimed at his mission and which, according to the account at the beginning of the synoptic gospels, arose from Jewish ideas of the Messiah. He conquered these temptations; his constant turning to God upheld him as the danger grew greater. We have all good reason to lay great stress on his faithfulness, his very personal and active self-abandonment to God.

He is only Christ if he resisted the utmost temptation, and otherwise he is not Christ. Consequently, the disciples know that their salvation is based on what was carried out in the life of one who was sinless. This is a judgement of faith, which is constantly produced by the encounter with Christ. His messianic work and sin are mutually exclusive. His power to bring us into fellowship with the Father depends on his *sinlessness*, that is on his own original, constant, and fundamental fellowship with the Father. The only judgement possible to one reconciled with God through his sacrifice is that he offered a spotless sacrifice. The very personality of Jesus leads to the unmistakable conviction that anyone who denies his own sinfulness is involved in a lie and a self-deception (Ullmann). This confirms our faith in the claim of Jesus that we shall all come face to face with him as our judge. Thus his work is a human act and the work of God at one and the same time, in an indivisible unity.

But we must look more closely into the *act of God in Christ*. It is true that Jesus committed himself totally to the saving will of God, and abandoned himself to God in complete freedom; but in doing this he did not merely receive the help of God in individual actions, but knew that he was completely taken up and penetrated by the power and love of God. It was his attitude of faith which made him conscious of being so imbued by God; this is a relationship to which we possess a distant analogy in the relationship of moral authority. The form taken by his personal life of faith and prayer is due to the way in which he is enfolded and enveloped by the Father. The traditional doctrine of the Church was wrong in denying personality to the human nature in Christ, but it contained one correct implication which it was unable fully to express with the conceptual means available: the will which receives and accepts from another knows that, by the reception and affirmation of what is given, it is rooted in the will of the giver. It is only possible for Jesus in his personal reality to convey to us the judgement and the grace of God directly, without our having to take a further step from him to God, because his personal life is one drawn from the innermost being and will of God, and because it has its real basis in God's innermost being and will. This basis and foundation in God is of course such that it guarantees the true freedom of Jesus's personal life, and is expressed in the form of personal faith. And it is an original relationship, not one which was first brought about by the bridging of a gap, but rather one in which the self-giving of the Father responds to the wholly pure self-giving of the Son. Our faith, which in turn is a personal self-giving, can understand the way in which this personal life can be drawn originally and fundamentally from God, however much it may be a mystery and a miracle to us. Our faith in this is strengthened by the statements in the Gospel of John that the Son carries out the works of the Father, and that his word is the word of the Father which he obediently carries out. The truth contained in Luther's doctrine of the *genus majestaticum* also becomes clear: if our picture of Christ presents us with a vision of the holy love of God, then it cannot consist merely of human virtues carried to a higher pitch; thus we must be able to look in it for the grace and the faithfulness of God making themselves available to us in the human figure of the Saviour.

It has been supposed that the only alternative to the traditional theocentric christology of the Church was an anthropocentric christology. For example, A. Ritschl (*cf.* II, 7c. above) sought to present the human personality of Jesus as the separate and independent embodiment of all his functions, and to see in the revelation of the grace and faithfulness of God no more than the content of the life of that personality. He suggested that, where the personal life of Christ was regarded as being continually embodied in God or the Logos, there was a danger of reducing it to a mechanism. This might perhaps be true in the case of a non-Christian concept of

God, similar to that of the ancient world. But in general, this is a view which once again brings an uncertainty into the religious evaluation of Christ, by subordinating it in some respects to a purely ethical evaluation, and letting the one replace the other. Both must originally form a unity. A revelation of God which is merely the content of a human life, and not its whole form, is not a *self-revelation* of *God*. In any case, the object of Christian faith is a revelation of God which, being a free act of God, requires to be identified with a personal human life giving itself in complete freedom. The traditional theocentric christology, based on the doctrine of the two natures, and fraught with great difficulties, cannot be replaced by an anthropocentric christology, but only by a theocentric christology which is nearer to the truth and which does justice to the testimony of the gospels.

Consequently, the unity of Jesus with God appears to us not merely as a unity of intention or will, to be understood in ethical terms; we have to speak of a *unity of being in the Spirit*, which is what makes the Son the representative of the Father to men. A prophet, of course, is equipped with the power of the Spirit by God for every task; but the Father makes himself accessible to the Son with his innermost being and Spirit, and gives himself directly, with his innermost being and Spirit, for fellowship with the Son, so that a relationship of mutual knowledge and love comes about; the Father is glorified in the Son, and the Son glorifies the Father. The Father gives himself to him, in order, in him, to give himself to sinful mankind, whom he loves in the Son, and thus in him to give his whole heart to sinful humanity. Christ is the historical and personal bearer of the Spirit of God, the saving will of God made flesh, the mediator in whom God carries out and realizes his self-giving to the world.

3. The Work of Christ

The mission of the person of Jesus is fulfilled in his work. The unity of his person is expressed in the unity of his work. The goal of the work of Jesus is the believing Church; its goal, in short, is faith. Faith sees this work in its proper context, and it also sees it as a present activity, complete and incomplete at once. It is widely accepted today that his life and his death form an intrinsic unity. His life itself was one of suffering; suffering shared with humanity for the sake of humanity, the bearing of a burden (of guilt), a sacrifice, a service, and a redemption; and his death was also such an act, an offering of himself to God, the highest act of faith—which does not mean that his death does not play a special part in the whole. As far as his *death* is concerned, there are two one-sided views which we must avoid. There is on the one hand the view which regards it in formal and ethical terms, as a test of Jesus's faithfulness to his calling, an act of pure heroism; and on the other hand there is the purely objective view, according to which the main effect was that of changing God's mind, as it were, by diverting the anger of God against men to Christ and so allaying it. In this purely objective view, the nature of the faith which is demanded in Christ is altered; it is intellectualized. But by contrast with the religious environment of the ancient world, the New Testament does not proclaim that God was appeased, but that God was at work in Christ to reconcile the world to himself.

We can sum up the work of Jesus in a single expression. It was *an act of holy love bearing our sins.* He has called us all to himself, because all are sinners. When as the emissary of the Father he pronounces the word of forgiveness, it applies in the first place to the individual whom he meets face to face. But before he invites all to come to him, he has identified himself with the distress of all in the baptism of his death. This is an assumption on which the pronouncement of forgiveness is based. As the servant of God he shares life and death with his people, and as the servant of God he desires to take the burden of his people on to himself; thus he accepts the cross as the necessary consequence of his actions. What some individuals heard personally from his own lips, we others experience in the cross, because it is the cross of the servant of God which speaks directly to us, and in which God deals directly with us. In his cross, Christ forcibly brings the holy love of God into human life for all time. And in the cross of Christ God reveals his holiness and his love to every heart. For Christ, the distress of his people is from the first the distress of humanity—and when the tempter tempted him, he promised him power over all the kingdoms of the world and their glory.

The *substitutionary part* played by Christ, by which he carries out what was not possible to others, must, according to the gospels, be understood in an inclusive sense. In the first place, he is the representative of God, in whose name he acts and suffers. Then he is the representative of those whom he unites with himself as their head. He takes on himself the lot of those who are burdened and in distress. 'For you' is the watchword of his life and death. This is the meaning of the service which he presents as the essential standard of the kingdom of God.

In his *willingness to die* the service carried out by Christ attains its highest form. He took the cup from his Father's hand and accepted God's purpose of salvation through his death, once he had become certain of the δεῖ, the intrinsic necessity of this, through the prophecy of the Old Testament and the guidance of God. The *cross* reveals how the love of God is separated from us and united with us; it reveals that the love and self-giving of God is absolute and utterly inflexible. The cross also asserts the inviolable sanctity of this love, which gives itself without reserve. Christ died on the cross so that he could enter into the deepest distress of human life, into the pain of death, the angry destiny which awaits all mankind. He, who is without sin, and who identified himself with sinful humanity, faced and shared in the reality of death as a judgement on human sinfulness; this explains how he came to be afraid in Gethsemane, and how on the cross he suffered abandonment by God, something which could only be overcome by a messianic faith ('My God!'). And by submitting to the destiny and judgement hanging over mankind, for our sake and in union with us, he sanctified the judgement of God through his faithful endurance, and at the same time made God's grace effective, and thereby both brought about the recognition of God's judgement and pronounced God's forgiveness, sanctifying the will of God in our sight and within us. In that one died, all are subject to death, but with him all also pass through death. We cannot explain this in all its profundity; we can only understand it as a mystery of the love which sacrifices everything and bears everything, the eternal love of God himself. And certainly the Son was never more enfolded by the love of the Father than in the hour when he hung on the cross abandoned by God.

The cross is the most characteristic action of Jesus, the act of him who is the king and ruler of history, and whose *obedientia passiva* is the highest degree of *obedientia activa*. Thus the love that bears our sins is present to us in his work in such a way that it cannot be debased or misused. The cross is the form which the saving activity of Jesus takes in the course of history, something established once for all, something final and yet not brought to an end, and something which is of fundamental value as the cross of the Son, who sacrificed himself διὰ πνεύματος αἰωνίου 'through eternal spirit', which is always present, and not merely something in the past, and which directly moves and conquers our hearts.

Rationalizing thought fails to recognize in the work, as in the person of Christ, this double content, with all its tension, and sometimes perceives in the cross only the love of God, and sometimes only his judgement. But this means either that the love is degraded and humanized, or that the judgement becomes superficial. Where there is merely judgement, the love of God can only be inferred; the disastrous consequence of this for the understanding of faith is clearly visible in Christianity. But in the cross, in the death as in the life of Christ, faith directly perceives both love and judgement together, love that submits to judgement and judgement which redeems and does not destroy, and which enhances the power of grace. In the cross, faith directly perceives not merely the anger of God, but the love and the anger of God together, redeeming anger and love that brings judgement, so that it can recognize the anger and cast itself into the arms of love. The holiness and the love of God are equally present and provide the basis of the living tension of faith, the unity of fear and trust, in which fear is constantly overcome by trust; this is the teaching of Luther, in which, in faith, man constantly stands before God as *simul justus et peccator*.

The cross cannot be understood in legal categories, for it goes beyond any legal relationship; it is only possible to conceive of it truly as an incomprehensible and miraculous act of the holy love of God, in new categories of thought based on the cross alone, and not in the terms of human legal practice nor even of a humanist ethos.

The cross, of course, is the source of salvation only because it is the cross of him who rose from the dead, just as the resurrection of Christ is that of the crucified. If we are not to forget this, we must describe the work of the love which bears our sins more closely from the two points of view of atonement and redemption. The work of Jesus brings *atonement*. On the cross he offers us forgiveness, but at the same time he offers atonement; he brings forgiveness, because he brings atonement and reconciliation. It is a great thing to forgive, but to bring atonement is even greater. To bring atonement means to prepare the way for forgiveness, to make it effective, and to bring it about effectively. Atonement expresses the creative, fundamental, and inexhaustible desire of God to offer us forgiveness. In theory, forgiveness and atonement could be brought about by two different persons. But here there is one person, God in Christ; God, who carries out his forgiveness in Christ in such a way that he sets up his holy will before our eyes, reveals our worthlessness to us, and leads us to acknowledge it in faith. Atonement is not an idea which God proclaims, it is not a fixed and universal truth which one can consider at some later time and so appropriate to oneself. Atonement is no less than the reconciliation of the individual whose conscience is humbled and set free in the encounter with the cross, and to whom faith in the holy grace of God provides an answer; atonement is in truth the reconciliation of the Church, which knows that in the cross it is encompassed by the holy grace of God. In the act of atonement Christ has come in person to meet the sinner who requires atonement, and meets every sinner, so that everyone can directly perceive and experience judgement and grace in his work. It is true that the atoning action of Christ lays claim to be no less objective than the payment of satisfaction in Anselm's theory; but of its very nature it does not possess an isolated objectivity, but an objectivity related to, and orientated towards, the subjectivity of faith, which is why it can be acknowledged by faith.

At the same time, and in the same action, Christ comes to us as the *Redeemer*. He placed this meaning on his work when he said that he came to give his life as a ransom for many. His work is concerned not merely with sin in so far as it isolates men from God, but also in the power of evil as a whole, extended over mankind. In his words when he was taken prisoner, 'This is your hour, and the power of darkness' (Luke 22.53), he was referring to evil in its objectivity, which was now to be revealed in full in his death, but which was also to be brought to ignominy and its power decisively broken. At this point, primitive Christian thought expressed in mythological form an important truth which in recent times has been neglected. Jesus himself regarded his messianic works as the subduing of the powers of evil, wickedness, and death, hostile to God, and as the liberation and redemption of the children of God languishing under the control of these powers.

We shall try to answer the question, how in this context his death can fundamentally be interpreted as the conquest of evil. A saying from the Sermon on the Mount, that one should not resist evil, that is with force, casts an interesting light upon his death. To use force always involves us with evil itself, and draws us into evil. But Christ gave himself up without resistance into the power of evil. This was only possible for someone who possessed the Spirit of God. Because he does not answer violence with violence, he remains outside the realm of sin. Thus his suffering—the suffering of one who was guiltless—is a judgement on the powers of evil. In the suffering of the messianic Son of God, the hour of darkness becomes a judgement upon the power of darkness. By the shedding of innocent blood, evil itself is condemned, and the power of evil, which works evil in the moral sphere, is given a mortal blow by the moral act of innocent and self-sacrificing love, passive suffering which offers no resistance. Of course, the acts of atonement and redemption are inextricably linked. Evil has power over man, because man is separated from God, lives under the anger of God, and lacks atonement. Atonement takes away from evil its rights over man. But at the same time, in the work of Christ, and especially in the cross, evil is directly attacked, and condemned in itself. That is why the redemption is not merely ancillary to the atonement; both together are gifts of God. Thus Christ is the Redeemer from the power of evil; one might also say, from the world, in that the term 'world', in the New Testament sense, includes everything hostile to God. As an objective force, evil or the world cripples our actions and fills us with doubt concerning God's rule over the universe. But the 'princes of this world' are deprived of their power by the work of the faithful servant (1 Cor. 2.6); they know that they have come under the judgement of God. Thus they must yield when we meet them in the power of Christ. And anxiety is removed from our hearts, and our courage is restored; we are able to carry on this struggle, for the outcome has already been decided in the work of the messianic Son of God. In the same way, Christ is the Redeemer from the bonds of death, from the fear of death, and from corruptibility. In his death he attacked the power of death, and his resurrection manifests his victory over death. Even death contains no fears for us. Christ, in short, redeems us into his kingdom, into eternal life. Redemption transplants us into the supernatural life of fellowship with God in Jesus Christ. Atonement and redemption also differ in this, that although both have already been brought about in essence, the redemption that has taken place within time points to redemption beyond all time; we also long for redemption from the body of this death, for the glorious liberty of the children of God that is to be revealed to us (Rom. 8.18 ff.); and here we are not reaching out into uncertainty, but into the certainty of the redeeming work of Christ (*cf.* Vol. I, *Eschatology* V).

Because he brings atonement and redemption, Christ also brings *revelation*; he makes known to us God and his holiness, and the nature of love and of love for enemies, that is, he carries them out in us. This revelation is in no sense concerned with a universal truth, which can be passed on to others as such; it is the personal testimony of God to himself, which is only accessible in faith to those whom he has apprehended. All intellectualism is at once excluded. If Christ the Redeemer is he in whom God's purpose of salvation is brought to realization, and if redemption is the perfecting of the creation, then Christian faith can seek to understand Christ as the mediator of the eternal plan of God for the world. The very last consequence of this final thought would be the setting up of a law; rather, faith becomes conscious that we can only have faltering words and partial knowledge, until the striving of faith is crowned with the vision of God.

GEORG WEHRUNG

3
Sin and Guilt

I SIN AND GUILT
IN COMPARATIVE RELIGION

1. Sin as Impurity

Perhaps the best starting point for the understanding of the concept of sin is the English proverb 'Cleanliness is next to godliness'. This expresses to perfection the fact that from the very first sin has been regarded as something which *defiles*, that is, that it possesses a material nature, and that this *material substance* is also a *power*, a force which works in the manner of a contagious and dangerous fluid (so that for example it can be conveyed not merely by men, but also by animals). This underlies attempts to remove it by 'wiping off' (the Indians describe the taking away of sins with the expression 'to wipe off someone's sins'), washing off or carrying away (e.g. the scapegoat). In this sense sin is similar to sickness, in that both are caused by a material substance which must be removed. This line of thought is continued in the view which is widespread even in higher religion (e.g. in Parseeism), that sin is a sickness; the later Jewish future hope looked forward to the healing of sin by the Messiah. But if sin consists of a contagious defiling material substance, it is obvious and natural that the sinner will be avoided; this idea is expressed, for example, in a prayer going back to an ancient liturgical formula: 'May the sinner be neither my friend nor my guest.' The acts the sinner commits, and especially murder, defile the country and demand an appropriate atonement. As is well known, the dominant concept of pure and impure is that of taboo. Thus sin is originally represented as the breach of a taboo, and in so far as taboo can be regarded as the oldest unwritten law of primitive society, the original concept of sin can also be described as an offence against the custom of this society (it is so regarded, for example, among the Tobabatac in Sumatra; and the words 'ethics', 'morality', and the German *Unsittlichkeit* ('immorality') are all derived from roots meaning 'custom'). From the importance which sexual taboo has within primitive custom, it can be seen that sexual sins were regarded from the earliest times as the principal sins.

2. *Sin as Transgression against God*

As long as sin is seen as exclusively a purely physical defilement it is possible to speak of it even at the predeist level of religion, and the same is true of the view, a higher view in itself, which sees it as a transgression against the order of nature or of heaven, as it is regarded in China. However, with the rise of genuine belief in God, the concept of sin takes on a new form: sin is no longer simply impurity, but impurity, say, in the sight of Apollo; the gods become the guardians of traditional custom and, as time goes on, even come to be regarded as having laid it down. Thus sin becomes the transgression of divine commandments, and therefore an act committed against the gods themselves. It provokes their anger and brings down their vengeance or punishment. This also means that it is foolishness—a frequently recurring point of view. Since this level of religion consists essentially of serving the gods in the particular way which is pleasing to them, the most grievous sins are in the first instance cultic, or at least purely religious in nature: the omission of ceremonies of worship, mistakes in the carrying out of rites, false oaths, where a god has been called upon as guarantor and avenger, and the profanation of property belonging to a god. This comes to be intensified in a positive sense, in the form of the view that for man to arrogate to himself what belonged to God was sin in a special sense—thus the Kharijites regarded acquiescence in the decision of a human court, instead of the decision of God in mortal combat, as a grave sin. Through this presumption, man falls prey to *hybris*, which the god will not tolerate, and perhaps cannot tolerate, out of envy. Ideas of this sort are familiar especially from Greece; but even the Jewish Satan will not submit to God. As belief in God gradually becomes *ethical*, acts committed by one man against another increasingly come to be regarded as acts against God. For example, injustice in court can be regarded as sin in the religious sense, because the god, as an incorruptible judge, is offended by every breach of justice, and is bound without question to oppose the guilty person. Sin is still regarded here as an *act*, and it is perhaps not difficult to see how extensively the older concepts of physical defilement were still at work: for example, in India contact with a member of a lower caste is a sin; the Persians consider it a sin to soil one's feet with one's own water, to lose one's seed or to cremate a body; according to Hesiod, it is a sin to touch water which has been used by a woman, etc. Naturally, the catalogue of individual sins provides a characteristic revelation of differences in the cultural status and the ideals of the people. For example, for the Chinese it is a sin to trample on written paper, though there, as elsewhere, a lack of filial piety is also a sin. Warlike peoples may condemn cowardice as a particularly grievous sin. Closed, tightly knit societies frequently place so high a value on mutual beneficence that they can regard meanness in almsgiving as the greatest sin, just as, on the other hand, almsgiving can remove sin, as for example in Islam.

A frequent custom is to list individual sins in more or less complete catalogues of sins or vices (*cf.* Chapter 125 of the Egyptian *Book of the Dead*, the 'Ritual of the Great Purification' of the Japanese, the Persian *Vendīdād*, and Hesiod). Where sin is regarded as a transgression against religious law, all sins are fundamentally the same, and this is also the Stoic doctrine. But for the most part distinctions are made between grave and lesser sins (thus the Chinese say that some sins shorten life by twelve years, and others by a hundred days), between premeditated and unpremeditated sins, and between forgivable, and unforgivable sins: the latter are known in Parseeism as *anâperetha*, and in Christianity as mortal sins, concepts behind which there is a long history. The list of seven such sins is typical, and is used by the Stoics, Posidonius, Horace (*1st Epistle to Maecenas*) and Hermetic religion; besides this, a widespread system of eight vices is found in the East. The most important step forward in the whole concept of sin is the transition from the objective to the subjective, from the evaluation of sin as an act, to its evaluation according to the *intention* (*cf.* the Parsee division into 'acts, words and thoughts'). This leads to the realization of human sinfulness as a chronic general condition, of which individual acts are only acute and intensified outbursts.

3. The Origin of the Idea of Sin

This view already contains an answer to the much-discussed question of the origin of sin. Here it is attributed to a particular human tendency, and advanced religions, in which theological speculation is practised, have frequently considered the idea that this tendency may be hereditary. Examples of this can be found in Babylonian hymns and prayers, in the idea of hereditary sin in Indian religion, and in hellenic religion. This view implies a return to the idea that sin is determined by natural causes. Other views, such as that of gnosticism, regard sin as having found its way from outside into a soul which was originally created pure and sinless; so it is possible to speak of a *fall* into sin. Thus, for example, the *Pistis Sophia* describes the ἄρχοντες εἱμαρμένῆς, 'the rulers of Fate', as the elemental spirits which forced man to sin, following in this view a series of widespread and often very ancient conceptions which derive all sin from the influence of evil spirits. These spirits are frequently associated with the planets, as in the thinking of the Peripatetic and Hermetic philosophers, according to which the soul descended from the realm of the spheres through disobedience against its creator, and in its descent took on the evil attributes of the planets, and would return them to the planets in the course of its future reascent (*cf.* also Servius on the *Aeneid* VI, 714). On the other hand, according to the Platonic view, the fall consists of the passage of the soul, brought about by desire (*eros*), into the world of phenomena, which must consequently be renounced through asceticism. We find a different explanation again in the Indian doctrine of *karma*, according to which man's actions and their consequences are subject to the law of an immanent necessity. However, in the religion of the Jains this *karma* is not so much a force as a substance, a kind of fluid, which flows into the soul and brings about either sin or merit. Although it is occasionally held that *karma* can be transferred from one person to another, in the concepts associated with *karma*, the individual is already dependent upon himself, by contrast with the earlier view of the solidarity of the family or clan; this is a breakthrough for individualism, which in a different way was characteristically championed among the Israelites by Ezekiel, and among the Greeks by Theognis (in contrast, for example, to Homer, Hesiod, and Pindar). But there cannot be a complete answer to the question of the origin of sin without a consideration of the problem of *God and sin*. Concepts exist which do not hesitate to make the gods themselves sinners (*cf.* for example the Egyptian Seth, or the Japanese Susanowo), and to regard them as the patrons of all kinds of sinners. The more sin is regarded as a force alien to the soul, the stronger the conviction becomes that like everything good and evil upon earth it comes from the omnipotent gods: thus men are holy or wicked according to the will of Zeus, a level of thought which was not unknown in the ancient religion of Yahweh, and was even more widespread in Islam, however much the Mu'tazilites opposed it. But the endeavour to avoid any connection between the deity and sin led inevitably to its being derived from some antagonist, hostile to God, such as Satan. In this context, the comparison between 2 Sam. 24.1 and 1 Chron. 21.1 is very instructive; in the latter passage the ancient concept returns, that sin is due to demonic influence.

4. Sin and Guilt, and their Removal

A consequence of the change in the concept of sin to a subjective view (*cf.* 2 above) is a more or less explicit *consciousness of sin*, which was sometimes expressed at a very early period as, for example, in the Babylonian penitential psalms ('the sin, which I know, which I do not know'), and even more clearly in the poems of Hindu poets such as Appar and Dādū Dayāl. Of course the consciousness of universal sinfulness can alternate with the view that there are sinless natures, as, for example, was held of Shi'ite *imams*. The consciousness of sin turns into the consciousness of *guilt*, which naturally anticipates that its sin will be punished. This punishment can be thought of in numerous forms; as misfortune and suffering of every kind, both in this world and especially in the world to come, or as the wandering of the soul into new bodies, even into the bodies of animals (here the idea that one is punished in the way one has done wrong is an important influence; for example, the covetous person becomes a beast of prey, etc.). On the other hand, it is well known that misfortune and suffering, and especially sickness, came at an early stage to be attributed to previous sins. The idea that sin is guilt is a major force in increasing the burden imposed upon the devout worshipper, and it can lead to the very considerable intensification of a pessimistic view of the world, and also to the equally certain expectation that the sin of the world will bring about the judgement of the world. It is because of these views that the endeavour of the devout believer in higher religions is directed towards *the avoidance of sin*, while the *confession of sin* serves as one of the principal means of removing it. This is found at the very earliest stages (e.g. even among American Indians) and at all subsequent levels (*cf.* e.g. Lydian and Phrygian inscriptions, and Buddhist and Manichaean ideas). The Persians made a confession of sin as a help at the time of death. All other devices used to remove sin (apart from those mentioned above) are partly *mechanical* in nature, such as reading or listening to the *Purānas* in India, or the use of the prayer wheel in Japan, where even the written letters have the effect of washing away the sins of the dead. *Spiritual* means of overcoming sin either take the form of *gnosis* (by contrast to the idea of sin as 'foolishness'), or that of turning inwardly towards God, and of mystical union with him. The forgiveness of sins is his work, and the divine grace can sometimes be so great that even the greatest sinner is not rejected: this, for example, is the teaching of the Japanese Buddhist 'Pure Country' sects; Shinran, the founder of the 'True Paradise' sects, goes even further than this, putting the concept of the help and mercy of Amida into the following paradoxical form: 'If the good can enter into life, how much more will the sinners do so also.' Because of the immense concentration of divine power in ascetics and saints, the ability to forgive sins can sometimes also be attributed to them—a last echo of the dynamist concept of sin.

ALFRED BERTHOLET

IIa SIN AND GUILT IN THE OLD TESTAMENT

1. Sin and the Demands of God

A characteristic of the religion of Israel is that in it the demands of God are set forth with particular emphasis; 'Thou shalt' is a theme that rings through the whole Old Testament, in worship, in the law, in custom and morality. Thus the idea of sin also plays an important role. The commandments of God were put forward with great force by the prophets in particular, and constructed into a whole system in the books of the law; this explains the increasing seriousness with which sin comes to be regarded.

2. Is the Concept of Sin More Objective or Subjective?

The first question is whether the emphasis is more on actual and objective sin, and even on unintentional transgression, or on the subjective evil intention of the sinner. At a lower level of religion, the first is usually the case, while higher religion and morality lay more stress on man's inner life. In the Old Testament both stages are found together even at the earliest period. This is shown in particular by the words for sin: apart from the word *ḥāṭā* to 'stray' from the right way, which refers to the objective aspect of sin, there are also words like *pāshā'* and *ma'al*, which mean 'to break faith'. Numerous

ancient stories show that the lower concept was the
dominant one during the early period. Thus in 1 Sam.
14.24 ff., Jonathan is subjectively completely innocent;
nevertheless, his deed was regarded as a grave transgression. And even at a later period the concept of the
unintentional sin or transgression (*sh^{e}gāgāh*) was a
familiar one. On the other hand, even at the early period,
evil intention was quite often taken into account. The
law distinguishes between manslaughter through in-
advertance and intentional murder. The ancient sagas
tell of misdeeds which were carried out in full consciousness that they were wrong: the people of Sodom were
warned beforehand by Lot (Gen. 19). The importance
given to intention was greatly increased as a result of the
preaching of the prophets; they regarded the real sin as
pride, unbelief, disobedience, unfaithfulness, and in-
gratitude; as early as Gen. 6.5 and again in the prophets
(e.g. Jer. 5.23) the site of sin is the *evil heart*. Consequently, they proclaim that at the end of time Israel
would be given a new heart (Ezek. 36.26); and the
psalmists prays for a pure heart (Ps. 51.10). But even in
the case of this profound understanding of sin, it is
taken for granted that the sinful heart is manifested in
sinful acts, and that it is acts which are ultimately at
issue.

3. What Kind of Acts are Sins?

Associated with this distinction is the question what kind
of acts are regarded as sins. The view which first appears
in the development of religion sees the essence of sin in
an offence against *the proper ordering of worship*. This
view is clearly evident in ancient Israel. The sin of the
sons of Eli was that they did not carry out the sacrifice
in the right way; the people of Beth-shemesh did nothing
more than look curiously at the ark; but both were
punished severely (1 Sam. 2 ff.; 6.19). The post-exilic

law, in particular, constantly repeats that anyone who profanes what is holy is liable to be punished by death: the sabbath-breaker, the uncircumcized, and even the person who eats the fat of an offering made by fire, or imitates for profane use the recipe for the incense offering (Exod. 30.38). This outlook certainly expresses a profound respect for the deity, but also reveals the influence, in the substance of the prohibitions, of numerous heathen superstitions. But higher ideas existed in Israel from the very first. Among those groups which passionately served Yahweh and which defended the religion of Yahweh, the essence of sin was considered to be to worship other gods in addition to Yahweh. And *moral* transgressions were also regarded from the first as sins against Yahweh, and great emphasis was sometimes placed upon them. Nevertheless, it is clear that in the early period cultic transgressions seem to have been worse than *social* sins (1 Sam. 2.25). The reverse is true in the prophets, one of whose greatest achievements was to condemn social sins with great force as an outrage against Yahweh.

4. Sin and Punishment

One element of the religious concept of sin is that it draws punishment upon itself. The fearful anger of Yahweh is provoked against anyone who profanes what is holy and transgresses God's commandments. This is an idea that is common to the whole Old Testament. How old this idea is can be seen from the words which describe it; many words for sin, such as *ḥēṭ'* and *'āwōn*, also refer to the religious consequences of the misdeed for the person who has committed it. This serious concept of sin and guilt might possibly have been overshadowed by the joyfulness of the cult, by the confidence of Israel in the national God; but the prophets forcefully impressed it upon the minds of the people. Everyday experience taught that punishment did not follow every sin at once (2 Sam. 21), and that God did not pass judgement every day, any more than the king. But faith was confident that sooner or later God's punishment was bound to come, once 'the iniquity . . . is complete' (Gen. 15.16). This was the origin of the concept of *guilt*.

5. Guilt

In understanding the view of guilt (*ḥēṭ*', '*āshām*, '*āwōn*) held in the ancient world, it is of fundamental importance that the word should not be taken in the subjective sense as *consciousness of guilt*, but in the objective sense as 'liability to punishment'. Guilt was like an overhanging wall, the fearful collapse of which would one day surely come (Isa. 30.13 f.). It was a burden, under which a person sooner or later collapses (Gen. 4.13); it was the outstretched arm of Yahweh, which one day would strike (Isa. 9.12); whether the guilty person was conscious of the fact was not of primary significance (Gen. 26.10; 20.9). When people were stricken by misfortune, the natural conclusion was that they were guilty in this sense, and that God had found out their guilt (Gen. 44.16). In such circumstances, the ancient Israelite was not easily persuaded to resist Yahweh's judgement, but rather was ready to find the guilt that brought about the misfortune in himself. In accordance with this view, anyone whose misfortune had turned into good fortune also believed that he had received the forgiveness of his guilt. Nevertheless, at an early period there was also a *consciousness of guilt* that was independent of a person's good or bad fortune. In particular, the prophets did not proclaim guilt once the punishment had come, but foretold in advance, with sublime pathos, the punishment of sins that had already been committed. The Book of Job gives a moving picture of one stricken by God, who nevertheless persisted in declaring his innocence and argued against the judgement of God, who seemed to be pronouncing him guilty. Of course such an attitude was only possible as an exceptional case.

6. *Atonement*

Because the ideas of sin and guilt were taken so seriously, an even greater emphasis was laid upon the many possibilities of atoning for guilt. Sometimes an attempt was made to discover the cause of God's wrath, and to purify the nation and the land, perhaps by killing the guilty person (2 Sam. 21); sometimes there was fasting and prayer, the carrying out of rites of atonement, the presenting of guilt offerings (1 Sam. 6.3 ff.), and atonement sacrifices, and the holding of feasts of atonement. Nevertheless, the effectiveness of such acts of atonement was limited by the idea that Yahweh decided according to his own free will: he took away the guilt or left it in being according to his pleasure. One of the marks of greatness in the prophets is that they would have nothing to do with rites of atonement or priestly mediation. All they demanded was the *conversion of the sinner*.

7. *The Universality of Sin*

We now come to a new line of development. At an early stage, that of popular religion, grave sin and the sinner were exceptions to the rule. But as the religious and moral ideal grew greater, devout worshippers grew increasingly conscious of the idea of the universality of sin, and the devout were more sharply distinguished from those who failed to obey the divine commands; thus there came into being the group or party of the 'godless', the 'sinners', who, the nature of man being what it is, formed the majority of the people. Thus the general outlook of the devout worshipper came to be that he was living in a thoroughly corrupt world. This development can also be traced within Israel. At the earliest period the distinction between two groups, the devout and the godless, was unknown; the official 'ecclesiastical' view was that the worshipping community was the 'congregation of the devout'. But from the time of the prophets this view was modified by another, which is particularly evident in the Psalms, and which contrasts the 'devout' with 'sinners', who resist the divine will. At the same time, there was an increasing consciousness of the universality and power of sin. Certainly it seemed natural from the very first to the Israelites that everyone, even the most devout, had a hidden, unconscious sin, which God might overlook; in fact, a deep sorrow over the corruption of the whole race can be seen in the story of the flood. But the devout only came to have a general feeling of sin at a later period. This was the consequence of the fierce preaching of the prophets, and also an impression produced by the terrible catastrophes which they had experienced. In their continuing misery, and under the influence of the universal pessimism which had overtaken the ageing nations of the East, this outlook became increasingly dominant in Judaism, and it was also influenced by the dualist religion of Parseeism, until ultimately this world as a whole was abandoned in desperation, and regarded as being in the power of sin.

8. *Reflections on Sin*

There had occasionally been some thought given to the question of the *origin of sin*, without the formation of any doctrine in the strict sense. The ancient myth of paradise tells of the first sin: it arose through the temptation of a demonic being in the form of an animal, which provoked mistrust of God and sensual concupiscence in man, who at that time was still childish in nature; but this story plays no part in the rest of the Old Testament. The thought of the ancient world easily led to the conclusion that man's sin resulted from the general imperfection of his being (Job 15.14 ff.; 25.4 f.; Ps. 143.2) and to the idea that this was connected with the impure way in which he is conceived (Ps. 51.5). That guilt could also be inherited was a familiar idea to the ancient Israelites: children often had to bear the guilt of their fathers. But the fearful idea that the burden of guilt incurred at the very beginning of man's history lay upon the whole human race, and condemned all succeeding generations, was still totally unknown in the Old Testament. Similarly the Old Testament could explain a sudden and terrible death as a result of the perpetration of a great sin, but did not derive *death* as such from sin. The Old Testament reflects at certain periods a burning desire for *redemption from the consequence of sin*, but not for a redemption from sin itself, since the general view persisted that man himself could avoid sin and do good. Nevertheless, some of the prophets, despairing completely of what man could do (Jer. 13.23), hoped that Yahweh himself would convert Israel at the end of time (Jer. 31.31 ff.; Ezek. 36.25 ff.), and one of the most profound of the psalmists prayed for such a redemption for himself (Ps. 51).

HERMANN GUNKEL

II*b* SIN AND GUILT IN JUDAISM

The idea which Ezekiel made one of the central themes of his preaching at the beginning of the Exile, that the sole subject of sin and guilt was the individual (Ezek. 18; *cf.* I, 3 above) was in essence maintained in the period that followed. He sought to refute the twofold belief that sin was a misfortune which existed in itself and was independent of the attitude of the individual, and that the effect of guilt, the liability to punishment, persisted regardless of what the individual did. Certainly this ancient conception returned occasionally, and even the form which Paul gave to it (*cf.* III, 3 below) drew a great deal from the Jewish thought of his time; the doctrine of the *evil impulse*, associated with an expression in the Bible (Gen. 8. 21), which is recognizable in Ecclesiasticus (37.3; *cf.* 21.11 and 15.14) may have been a step in this direction. However much human associations and entanglements were included in the concept of sin and guilt, once Ezekiel's idea had been conceived, it remained decisive. The Deuteronomic idea of ethical *freedom of choice* (Deut. 11.26 ff.; 30.15 ff.; *cf.* Eccleus. 15. 11-20), which was always maintained, exercised an influence in this direction; in accordance with this idea, it was said of the evil impulse: 'You yourself make it into the evil impulse' (*Tanchuma* on Gen. 3.22). The firmness with which the concept of original sin was rejected is shown by the Targums, which were used in popular instruction; for example, they translate the saying of the second commandment, concerning the avenging of guilt unto the third and fourth generation by the phrase: 'Who avenges the guilt of wicked fathers in their rebellious children . . . if the children continue to sin like their fathers' (Targum on Exod. 20.5 and Deut. 5.9; *cf.* the Targum on Jer. 32.18 and also *Berachot* 7a). Through Rashi's commentary on the Bible ('If they persist in the act of their fathers'), this interpretation became the standard throughout the Middle Ages. The saying of Eleazar (third century A.D.), 'Repentance, prayer and good works take away the condemnation' (*Tanchuma* on Gen. 8.16 and parallels), came to be of equal importance, as a result of being placed at the centre of the worship of the New Year and the Day of Atonement as a solemn introduction to the Trisagion of the *mussaph* prayer.

The fall of the first man was represented in numerous legends, and death was sometimes regarded as resulting from it in the Apocrypha (Ecclus. 25.24; *Apoc. of Baruch* 23.4; 2 Esd. 3.7), and also in the Midrash (on Deut. 31.14).

But however much the remoteness of man from God is emphasized, Judaism never came to believe in the conception of original sin, sin as a metaphysical necessity resulting from a radical change in human nature through the first sin. The idea of the *conversion* (*teshūbā*), which was always possible to man, so that 'he becomes pure before his Father in heaven, and he lets him become pure' (*Yoma* VIII. 9) was fundamentally opposed to it. The Targum is also significant; for example, on the biblical text 'surely there is not a righteous man on earth who does good and never sins', it adds at once: 'But God shows the person who becomes guilty in his sight the way of conversion, before he dies' (Targum on Eccles. 7.20). The idea of conversion, and the idea it implies of a direct access to God, who alone forgives, increasingly became one of the central ideas of Jewish religion, especially in opposition to Pauline theology and later to the fatalism of Islam, and assured for the Day of Atonement a central place in the Jewish calendar. When medieval mysticism, with its doctrine of the 'shells', the elemental forces of evil (*cf. Mysticism* III, 2 p. 366 f., below), renewed older concepts of guilt, it nevertheless maintained the old meaning of 'conversion' as the freely exercised power of man to raise himself and others above sin, and even gave it a cosmic significance as the co-operation of man in the redemption of the sinful world.

The content of sin, in which the original cultic and ritual concept was mingled with an ethical view (*cf. Mishna Keritot* I), came in the course of the development to have a specifically moral character. Once again, Ezekiel is typical: in his account of sin (18.5-19) he retains, apart from his worship of idols, only purely ethical sin. In accordance with this development, the Talmudic period regarded as cardinal sins the worship of idols, unchastity, and the shedding of blood (*Sanhedrin* 74*a*.). Later on, the content of the confession of sin, which had become canonical, was exclusively ethical, both in the original shorter form and in the longer form; it lists every aspect of the moral conduct of life, but no ritual or cultic matters.

LEO BAECK

III SIN AND GUILT IN THE NEW TESTAMENT

1. Sin as a Fact

The New Testament contains no theoretical discussion of sin, but takes for granted its *reality* from the start (*cf.* the Sermon on the Mount, Rom. 1-3, the 'catalogues of vices', and the descriptions of pagan or antinomian conduct). That *Jesus* has no 'doctrine of sin' is unquestionable; but even the most fundamental utterances of the epistles always refer, either directly or indirectly, to the concrete situation of sinful man. They never speak of the 'concept' of sin in the general sense of a definition (not even Rom. 14.23). Gnostic speculations concerning the origin of evil are totally absent, even in 2 Pet 2.4. Though *Paul* regards the 'flesh' as the realm of sin (e.g. Rom. 8.3) and the body with its limbs and active organs as the sphere in which it takes effect (e.g. Rom. 6.12 f.; 7.5; Col. 3.5), he is not trying to 'explain' it on the basis of physical 'material' or of sexual desire; for the idea of the flesh denotes fallen man as a whole (Rom. 7.14; Col. 2.18), and the body is not only the 'body of sin' (Rom. 6.6), but also the 'temple of the Holy Spirit' (1 Cor. 6.19). And above all, when *Johannine texts* describe the connection between sin and the Satanic powers of temptation (e.g. John 8.44f.; 1 John 3.8 ff.; Rev. 12.9; 20.2 f.), there is no intention of deriving sin from the devil in the sense of *objective* causality. Even the occasional comments on the psychology of sin (Mark 7.21 f.; John 8.34 f.; Rom.

7.7-23; James 1.14 f.) have nothing to do with the problem of its first origin. Instead, the sinister reality of sin, which is also reflected in linguistic usage, is brought to mind even more forcibly by these passages. Sin remains wholly inexplicable as something which is not bound to exist, and is nevertheless real; that is, it is taken seriously as *guilt*.

2. Sin as Guilt

According to the New Testament, man is absolutely obliged to obey the will of God. Consequently, his whole existence is subject to the decisive judgement of God. Every wrong act makes him guilty in the sight of God. This condition of guilt, frequently represented by the image of a monetary debt (Matt. 6.12; 18.21-35; Luke 7.41-43), is most forcibly expressed in the expectation of the future judgement. Here the New Testament continues the thought of the Old Testament and late Judaism. But the certainty of judgement only becomes inexorable in the light of the New Testament day of salvation (e.g. Matt. 5.25,29 f.; 11.20-24; 23.32 f.; Rom. 2.1-11; Heb. 2.2 f.; 10. 29 f.; 12.25).

That sin can be taken seriously as guilt in this radical way assumes the *responsibility of man*. The 'truth of God' is accessible to him through the creation (Rom. 1.19 f.; 1 Cor. 1.21; Acts 14.17), and to the Jew, over and above this, through the written law (Rom. 2. 17-20), besides which even the Gentile has a kind of law in the form of his conscience (Rom. 2.14 f.). The nature of sin and guilt is not put in question by the fact that *Jesus* distinguishes different degrees of responsibility (Matt. 11.22 ff.; Luke 12.48; John 19.11), occasionally compares sin to sickness (Mark 2.17; *cf.* Rom. 5.6) and regards a deficient awareness as a mitigating circumstance (Luke 23.34; *cf.* also Acts 3.17; 17.30; 1 Tim. 1.13; Heb. 5.2; 1 Pet. 1.14). Nor is the responsibility of the individual removed

by the fact that Paul sees it in the context of the common
fate of man to be condemned for his guilt (Rom. 5.12 ff.),
and regards the uncontrollable nature of human desires
and emotions as a sign that he is abandoned to his
delusions as the result of the exercise of God's judgement
(Rom. 1.24-32).

It is typical of the strictly *religious* and strictly *personal*
way in which sin is conceived of as guilt, that the
fundamental sin consists of the rejection of God (Rom.
1. 21-23), with whom one is concerned in the first and last
instance both in relationship to oneself and to others.
The perversion of man's fundamental ethical condition
is merely a necessary consequence of his primary disobedience against the 'truth of God' (Rom. 1.25, 28).
Accordingly, Jesus explicitly rejects the material view
of sin as a physical defilement, and sees its sole source in
the heart of man, as the centre of man's being (Mark 7.
14-23), in the same way as Paul makes the 'conscience', or
alternatively 'faith', regulative for right behaviour (1
Cor. 8.7,10,12; 10.25-29; Rom. 14.23). Consequently,
for *Jesus*, what matters is always the concrete act which
also includes words (Matt. 12.36 f.) or their neglect
(Matt. 25.42 f.; *cf.* James 4.17); but it is invariably
important as the expression of an attitude of the heart
(the tree and the fruit, Matt. 12.33-35; *cf.* also 3.10).
Even in *Paul* it is always 'works' which make man guilty
(e.g. Rom. 2.6; Gal. 5.19 ff.; Col. 1, 21); but they do this
because they are entirely his own acts (2 Cor. 5.10).
The abstract idea of 'intention' is not relevant to the
substance of sin as the New Testament sees it; for 'good
and evil' only exist there with regard to the judgement of
God, while the concept of 'intention' is consummated in
itself. 'Intention' only takes into account man's time on
earth, while the New Testament looks forward to the
abrogation of earthly time in eternal time.

3. Sin as a Human Force

In this sense, sin is the *transitory* mark of human existence. For John the Baptist and Jesus the situation of the Gentiles lies at the very edge of their purview (Matt. 5.47; 6.7; 8.11; 26.45). This makes it all the more evident that Israel *as a whole* is guilty in the sight of God (Matt. 3.2,7; 4.17; 6.12; Luke 13.3,5). Thus the Pharasaic *distinction between the 'righteous' and 'sinners'*, based upon empirical facts, was accepted by *Jesus* and not made the subject of his ironical attack. But since he deliberately aimed and limited his mission to sinners, he thereby made the contrast a relative one, that is, he took away from it the absolute value which it had in the minds of the Pharisees for the relationship between man and God. Furthermore, sinners are given precedence over the righteous, in so far as they alone are included in his call, and the righteous excluded from it, so long as they continue to maintain as absolute the distinction between themselves and sinners (Mark 2.17=Matt. 9.12 f.=Luke 5.31 f.). The parable in Luke 7.41-43 expresses the relativization of the distinction between 'sinners' and 'the righteous' by showing that both need the remission of their sins, although their guilt may vary. The preference shown to the sinner is made visible in his greater love, due to the greater remission of guilt, and this expresses another deficiency on the part of the righteous, which makes the difference between them and sinners relative from another point of view. The *ultimate* standard of the status of the righteous and sinners in the sight of God is seen to be the positive or negative attitude of both to Jesus, and of Jesus to them both. The parables in Luke 15 also maintain a relative distinction between sinners and the righteous (vv. 7.10,12 ff.). But the greater joy of heaven over the repentant sinner shows how differently they are valued from the point of view of God. The attitude of the elder brother to the returning prodigal reveals the limits of his righteousness by contrast with the love of the father, which transcends these limits.

Paul is equally concerned with the situation both of the *Jews* and of the *Gentiles*. He has a strong sense of the different nature of the 'Gentile sinners' (Gal. 2.15; 1 Thess. 4.5; Eph. 4.17 ff.); but the impartial and inexorable nature of the divine judgement and retribution places both Jews and Gentiles without distinction 'under sin' (Rom. 2.11 f.; 3.9,21; Gal. 2.17; 3.22). Even the law, as a revelation of the divine will, brings no advantage from the point of view of actual 'transgression' in God's final judgement of man's actions (Rom. 2.17-29). Thus the relativization of the distinction between 'the righteous' and 'sinners' within Israel by Jesus is as it were repeated in the relativization by Paul of the similar distinction between Jew and Gentile. He summarizes the fact that the whole world is subject to sin (Rom. 3.19 f.; *cf.* John 1.29), in the light of God's reaction to it, as an effect of the power of sin which, since the fault of the *one* man, Adam, controls the whole of mankind, brings with it condemnation and death, and produces effects far beyond single individuals (Rom. 5.12 ff.).

4. Sin and the Law

In this all-embracing rule of 'sin' the law plays an important part. Paul calls it the 'power of sin' (1 Cor. 15.56). Because it turns 'sin as an act' into 'transgression' and so increases it, it brings into being its true nature, and becomes an instrument by which 'sin as a force' takes over the desires of 'man under the law' and makes him a helpless prisoner of the 'law of sin' which dwells in his members (Rom. 5.13 f.; 7.7 ff., 13,23; *cf.* 3.20). This paradox, which can only be resolved by 'grace' (Rom. 5.20) is presented by Paul as the ultimate meaning of the law in the context of the divine act of salvation (Rom. 5.20; Gal. 3.19-24; 4.1-3); but it is implicitly present in the gospels where Jesus, demonstrating the sin of Israel in concrete terms, demonstrates the completely corrupt religious position of the strict followers of the law in particular. Nevertheless, the law, as the divine 'legal ordinance' with an absolute claim within its own sphere, continues to be valid; in fact, this validity is the premiss for the part it has to play in history and salvation as the 'power of sin' (Rom. 7.12,14; *cf.* 8.4; 3.21; Gal. 3.12; 1 Tim. 1.8; Matt. 5.17 ff.; *cf.* also the frequent characterization of sin as 'lawlessness', e.g. Rom. 6.19; 2 Cor. 6.14; 2 Thess. 2.3,7; Titus 2.14; 1 John 3.4).

5. Sin and Death

Hand in hand with the rule of 'sin' over mankind goes the rule of death brought about by sin, which is likewise universal; it too results from the 'trespass of the *one*' (Rom. 5.12 ff.). Here death is understood not as a physiological, but as a metaphysical event, in so far as earthly death is a token of eternal death as the 'wages of sin' (Rom. 6.23), which is consequently its 'sting' (1 Cor. 15.56). The whole pattern of 'transitory existence' is a *consequence and punishment of sin*, which as such excludes man from the 'glory' and the 'life' of God (Rom. 3.23; 7.10; Eph. 2.1; 4.18). The effect of this judgement can be manifested even during earthly life in sickness and sudden death, as the 'destruction of the flesh' (1 Cor. 5.5; 11.30 f.; Rev. 2.22 f.; John 5.14; but *cf.* 9.2 f. and Luke 13.1-5); it is consummated in the 'perishing' of those who are 'still in their sins' (1 Cor. 15.17 f.) on the 'day of wrath' (Rom. 2.5 ff.). This death as the result of sin is not limited to the explicit 'transgression' of the law (Rom. 5.13 f.), for the man who is 'under the law' already experiences it in his living body, in the purely negative fate to which his life is subject (Rom. 7.9 f.).

The connection between 'sin' and 'death' is only worked out in detail in the Epistle to the Romans;

but it is also referred to elsewhere in the New Testament
(Luke 13.3,5; John 8.21, 24; Heb. 2.14 f.). Above all,
however, throughout the whole of the New Testament
from the gospels to Revelation it is the 'second death'
(Rev. 21.8) which is presented as the inexorable
effect of the judgement upon sin, the 'eternal punishment' (Matt. 25.41) which through the judgement pronounced by God or by Christ brings exclusion from
'eternal life'. The images in which this conception is
advanced (Matt. 3.12; 13.42; 22.13; 25.11 f.; Mark 9.
48; 2 Cor. 3.13 f.; Gal. 6.8; 2 Thess. 1.9; Heb. 10.27;
12.29; Rev. 20.8) state unambiguously that this 'destruction' is final.

6. *Christ and Sin*

Within this world of sin and death Jesus, the 'holy one of
God' is the only one who 'knew no sin' (2 Cor. 5.21).
That he was innocent and pleasing to God is not merely
one of the fundamental certainties of primitive Christianity (Heb. 4.15; 7.26 f.; 1 Pet. 2.22 f.); it is also an unmistakable element of his own consciousness (Mark 1.11;
Matt. 11.27; John 8.46). From his authentic knowledge
of the will of God he describes certain specific attitudes
as sin, on the basis of an interpretation of the commandments (Matt. 5.21-48), and shows by specific examples
the nature of true 'righteousness'. Since in his words he
himself effectively becomes the divine standard of what is
'good' and 'evil', he reveals in concrete situations that the
Pharisaic practice of devotion is self-deceiving godless-
ness (Matt. 6.1 ff.; 23.13 ff.; Luke 16.15; John 5.44),
and elsewhere, pointing out the sin of Israel in concrete
terms, reveals the human situation in the light of God.
This unrelenting revelation of the sin of the very persons
who were held to be devout Jesus then extends to the
point where the sin and guilt of the chosen people is
concentrated and fulfilled in him, the Christ (Mark

12.6-9; Matt. 23.37; John 16.9). By 'enduring from sinners such hostility against himself' (Heb. 12.3; *cf.* Matt. 27.40-44) to the point of death, in the obedience of the Son, and allowing himself to 'be made sin' (2 Cor. 5.21), he became the place of God's forgiveness for the 'sins of the whole world' (1 John 2.2).

7. *The Christian and Sin*

Primitive Christianity knew that, as a result of the forgiveness of sin as guilt, men were also *redeemed from the rule of sin as a power*, as is clearly shown in the utterances of Paul (Rom. 6.2,6,11 f.; 7.4,6; 8.4,9,12 f.; Gal. 5.16,24). Not that the Christian who was 'in Christ' was made actually sinless (1 Cor. 3.1-3; 10.12; Gal. 5.17; 6.1; *cf.* James 3.2); rather, his struggle against the Satanic powers of temptation was if anything increased (1 Cor. 7.5; 2 Cor. 2.11; 11.3; Eph. 6.10 ff.; 1 Pet. 5.8), and the constant threat of the ability to sin led often enough to actual sin (Gal. 2.11 ff.; 2 Cor. 12.21; Acts 5.3). Thus there is quite often mention of *repentance* within the Church (2 Cor. 7.9 ff.; 2 Tim. 2.25; Rev. 2.5,21 f.; 3.3,19; Acts 8.22). Thus even after baptism, Christians still needed and received the forgiveness of sins, although there were limits which could not be exceeded (Heb. 6.4 f.; 10.26; 12.17 (?); 1 John 5.16 f.; *cf.* Mark 3.28 f. and parallels). This is why there are so many urgent exhortations in the New Testament epistles. But these imperatives assume that the old subjection to sin has been replaced by a new subjection to God (Rom. 6.18 ff.), on the basis of the union in the spirit with Christ, who dies once for all to sin, and now lives forever to God (Rom. 6.1-11).

Paul's judgement on himself is characteristic of the situation. We look in vain for an explicit admission of his own present sin, unless Rom. 7.14 ff. is to be regarded as such. Furthermore, the clear conscience of the apostle is expressed so frequently and so forcefully (e.g. 1 Cor. 4. 3 ff.; 2 Cor. 1.12; 1 Thess. 2.3 ff.; 2 Thess. 3.7 ff.), that Luther's formula 'righteous and unrighteous at the same time' is foreign to his usage. But as a result of this, his 'life in the flesh' is continually marked by the fact of forgiveness (Rom. 8.1; Eph. 1.7), and by the threat of being 'disqualified' (1 Cor. 9.27). Reaching out with all his soul to the goal that lay before him (Phil. 3.12 ff.), he was as far removed from the delusion of the perfectionist idea of sanctity as from the subtle self-satisfaction of the false humility of the sinner who will not seek holiness.

The dialectic of faith in the attitude of the Christian to sin is most clearly expressed in the *First Epistle of John*, which regards the consciousness of freedom from sin as self-deception, and takes account of sin as a possibility repeatedly realized in the Christian condition (1.8-10; 2.1; 5.16,21), but at the same time considers it an indispensable mark of one who is born of God that he 'does not sin' (3.8 f.; 5.18 f.).

OTTO SCHMITZ

IV SIN AND GUILT IN THE HISTORY OF DOCTRINE

1. The Stage before the Problem was Recognized
The concept of 'sin' plays a fundamental role in Christianity, and this is expressed above all in the Christian pattern of life, in worship and in the penitential system. In the very *earliest period* a Christian received the forgiveness of his previous sins in baptism and regarded himself as obliged to avoid new sin, but asked pardon in an *exhomologesis* to God and to the Church for the lesser sins which he had nevertheless committed, and for more serious sins was subject to the discipline of ecclesiastical penance, which gradually grew more lenient. There was

no lack of *theoretical* consideration of sin (Rom. 7; *cf.* III above). But it never led to any discussion that was dogmatic in purpose. Christians of that period were not dominated by the feeling that they were miserable sinners; their basic outlook was provided by the good news of the forgivenesss of sins and of redemption.

2. The Gnostic Theory of Sin and its Rejection

The first reflection on the subject began with gnosticism. Here the question of the *origin of sin* was posed, and it was located in matter, as something essentially evil. Here sin became a physical substance. But this view was forcibly rejected by the *early Catholic Fathers*: Clement of Alexandria emphasized the moral neutrality of the soul, which was not good 'by nature', and also that of the body, which was not evil 'by nature' (*Stromateis* IV, 36), and Origen declared the thesis that ὕλη, matter, was the cause of evil to be an unchristian proposition (*contra Celsum* IV. 66). For Clement, sin was an offence against reason due to error or weakness, something παρὰ τὸν λόγον τὸν ὀρθόν (*Paedagogus* I. 13), or, to translate his words from the language of Stoicism to that of Christianity, disobedience against God. For Origen sin was fundamentally something οὐκ ὄν, something ἀνυπόστατον, something unreal, because it was only a transitory condition; for none of the rational souls was evil when it came from the hand of the creator, and at the end they would all return to God. Divine providence had created the world of experience as a place of purification for the spirits who, before the beginning of time, had fallen into the misuse of their freedom to develop, and had been incorporated in more subtle or more coarse matter according to the extent of their fall into sin. Gnostic dualism, together with its physical view of sin, then underwent a revival in *Manichaeism*.

3. The Development of the Doctrine of Original Sin in Tertullian and Augustine

Tertullian was the first of the Church's theologians to recognize that sin was a condition which went beyond the actual sins of individuals. He regarded sin as the natural condition of the posterity of Adam, which was derived from the *vitium originis*, that is, from the inferior nature of human reproduction *(ex stupri affinitate)*. Thus Tertullian introduced the doctrine of hereditary, *original* sin, and also regarded what was inherited as something physical. That he never developed his theory to its logical conclusion can be seen from the fact that he speaks of an *innocens aetas*, and regards the early baptism of infants as incomprehensible *(De Baptismo* 18; *cf.* Vol. I, *Baptism* II, 1). He saw hereditary sin as a *contagium*, not as guilt.

During the periods that followed, Tertullian's theory of original sin was considerably elaborated in the West. Though *Augustine* had rejected Manichaeism, he maintained its hostility to the material world, and was a champion of the monastic ethic, which regarded sinful concupiscence as essentially taking the material form of sexual pleasure, whereas in paradise the organs of reproduction had functioned without sensual pleasure, responding only to the will to carry out their appointed purposes. Thus in practice his concept of sin amounted to the view that it was physical in nature, although he endeavoured to present *superbia* and *amor sui* as the essence of sin in theory, and in the *Enchiridion* (Ch. 11) describes sin in a Neo-Platonic way, like Origen *(cf.* 2 above), as something purely negative, a *privatio boni*. In the struggle against *Pelagius* and his adherents the specifically Augustinian doctrine of sin was consolidated. Pelagius argued against original sin, saying that Adam had only given a bad example, and had not transmitted any seed of original sin; death was man's natural destiny, and not the consequence of an original sin. But if the sin of Adam's posterity was only the fault of their own will, and not an inherited natural deficiency, this reduced the value of baptism, which would then only signify the remission of actual sins. Here we can see the support which Augustine's theory received from the sacramentalism of the Church. His doctrine of original sin took on the following form: through the fall Adam lost his free will (*liberum arbitrium*), as well as the *adiutorium gratiae* (*cf. Grace* IV, 1 p. 215 below), through which he would have been able to persevere in the good (*potuit non peccare*). He became subject to death, and incapable of doing good (*non potest non peccare*). In Adam all men had sinned. This hereditary sin had tainted both the body and soul of mankind, so that mankind had become a *massa perditionis*. The African synod of 418 turned Augustine's basic ideas into dogma, with the support of the Pope and the Emperor; however, it did not lay down the complete inability of the natural man to do good.

4. The Treatment of the Problem of Sin in the Eastern Church

The Eastern Church showed no concern for the Western dogma of sin. Since the Pelagians who fled from the West were received by Nestorius, they were involved in his fall, and included in the condemnation of Ephesus in 431; nevertheless, the East maintained the ancient doctrine of the freedom of will. In a certain sense, Irenaeus, who came from Asia Minor, can be regarded as having prepared the way for the doctrine of original sin, in so far as he advanced the theory of the mystical unity of man in Adam on the one hand, and in Christ on the other; in Adam humanity had become disobedient, and subject to death. But Irenaeus was not concerned with the ethical consequences of the fall; he did not teach that sin was hereditary. Clement of

Alexandria rejected both hereditary sin and hereditary guilt, as explicitly as he rejected the gnostic thesis of the origin of sin (*cf.* 2 above); and the passages in Origen's homilies which seem to favour a doctrine of original sin (e.g. *in Leviticum* VIII and XII) are to be interpreted on the basis of his theory of a fall before the beginning of time (*cf.* 2 above); when he speaks of *quaedam contaminatio in patre et matre*, he is speaking as an ascetic, and is not advancing a theory of original sin. The later Greek doctrine did recognize that the sin of Adam had had harmful consequences for the human race—mortality, the disturbing of the νοῦς (*nous*) and the ψυχή (*psyche*) (Gregory Nazianzen), and the weakening of the moral powers—but did not consider that it had caused a total corruption. Athanasius regarded many saints as free from any sin and removed from man's normal sinful condition (*contra Arianos Oratio* 3); Cyril, etc., asserted that the beginning of man's life was without sin; Chrysostom warned against making the sin of Adam an excuse for one's own sins; John Damascene was acquainted with the purely negative concept of sin as ἀναχώρησις τοῦ ἀγαθοῦ (*anachorēsis tou agathou* 'withdrawal of good').

5. *The Western Scholastic Doctrine of Sin*

The doctrine of sin in Western medieval scholasticism is characterized above all by the development of the legacy of Augustine. Thus Augustine's purely negative concept of sin is also found in John Scotus Erigena, Hugh of St. Victor, etc. On the other hand, in some respects Western scholasticism departed altogether from Augustine. Thus Anselm of Canterbury not only opposed the placing of the main emphasis on sensuality, but also the imputation of the sin of Adam to all mankind, and although he did not deny the hereditary nature of the sin which makes man guilty, he did deny original guilt. Abelard departed even further from Augustine, recognizing merely a hereditary punishment. The followers of Duns Scotus put forward a form of Neo-Semi-Pelagianism, which regarded original sin merely as the loss of the *donum superadditum* of grace, but not as *corruptio naturae*, while the Thomists followed Augustine more closely. Thomas Aquinas coined the following definition: *peccatum originale materialiter quidem est concupiscentia, formaliter vero est defectus justitiae originalis (Summa Theol. Ia IIae, lxxxii 3c.)* A special problem that arose was whether the Virgin Mary shared in the original sin of mankind (the immaculate conception).

6. *The Restoration of a Religious and Personal Content to the Doctrine of Sin at the Reformation*

The Reformation introduced a more spiritualized and religious concept of sin, which, based on the new understanding of *Luther* (*cf.* Vol. III, *Luther* 2*b.*, *c.*), also dominates the Protestant confessions of faith. The classical formulation in the Augsburg Confession is due to *Melanchthon*, who, by a process similar to the way in which *gratia infusa* was replaced by the *favor Dei* (*cf. Grace*, IV, 3 pp. 218 ff. below), took away from the concept of sin the material form it had possessed in Catholicism, describing the nature of sin as a religious deficiency. While the preparations for the Augsburg Confession and the Schwabach and the Marburg Articles (Ch. 4) were limited to the anti-Catholic and anti-Zwinglian thesis that original sin was 'not merely a lack or deficiency', but a sin which truly brought about damnation and separation from God, in Article II of the Augsburg Confession Melanchthon put forward the definition that the nature of original sin lay in being remote from the fear of God, the love of God and trust in God. And the *Apology* derided the scholastics, who concerned themselves with problems of no account, but failed to observe the *graviores morbos*, ignorance of God, contempt for God, hatred of the judgement of God, despair, and trust in visible things. As early as the *Loci* of 1521 Melanchthon had denied that the sinful tendency was rooted only in the faculty of *sensual* desires; the biblical *caro*, flesh, did not refer to the body alone, but to the whole man, whose 'false virtues' were revived through self-love. Thus even the expression *cum concupiscentia* in Article II of the Augsburg Confession must not be read with the monastic implication of sexuality, or understood as a mere *corruptio qualitatum corporis*, but must be seen as a fundamentally *religious* concept: an endeavour to establish one's own wisdom and righteousness, and trust in them, in contempt of God. This religious content given to the content of sin is expressed in paradoxical terms in Luther's Schmalkaldic Articles, when he writes: 'Such original sin is so much a deep and evil corruption of nature, that no reason can know it, but it must be believed from the revelation of scripture'. These words do not express a heteronomic moral principle, as though we only recognize what is *morally* evil to be such on the basis of the authority of scripture, but assert that we can only be conscious of sin as a *religious* deficiency through the scripture. For Luther as for Melanchthon sin is the opposite of the attitude expressed in his explanation of the first commandment: 'We must fear, love and trust God above all things.' Here the religious point of view is expressed much more acutely than the definition which had been most common since 1 John 3.4 asserted that sin was a straying from the divine law ($\dot{\alpha}\mu\alpha\rho\tau\acute{\iota}\alpha = \dot{\alpha}\nu o\mu\acute{\iota}\alpha =$ *hamartia = anomia =* 'sin = lawlessness').

7. *The Attitude to Original Sin of Early Protestantism, the Council of Trent, Post-Tridentine Catholicism and Seventeenth-Century Protestant Orthodoxy*
a. The treatment of the dogma of original sin on the part of the Lutheran and Calvinist Reformation was clearly

aimed against the scholastic theologians, who watered it down by reducing the corruption of human nature to the loss of the additional supernatural faculty bestowed upon normal human nature in paradise. However, *Zwingli*, without affecting the Reformed Church creeds, shared this tendency to water the doctrine down, in so far as he treated original sin not as a sin which brought guilt with it, but only as a 'natural deficiency', 'which one has from birth, through no guilt of one's own, or acquired by accident'. All the reformers, including Zwingli, described the sinful condition of man in gloomy terms, in order that the grace of redemption should shine all the more brightly against this background; they regarded Pelagianism as lessening the honour of Christ. Here they overlooked (with the exception of Zwingli) the fact that the concept of hereditary sinfulness took away the responsibility of the individual, and that the assertion of man's complete lack of freedom reduced the guilt of sin. It is true that they laid less emphasis on the *inherited* nature of original sin than on its damnable nature as *sin*. What was merely inherited, together with hereditary guilt, was regarded as removed by baptism; but the present guilty reality was a continuing affliction.

b. The theologians of the period which followed the *Formula of Concord* expressed at length the serious Reformation attitude to sin, which, however, in Luther had always been linked with the sublime realization of redemption (*pecca fortiter!*). They revelled in gloomy descriptions of unregenerate man, whose moral value was less than that of stocks and stones. The Slav *Flacius* went even further with the thesis that original sin was the substance and nature of corrupt man. By contrast, even the *Formula of Concord* regarded sin as an *accidens*, because it was not something independent in itself, but was attached to something else (*in substantia haeret*), and it recognized a distinction 'between the nature of man . . .

who even after the fall still is and remains a creature of God, and original sin, and this distinction is as great as the distinction between the work of God and the work of the devil'.

c. In the face of the Protestant position, the *Council of Trent (Session* V) held firmly to the following propositions. First, that Adam at the fall became worse in 'body and soul' (*in deterius commutatum esse*); the physical view of sin was maintained in the conception of the pollution of infants by original sin. Secondly, an anathema was pronounced against Luther's limitation of the effects of baptism to the removal of original sin; it was true that concupiscence remained in the baptized as a tinder ready to flare up, and as an incentive to struggle, but in spite of Rom. 6.12 ff. this was not to be regarded as sin *vere et proprie* in itself. In reaction against M. Baius and against Jansenism, *Post-Tridentine Catholicism* developed a milder doctrine of sin, which rejected harsh opinions, such as the idea that all works carried out by unbelievers were sinful, or that life-long penance had to be done for mortal sin.

d. The *early Protestant scholastics* of the period following the Formula of Concord added little to the doctrine of sin by their definitions and distinctions. By contrast to the genius of the Reformers, whose attention was firmly concentrated on the present power of sin, they produced banal speculations, such as Quenstedt's division of *peccata actualia* from seven points of view, or the detailed description of *iustitia originalis* in man's original condition, and of its loss by the fall of man's first parents. Hollaz emphasized the transmission of original sin *per carnalem generationem*; in this, he was in accord with the Formula of Concord (*Solida declaratio* I. 7). Thus these earlier dogmatic theologians, appealing to Luther, developed a doctrine of traducianism.

8. The Modern Development of the Doctrine of Sin

The modern development of the doctrine of sin is characterized by two features.

a. THE DECLINE OF THE DOGMA OF ORIGINAL SIN. The dogma of Original Sin was first criticized by the *Socinians*. This criticism was not yet very well considered. They denied the corruption of human nature through the sin of Adam, but as a result of their outward biblicism left untouched a remnant of the Church's doctrine of original sin, by deriving from the fall of Adam at least the necessity of death for the human race. In fact they accepted a gradual depravation as a result of the regular practice of sin, and a sinful *habitus*, which considerably hampered the decision of the will, which was still free to choose the good. The *Arminians* were more logical, denying not merely hereditary guilt, but also hereditary punishment. In addition, they agreed with the Socinians in teaching that a propensity to sin was inherited not from Adam but from one's immediate parents. Neither succeeded in rejecting the element of sensual concupiscence in the theory of hereditary sin. It was the *Enlightenment* which first comprehensively rejected the Church's dogma of original sin. Its attitude is foreshadowed in this saying of Gottsched: 'Reason knows nothing of the fall of Adam. It accepts man as it finds him, coming into the world weak and simple, but gradually becoming capable of doing much that is both good and evil' (*Phil. Abhandlungen* 2, 1732). Then the moral psychologism of rationalist 'neology' began its onslaught. In 1745, the first shots were fired in the sermons of Jerusalem, who remained conservative with regard to the rest of the Church dogma; the main attack was launched in the 1770s, led by the *New Apology of Socrates* by J. A. Eberhard in 1772. Even the orthodox advocate of the doctrine of the Trinity and of the atonement, G. F. Seiler, was less faithful with regard to this doctrine. Genesis 3 was regarded as a moral parable, and Adam as the original model whose development was repeated in his posterity. The doctrine of hereditary sin was regarded as offensive from the religious and moral point of view. 'Every creature of God is good'; to except from this statement the noblest race of the visible creation would be to degrade God's omnipotence. It was true that an empirical judgement gave a gloomy picture of mankind; but the beneficent influences of the divine light produced undeniable effects, and residual traces of natural goodness were still to be seen in the nature of the most depraved persons. It was never the intention of Jesus to condemn human nature; he did not seek to torment it, but to sanctify it. At the period of the doctrine of 'neology' Augustine attracted the utmost dislike, because he had done the greatest damage to the idea of human dignity. His pessimistic view of sin was replaced by a belief in the possibility of educating human nature. According to this, man was not virtuous from birth, but was born capable of virtue, and was able to develop towards a state of virtue not merely as a result of the special assistance of grace, but even on the basis of his original natural condition. The culmination of the idea of the complete conquest of sin is found in later *pietism*, as represented by the 'beautiful soul' in Goethe's *Wilhelm Meister*, and in Schleiermacher's *Monologues*. In his 'doctrine of faith' the latter essentially replaced the idea of original sin by that of universal sin; following the same line of thought, A. Ritschl arrived at the concept of a 'kingdom of sin'.

b. A NEW EVALUATION OF SIN IN GENERAL. The second characteristic of the modern development is a completely different evaluation of sin. Sin is no longer merely regarded as bringing guilt, and as worthy of punishment, but appears as a positive factor in moral development. It is no longer treated merely as something which should not exist, but as something which is bound to exist as a preliminary or transitional stage, and is thereby included in the divine plan for the world. The first who dared to see the *primus auctor peccati* not as the devil, but as God, was Zwingli. The idea that God was at work in all things seemed to him to demand a determinism even with regard to evil. On the other hand, God was to be thought of as free from all evil, and human sin remained guilt. God forced man, as his instrument, to do evil; on the other hand, he had set up a table of prohibitions which condemned those who transgressed the law as guilty. 'One and the same action, for example, adultery or murder, is no crime in so far as God instigates, incites and provokes it; but in so far as it pertains to man, it is a crime' (*Sermon on Divine Providence*, 1530). Zwingli tried to reconcile these opposing ideas in three propositions. First, that God was outside and beyond the law; thus he did not sin if he caused a murder to be committed. Secondly, God revealed his goodness by causing a fall, in so far as this was the only way in which man could come to know the righteousness of God, so that the fall had been to his good. Thirdly, God drove the murderer to kill, but also the judge to condemn the criminal. One must not look only at one aspect of reality. Though the position of sin in God's plan for the world is still burdened in Zwingli by a *complexio oppositorum*, in the period that followed this idea was expressed with less and less restraint the more sin came to be regarded from a purely natural point of view. Leibniz wrote a *Theodicy*, in which evil was presented as a lower degree of good, that is, good and evil were no longer regarded as absolutely opposed, but became relative. As the *Enlightenment* progressed, it came to regard man's sensual nature (not in the sexual sense) as the cause of man's fall, but also as a blessing. The perceptions of the senses are the primary means by which we maintain ourselves; they make possible our thankful recognition of the beauty of the divine creation. Furthermore, 'we have no more · faithful friends than our inclinations and passions' (Justus Möser, *Patriotische Phantasien* III, p. 58). 'What the winds are to nature, so are our desires to human society. Without the movement of the air everything would rot and stifle, and without desire everything would fade away into a void without feeling' (Jerusalem's *Sermons* II, p. 219). What was previously abominated or lamented was now considered a factor urging man to higher things. This was the meaning of the saying of Hegel that, without the fall, paradise would have remained a park for animals; of Goethe's 'reverence' even before sin; of the title of the novel of Baron J. von Grotthuss, *The Blessing of Sin(Der Segen der Sünde*, 1897). The belief of the philosophers of neology in the goodness of human nature, as it was expressed in Zollikofer's collection of sermons, *On the Dignity of Man* (1874), or in Herder's idea of humanity (that is, the dignity of man), was of course distorted in Rousseau's portrayal of man's natural condition as that of paradise, and in the unpretentious pedagogical theory put forward by the 'Philanthropinists'. The third stage of the Enlightenment, that of rationalism, actually brought back the concept of original sin, but interpreted it in a speculative sense (*cf.* Lessing's *The Education of the Human Race*, 74). Kant spoke of a 'radical evil' as a generic deficiency of mankind, but he meant by this merely a natural propensity, which it was improper to ascribe to an inheritance from Adam.

A characteristic of the spirit in theology which followed the Enlightenment is the return to the straightforward condemnation of sin, first found in A. Tholuck, *The Doctrine of Sin and of the Atoner, or the True Inspiration of the Doubter*, 1823. For the rest, what was written about sin in the *nineteenth century* gave rise to no new doctrinal ideas, and so does not belong to the history of doctrine, but to the history of theology.

KARL ANER

V SIN AND GUILT IN DOGMATIC THEOLOGY

1. The Theological Problem

The *concept of sin* is specifically *religious*: a particular attitude of man is regarded as improper because it runs contrary to his calling to salvation. In Christianity, sin signifies the attitude on the part of man that is opposed to God's saving will. When the Bible speaks of sin, it sometimes means individual wrong acts and omissions on the part of man (everyday, actual sin, *peccatum actuale*), and sometimes the fundamental sinful attitude of man (his sinful nature, sinfulness, *peccatum habituale*). The emphasis in the Catholic doctrine of sin is upon actual sin, while the reformers base their doctrine of sin, in a somewhat one-sided way, on the essence of sin (*cf.* IV, 6. 7*a* above). Thus the theological task of the present day is that of achieving a balance between these two approaches. In fact from the basic reformation point of view, the distinction between good and sinful works on the basis of their actual content is incomprehensible. The reason for this confusion is an inadequate definition of the relationship between the formal and material norm of faith.

2. The Phenomenology of Sin

Man's destiny is fellowship with God, that is a full acceptance, in his whole person, of the divine teleology of salvation. This demands from man, on the one hand, an appropriate attitude, that of faith, which is a trusting and obedient self-surrender to the activity of God, and on the other hand the realization of this attitude, in a way corresponding to the divine purpose, in his individual acts. In practice, this means the existence of *two different norms* for the recognition of sin. The aim of the teleology of salvation, which is also the goal of the attitude of faith, is shown to us through the Bible, especially in the life and teaching of Jesus. But the substance of the norm for our attitude in concrete circumstances, which points towards this goal, cannot be derived directly from the Bible; it has to be worked out through the personal understanding of faith, attempting to do justice to the demands of a given situation. Consequently, there can be no human ideal of classical significance for all periods; rather, the perfection of man lies in his co-operating, in his whole person, in the teleology of salvation, according to the stage of development which he has reached. Therefore, depending upon the progress of revelation and the understanding achieved by faith, the will of God has been equated with different concrete norms at different periods and in different places, and this continues to be the case. Consequently, widely varied judgements have been made as to what is to be regarded as sin. But sin is always present wherever man acts against the norms of the teleology of salvation which he acknowledges in his conscience. And since the will of God comprehends the whole of reality, sin is also found in every sphere of life, and in all aspects of life, and not merely in the sphere of religion or morals. Even our attitude to our destiny and life can be sin.

Thus the *essence of sin* can be regarded as man's essential tendency to sinful actions. Since an individual action derives its sinful character from the intention of the doer, it is only possible to speak of actual sin (as the opposite concept of that of good works) in the case of a believer, while all actions of an unbeliever are sin, even though they are equivalent in content to the right acts of the believer. The classification of actual sins is of more importance for practical pastoral work than for theology.

3. The Essence of Sin

Since sin is a wilful violation of the will of God, it is usually regarded as a form of *disobedience*. If the nature of sin were disobedience, then man himself would have to be regarded as the source and principle of hostility to God in the world. Against this, it can be argued that human reason only regards positive values as original. Thus the nature of sin is rather to be seen as a form of *doubt*, or, to be more precise, it is the basic form of doubt (existential doubt). It consists of man's inability, in the face of the reality of evil, present in the world independently of himself, to condemn it on principle. He considers it possible to set up a meaningful order out of the chaos in and around himself, which has been brought into being by evil, through the means offered by this chaos (his own powers and those of the world). This is the 'love of the world' of the Bible. In concrete cases, this is sometimes expressed by ignoring the divine teleology, and sometimes by the tendency to transgress positive norms.

4. The Principle of Sin

The essence of sin is not to be explained simply by the lack of essential attributes necessary to human perfection (a lack of trust in God, of love for God, or of fear of God), nor as weakness (e.g. a weakness of the reason by comparison with the senses); rather, it requires a principle of its own. But from the way we have described sin it will be seen that this cannot be regarded as a tendency towards evil (*concupiscentia*), nor as man's desire for happiness, which is rather a natural correlative of his indigence as a creature; it is man's over-estimation of his own value (*superbia*), the fact that he does not acknowledge his created condition and his associated subjection to values laid down objectively from outside himself, but regards himself as the creator of his own values. Although the structure of his reason obliges him to accept an objective and imposed system of values, his own arrogance cannot tolerate the fact that it is not possible for him to make his own laws (autonomy), especially since all life experiences its content as something produced by itself. But this pride, which only attains the possibility of realization through the reason, is to be distinguished from the self-assertion of every individual, which is the prerequisite of sin, and also from egoism, which is a manifestation of sin.

5. *The Universality of Sin*

This fundamental doubt is a *generic quality* of mankind which is inseparable from the personal nature of man, and which we possess from birth (original sin). Thus as soon as personal life is possible, it is manifested as actual sin, and is expressed in every sphere of life, both in the body and the mind, in conscious and unconscious acts. It is also impossible for man to free himself from his essential sinfulness in the course of his life; for he can never avoid the tension between the imposition of values from outside, and his desire to rule his own life. It is true that all men have an inkling of the will of God; this is revealed in the activity of reason, and most forcibly in moral understanding. But his understanding alone cannot preserve him from fundamental doubt (the bondage of the will). Even a believer cannot wholly escape from sin; he constantly remains under its influence (*iustus et peccator*). However, he is no longer under its control. God gives him through his grace a readiness to acknowledge the exclusive validity of positive values, so that he is no longer far from God (*impius*); in faith and repentance he is able to condemn his actual sins as against the will of God.

6. The Origin of Sin

Sin must not be seen as a biological quality acquired in the course of human history, but as an *essential attribute of man*: as soon as rational man (*homo sapiens*) appeared in the course of evolution, he manifested a fundamental doubt. Consequently, the act of *conception* is only the instrumental and not the real cause of its universal extent. The pleasure associated with conception cannot be the reason for the sinfulness of man's posterity; for this pleasure is on the same level as eating and sleeping or as intellectual activity, and as an individual act it can be wholly justified. The desire to conceive is closely associated with sin, only in so far as it is the most tangible expression of an unreserved acceptance of this world, and of the present nature of man. Original sin is not spread by the inheritance on the part of subsequent generations of the attributes of their parents as a consequence of conception—the most we inherit in this way is individual weaknesses and imperfections—but by the continuance in the individual, in association with conception, of the essential generic attributes of man. The *kingdom of sin* (A. Ritschl) is to be distinguished from sin as a generic attribute of man; it refers to the universal taint of actual sin brought about by the fact that men live together in society: through our example, and the wrong that we do to other men, they are also led into actual sin.

7. The Guilt of Sin

The fact of sin cannot be explained in purely biological terms as, for example, a dominance of the natural side of man over the spiritual. If this were so, it would be no more than a stage in evolution, which could gradually be overcome. But the basis of sin is not that the intensity of the rational is too weak, but that there is an opposition between the natural will of man and the meaning of life provided by his reason. Even outside Christianity, when man looks into his heart, he experiences the contradiction between his fundamental doubt and his human destiny. This opposition only becomes comprehensible if one accepts the existence of the independent reality of evil in the world, to which man, like everything, has fallen prey (the fall). Man's fundamental doubt is his natural reaction to the inadequacy of the world, the non-teleological nature of events, and the general imperfection of our life. Thus our sinfulness is in the first instance our *fate*. But in spite of the character of sin as the destiny of man, sin, including the basic sinfulness of man, also involves guilt. It can be objected that it is only possible to speak of guilt in the case of a conscious transgression of the law, but not in the case of something inherited, which has come about without our will (J. Kaftan, T. Haering). But this assertion ignores the attribute of individual personality. It is true that the human person is something that has come into being in so far as it arises from the union of two separate individuals in the act of conception, and receives its attributes from them; but at the same time, it is the originator of all its own acts. Thus while original and fundamental doubt is inherited on the one hand (original sin), on the other hand it is the fundamental pattern of activity of the personal life of the self. When man takes earthly life upon himself, he also takes on—not in a conscious act, but from the very depths of his being—responsibility for his life, and thus also for his fundamental doubt (*reatus culpae*). We call this responsibility the guilt of sin, though it must be distinguished from guilt for an actual wrong act. Thus the concrete nature of earthly life is in itself that of a single great guilt in the sight of God: it brings into question the meaning of our life as it is laid down by God. This guilt is also individual personal guilt, because everyone is the centre of his own life; and it is also hereditary guilt, in so far as the life of the whole species is manifest in each individual.

8. The Reprehensibility of Sin

The guilt of sin is reprehensible (*reatus poenae*). The view
of idealism, that the fall of man was the most fortunate
event in the history of the world, because it was through
the fall alone that the good became a reality, failed to
recognize that the believer does right not because he is
provoked into doing so by resistance to evil, but because,
in spite of the fundamental sinfulness of his nature, an
urge towards the good still exists within him. Thus the
essential sinfulness of man is not a principle of evolution,
but a fundamental hindrance imposed upon human
nature. Even when man succeeds in overcoming all the
external difficulties which tend to hinder him from
achieving his destiny, he is still faced with the fact that
he continues to destroy this destiny himself through the
fundamental doubt that arises from the very heart of his
personality. Because it destroys the meaning of personal
life, the guilt of the essential sinfulness of man is an
absolute and unqualified guilt. Consequently, it is impossible for it to be equated with the guilt or rightness of
individual actions, which only endanger or promote the
particular relative significance of any given situation.

9. The Consequences of Sin

Sin is possible, because man, like every created being,
possesses a relative independence of God. But because he
is not independent of God his sinful attitude still remains
within the framework of the teleology of salvation of the
whole creation. God permits the sinner to experience the
consequences of what he desires. Thus the destruction of
the meaning of life through his fundamental doubt leads
him into the realm of the inadequacy and instability of
cultural values, and ultimately to the collapse of his
outward existence in *death*.

In addition to this general judgement, which also
affects the believer, because he has not completely freed

himself from the influence of sin, there is also a *special judgement upon actual sin*. While the actions that come from faith reveal themselves as a force for unity, continuity, and order in the world, the works of sin, however powerful they may be, are factors in the isolation, decay, and destruction of the person who carries them out, and of his environment. Man is no more able to free himself from the guilt of sin, than he is to escape from the bondage of sin (*cf.* 5 above), other than by the grace of God. If his life has any absolute meaning, this is only because God has given it this in spite of his guilt.

10. The Removal of Sin and Guilt

If one speaks of the guilt of a person's sin, one must consider his fundamental guilt and the guilt of his actual sins as a unity. The meaning of a person's life and its eternal destiny are not measured by an absolute standard, but depend on the relationship between his ability (or understanding) and his achievements. Consequently, the same attainments are not expected of a child as of an adult. That God does not desire the eternal destruction of men (that is, that he forgives our fundamental guilt), he makes most tangibly evident to us through the activity of the community of salvation, the Church. God's readiness to *forgive sins* is also shown in the fact that he gives man not only the knowledge but also the power to recognize his will as universally valid. It is the person, as the subject, who carries out this recognition, not through his natural humanity, but by grace. If the believer attains to *eternal life*, therefore, it is not by his own merit, but by the loving kindness of God, that his tendency to fundamental doubt, never entirely lost, is not imputed to him as guilt (*cf. Grace* V, pp. 221 ff. below).

OTTO PIPER

4
Grace

I GRACE IN THE HISTORY OF RELIGION

Grace is attributed to the deity wherever it is thought possible to be reconciled with him by means of a sacrifice, or where there is a belief that he forgives sins even without a sacrifice. Sometimes the *Greeks* express the grace ascribed to their gods; thus in the *Oedipus on Colonus* of Sophocles (1275 ff.) Polyneices says:

'Compassion even shares the throne of Zeus, to heal what has gone by; so, father, let it be with you'.

But it is in certain forms of Hinduism in particular that we hear of the grace of the deity, either of Shiva or of Visnu particularly. The most developed doctrine is found in the *Marjāranyāga* or Cat Rule, according to which the soul can leave everything in the hands of God, who will lead it to salvation, just as the cat bears its young without their having to do anything about it. Later on, in *Buddhism*, the deity, and particularly Amida, was thought of as gracious, in that it was only necessary to call on him in order to enter paradise. In Islam, too, Allah is frequently called the Merciful, but it is actually expected that by his grace at the last judgement he will permit the prophets, saints, and teachers to intercede for the faithful, and will then set sinners free from hell so long as they are not unbelievers or hypocrites. Wherever religions of redemption have developed a systematic theory of redemption, the question of the relationship between divine grace and human co-operation has always been raised, even outside Christianity.

CARL CLEMEN

II GRACE IN THE OLD TESTAMENT AND JUDAISM

1. The Earliest Times

From the earliest times it was the repeated experience of Israel that Yahweh was a God who was to be feared. Sometimes, he treated his people cruelly, without any reason, but simply because it was his pleasure. Quite often, it is true, he had every reason to do this, when he was punishing the sins of the people or the sins of individuals. But a much more frequent experience was that Yahweh was the grateful and merciful God who was to be loved. He had redeemed Israel out of Egypt (Exod. 3.7 ff.; 15.21; 18.8 ff.), and given them Canaan as their possession (Gen. 12.1 ff.; Exod. 3.8; 33.1 ff.). Israel's enemies were his enemies (Exod. 17.16; 23.22; Num. 10.35; Josh. 10.14; Judges 5.31), and woe to anyone who should injure them. He watched over individuals in Israel in the same way. He delivered them from the utmost distress (Gen. 48.15 f.; 2 Sam. 4.9; 1 Kings 1.29), let them reach a ripe old age (Exod. 23.26), preserved them from sin (Gen. 20.6; 1 Sam. 25.26,34,39), and rewarded them for their righteousness and faithfulness (Exod. 20.6; 1 Sam. 26.23).

2. The Period of the Great Prophets

During the period of the great prophets, the prophets of salvation expected above all that God in his grace would bring about a miraculous and glorious transformation of the future of the people. The effect of their teaching was that people began to long for the 'day of

Yahweh', which would bring to an end all the distress of the present time (Amos, 5.18; *cf.* Vol. I, *Eschatology* II, 2.3). In contrast to them, the *prophets of doom* proclaimed that Yahweh was in the first place the God of righteousness (Isa. 30.18; Zeph. 3.5), who insisted on unconditional obedience from his people (Amos 3.2). If this was not given, the people would be destroyed without mercy (Isa. 1.19 f.). But even the prophets of doom ultimately arrived at the idea of a gracious God. In general, they proclaimed that the people would be destroyed because of their sins. But from time to time they expressed the hope that perhaps the whole people (Isa. 1.16 f.; Jer. 3.21 ff.; 7.1 ff.; Ezek. 18.30 f.; Amos 5.4 ff.; Micah 6.1 ff.), or at least a remnant of the people (Isa. 7.3; 10.20 ff.) might repent, and receive as their reward the fullness of earthly and heavenly blessedness which is to be found in God. But the prophets themselves finally shattered the belief that the remnant of Israel would repent. The people's habitual sinfulness went far too deep. In the distress that this realization caused, the prophets attained to their final and most profound idea. The end cannot be death, the end can only be life. But life without purity of heart is impossible. If men can not attain purity of heart by their own powers, then God will work this miracle and create pure hearts in them, so that men can live a life of blessedness (Jer. 24.4 ff.; 31.33 f.; 32.36 ff.; Ezek. 11.19 f.; 36.25 ff.; Zeph. 3.8 ff.). If this is so, he is not merely a God of righteousness, who demands unconditional obedience. He is also a God of grace, who frees men, who cannot save themselves, from the bonds of sin. The salvation then enjoyed by men set free by God is no more than a consequence of redemption.

3. The Exile and the Post-Exilic Period

The effect of the exile on those who endured it was first of all to confirm the idea of the God of righteousness who insists on absolute obedience from his people. Everything had happened as it was bound to do. But during the exile itself, and in the post-exilic period, the idea of the God of grace also came powerfully to the fore. God is not merely a God of righteousness; he is also a God of grace, and in particular, he never rejects those who repent. This idea was enthusiastically received by everyone who still had hopes for the future of the nation (Micah 7.7 ff.; Ps. 126). The prophets of that period strengthened the longing of the people for a miraculous future transfiguration by extravagant prophecies (Isa. 40 ff.; 24 ff.; 30.18 ff.; 33; 56 ff.; Micah 4 ff.; Haggai 1 f.; Zach. 1 ff.; Mal. 3). Likewise, in *individual devotion* in the *post-exilic period* there was an increasing emphasis on the idea that God is above all a God of righteousness, who recompenses everyone according to what his deeds deserve. When pious individuals suffered any distress, they appealed to the God of righteousness, since for the most part they regarded themselves as innocent. They felt he would surely not let the innocent suffer. But the idea that God was also a God of grace was not forgotten as a result. All those who submitted to the view that suffering was a punishment for sin, and who saw in the evil that had come upon them a just recompense, appealed to the grace of God (Pss. 6; 25; 38; 39; 40.13 ff.; 51; 69; 130; 141; 143). In general they besought the God of grace for the forgiveness of their sins and for deliverance from their suffering. One asks more of him: the author of Ps. 51 prayed also for a clean heart and a new and right spirit.

4. Late Judaism

Late Judaism remained strongly under the influence of the idea of the justice of God. All good fortune was regarded as a reward, all misfortune as a punishment. Anyone who did not receive a just recompense in his lifetime could be sure that it would be given him on the day of judgement, at which he would be present as a result of the resurrection. On the other hand, late Jewish writings constantly stress that God is also gracious (the *Letter of Aristeas* 192; Jubilees 23.31; Ps. Sol. 2.36; 9.6 f.; Enoch 50.3; 61.13; 4 Ezra 7.132 ff.; 8.31 f.). The godless are excluded from his grace, but everyone else can count upon it. On the day of judgement the merciful God will overlook, through his grace, anything in which his people have failed to deserve blessedness (Ps. Sol. 14. 9; 15.13; 18.5; Apoc. Baruch 84.11).

EMIL BALLA

III GRACE IN THE NEW TESTAMENT

1. *The Gospels*

The word χάρις has a very wide meaning in Greek. It means thanks, charm, kindness, and favour, and is also used in the New Testament in this sense, that is, without its specifically religious meaning. It is not very frequent in the gospels; it does not occur in Mark and Matthew, while in Luke it occurs a few times with the significance 'thanks' (6.32 ff.; 17.9) and in the Old Testament expression 'he found favour with God' (Luke 1.30; Acts 7.46, etc.), as well as in a few expressions influenced by Pauline usage. In John the word occurs only in the Prologue, where the thankful disciple says of Jesus that we have beheld his glory, full of grace and truth, and that from his fullness we have received grace upon grace (1.14,16,17).

We cannot of course conclude from this that the idea of the grace of God was unknown to the evangelists or to *Jesus* himself. In fact the gospels give us a picture of a gracious Saviour who has mercy on the sick and suffering (Mark 5.19; 10.47 f., etc.), brings the forgiveness of sins to men (Mark 2.1 ff.), received sinners with

kindness (Mark 2.13 ff.), and with God's forgiving love
in mind, constantly demanded forgiveness and mercy
from men (Matt. 5.7; 6.12; 18.12 ff., 21 ff.; Mark 11.26;
Luke 10.25 ff.; 15, etc.). Both the portrayal of the merciful Saviour and his message of God's merciful and forgiving love are characteristic of the gospel tradition.
Consequently, there can hardly be any doubt that both
are genuine reflections of the historical Jesus (*cf.* Vol. I,
Jesus Christ).

2. *Christianity as the Religion of Grace*
It is true of course that the familiar conception of
Christianity as the *religion of grace* is first clearly expressed
by Paul. The word 'grace' is one of his favourite terms,
and he came to regard grace as the essence of Christianity.
An effect of the miraculous grace of God in his own experience was the fact that he, who had persecuted
Christianity, had been called to be an apostle and a
highly successful missionary (Rom. 1.5; 1 Cor. 15.10;
Gal. 1.15; 2.9); but he regarded not only his apostolate
but Christianity as a whole as a consequence of divine
grace, which calls man to receive salvation, to become
a son of God and to share in the messianic heritage. The
grace of God is here identical with the grace of Christ,
and is linked with the saving acts of the cross and resurrection (Rom. 3.24); the grace of God, in which a
Christian stands, presupposes this work of salvation
(Rom. 5.1). Thus at the beginning of these letters, in the
solemn formula greeting which transforms the usual
Greek greeting ($\chi\alpha\iota\rho\epsilon\tau\epsilon$, related to $\chi\alpha\rho\iota\varsigma$) in a Christian
sense, the grace of Jesus Christ appears side by side with
the grace of God. This signifies not only that grace is
procured for the Christian through Christ; it is a continual activity of the exalted Lord, in which he can take
comfort in suffering and sorrow (2 Cor. 12.9); and
because Christ is at work in the Church through his

Spirit, the various effects of the Spirit (knowledge, faith, miracles, speaking with tongues) are necessary expressions of the grace given to the Christian (Rom. 12.6 ff.; 1 Cor. 12), as is signified by the term used to describe them, gifts of grace (χαρίσματα). In so far as life in grace, which in substance amounts to a communion with Christ, begins with baptism (Rom. 5.1 ff.), Paul contains at least the seeds of the later Catholic conception of grace, in which grace is regarded as an effect of the sacraments.

But for Paul grace is *opposed to the law*, which for the Jew was a means of obtaining grace. By fulfilling the law, the Jew hoped to win righteousness and grace; for the apostle grace is imparted to men without the fulfilment of the law, and without merit gained by works; otherwise grace would no longer be grace (Rom. 4.4; 6.14; 11.6). The view of Judaism, according to which God imparted his grace and mercy to the devout worshipper who had faithfully kept the law, was turned completely round by Paul: the law and grace exclude each other (Rom. 6.14; Gal. 5.4); only by believing in Christ, who brings grace, can one be justified on the basis of this faith, and so receive the grace of God. 'By grace alone' means through Christ alone, and this in its turn means not through the law, which for Paul merely has the task of preparing for the fullness of grace that comes in Christ (Rom. 5.17,20).

3. Later New Testament Literature

The language and doctrine of later New Testament literature was based upon Paul's view. The sharp opposition between the idea of grace and the piety of the law is certainly much less prominent; the freedom from the law for which Paul had fought was not firmly established in the Church until a later period. There are only occasional echoes of it (*cf.* Eph. 2.5,8; 2 Tim. 1.9; Titus 3.5). But the concept of Christianity as the consequence and epitome of divine grace was not disputed. The appearance of Christ on earth, and his crucifixion in particular, were regarded as the effect and revelation of the grace of God (*cf.* Titus 2.11; John 1.14,17,18; 1 Pet. 1.10,13; Heb. 2.9); through Christ the high priest we have access to the throne of grace (Heb. 4.16); Christianity is simply the grace of God, in which we have to continue (Acts 13.43); faith comes into being through grace (Acts 18.27), and the Christian preaching is the word of grace (Acts 13.43; 14.3); this grace justifies (Titus 3.7), and one must be strong in it, be firm in it, and grow in it (2 Tim. 2.1; 2 Pet. 3.18; Heb. 13.9); furthermore, grace must not be neglected (Heb. 12.15) or perverted by false doctrine (Jude v.4). As the grace of life (1 Pet. 3.7 according to good manuscripts) it contains the promise, and God, who gives grace, is the God of all grace, who has called Christians to his eternal glory (1 Pet. 5.10); thus the faith and the hope possessed by Christians are united in the idea of grace.

WILHELM MUNDLE

IV THE HISTORY OF THE DOCTRINE OF GRACE

1. *The Foundations of the Doctrine of Grace in the West in Tertullian and Augustine*

As an essential religious concept comprehending the love and favour of God and Christ, both in their general expression and also as they are imparted to the individual, the word grace is prominent throughout the whole history of Christianity. The doctrine of grace as a subject of dogmatic theology was created in the West. The Greek Fathers were preoccupied by metaphysical problems (*cf. Christology* II pp. 90 ff. above); as far as man was concerned, their interest was only in the hope of deification, that is of obtaining ἀθανασία (*athanasia*, 'immortality') or ἀφθαρσία (*aphtharsia* 'immortality', 'incorruption'; *cf.* Vol. I, *The Eucharist* II, 1a., etc.). The more practical Western outlook led to soteriology in its moral aspect being treated as a part of dogma of equal importance to metaphysics. But this meant that the naïve moralism of the Apostolic Fathers and the Apologists, who followed the view of the ancient world in basing human action essentially on man's own intrinsic freedom and power, became inadequate, and it was necessary to turn to the fundamental principle of grace.

The first to consider grace in this sense in theological terms was *Tertullian*. It is true that he was never able to shake off the influence of the Apologists and moralists; he held firmly to the idea of reward in considering the relationship between God and man, and he considered that the forgiveness of sins obtained in baptism had been earned by the repentance effected in conversion; but, besides the *gratia a Deo offenso* present in the forgiveness of sins, he also affirmed the existence of a special *vis divinae gratiae potentior natura* which was the support and assistance of the Holy Spirit, given in baptism and accompanying the Christian in his life, which, following Stoic ideas, was thought of as the breathing in (*inspiratio*) of a divine substance of divine power. This concept of *grace as a substance* became predominant in Western Catholicism. The following rule was laid down by the General Synod of Carthage in 418: 'If anyone says that the grace of God, by which man is justified through Jesus Christ, avails only for the remission of sins already committed, and not for assistance to prevent the commission of sins, let him be anathema.' Meanwhile, *Augustine* had developed a fuller doctrine of grace. This doctrine emphasized the exclusive necessity of grace in the regeneration of man. It is true that his freedom was not entirely denied; but it remained a purely formal concept which, since the Fall that took place through the sin of the first man, could mean nothing more than the will to do what was morally reprehensible. Mankind, sunk in selfishness and sensuality, could only be given the ability to do good through grace, which was responsible both for the will to do good and the carrying out of good acts. He says: 'He begins his influence by working in us that we may have the will, and completes it by working with us when we have the will.' (*De gratia et libero arbitrio* 17.33). Grace brings faith and love, sets man free from *concupiscentia mala* and gives to the *certus numerus electorum* the *donum perseverantiae*, which *invictissime* enforces perseverance. The idea of the effectiveness of grace alone was taken from Paul (Rom. 9.16; *cf.* III, 2 above); but Augustine departed from Paul in according to the grace of forgiveness a purely preparatory role, and basing the true *sanatio* on the infused, dynamic substance of grace, the *gratia infusionis* (*cf.* above). He did not regard this *gratia infusa* as won by Christ; it had been imparted to the human nature of Christ himself, 'that men may understand that they are justified from their sins by this same grace by which it has come about that the Man Christ can have no sin' (*Enchiridion* 36.11). 'There is no more signal illustration of predestination than Jesus Himself' (*De dono perseverantiae* 24.67). The thought of Augustine's opponent Pelagius followed that of the East, of which this saying of Clement of Alexandria is characteristic: 'And as the physician provides health for those who co-operate with him for health, so also God provides eternal salvation for those who co-operate with him for knowledge and right action' (*Stromateis* VII, 7). He regarded moral freedom as a *bonum naturae* which had not been lost in spite of the Fall, and regarded grace as a second, co-operative factor; he saw it as the grace of creation (the *posse*) and *gratia auxilii*, teaching man through the law and example of Christ, and not as *gratia inspirationis*.

Augustine perfected his doctrine of grace in conflict with Pelagius; it defeated his opponent, but never became official ecclesiastical doctrine in its totality.

2. *The Development of the Doctrine of Grace*

a. IN POPULAR CATHOLICISM AND SEMI-PELAGIANISM. Its main assertions were already blunted by the Synod of 418 (*cf.* above), which did not mention the idea of the total inability of the natural man to do good, the unmerited nature of grace (asserted in Augustine's expression *gratia gratis data*), the necessity for it to precede the will, its irresistibility, and a predestination not affected by foreknowledge. A similar attitude was taken by Augustine's colleague in the conflict against Pelagianism, Jerome, who had been drawn to his side principally by the anti-sexual emphasis in Augustine's doctrine of sin. The aspect of the Augustinian doctrine of grace which was regarded with suspicion by *popular Catholicism* can be seen in the misunderstanding of a community of monks in Madrumetum, who thought that God would not judge in the future *secundum opera*. Augustine himself did not go as far as this; he always insisted on the necessity of good works: 'through grace we obtain the meritorious qualities which lead to everlasting life' (*De gratia et lib. arbit.* 1.1) All the same, he was far from being logically consistent; the exclusive effectiveness of grace, which he taught, completely removes any human merit. But Augustine, as an advocate of monasticism and a cleric, was firmly rooted in the sanctification by works typical of popular Catholicism. The opposition of strict ecclesiastical circles in southern Gaul (Vincent of Lérins, Hilary and John Cassian) developed into Semi-pelagianism, which in contrast to Pelagius maintained the idea of *gratia infusa*, but like him accepted the cooperation between universal grace, which he did not even regard as always being prevenient, and human decision (*nostrum est velle, Dei perficere* 'it is for us to will, for God to perfect'); its most significant literary advocate was Faustus of Riez. The synod of Arausio (Orange) in 529, the importance of which was increased by the Pope's ratification of its decisions, did take a firm stand against Semi-pelagianism, under the guidance of the true Augustinian Caesarius of Arles; but it did not mention the irresistibility of grace and predestination. A similar attitude is found in Gregory the Great, who was the most widely read author of the Middle Ages, and gave to that period an Augustinianism watered down into a concealed Semi-pelagianism; the Church could not adopt a wholly Augustinian position if it was not to deprive its means of help and salvation of all value.

b. IN SCHOLASTICISM. Scholasticism firmly maintained the concept of *gratia infusa*, including the idea of its absolute necessity. But there were nuances in the way the received teaching of Augustine was handled by individual teachers. The most thorough-going Augustinian was *Thomas Aquinas*, who even accepted the idea of the irresistibility of grace. For him, *gratia infusa* is the *gratia prima*, which with the simultaneous *remissio culpae* is what forms *iustificatio*; by *gratia gratis data* Thomas means a particular charismatic endowment given for the service of one's neighbour. Nevertheless, his acceptance of a special *auxilium gratiae*, in addition to *gratia habitualis*, as well as the expression *cooperari*, implies concessions to a hidden Semi-pelagianism. The doctrine of grace taught by the *Franciscan scholastics* (Alexander of Hales, Bonaventure, Duns Scotus) took a firm Neo-semi-pelagian line, asserting that after the beginning of the process of conversion through *gratia gratis data (disponens)*, a natural endowment scarcely to be distinguished from the grace of creation, one could obtain, by the use of this grace on the part of the free will, the meritorious *gratia proprie dicta* (that is, grace properly so-called), by which they meant *gratia habitualis* and *gratum faciens*. The *nominalist* scholasticism of the late Middle Ages (Occam, Biel) fell back completely into Neo-pelagianism. As a result of the high value they placed on the human will, the natural man was accorded the power, of himself, even without grace, of doing *bonum morale*, and also the power to *diligere Deum super omnia* 'to love God above all things', and they accepted only as an ordinance of the divine sovereignty, that only good works carried out by means of *gratia infusa* could be regarded as *meritum*. This Pelagianism did not remain undisputed; but neither Thomas Bradwardine, nor Gregory of Rimini, nor Wycliffe, nor any other of the 'predecessors of the Reformation' could overcome the Catholic concept of the infusio of grace and the resultant devaluation of grace.

3. The Protestant Doctrine of Grace

This was the work of the Reformation. Melanchthon was the first to abandon the concept of grace as a substance, when in his *Loci* of 1521 he suggested that the expression *gratia* should be replaced by *favor*. This implied the rejection of the concept of a dynamic substance, and the consciousness, more appropriate to a living religion, of a *personal* attitude on the part of God. The impulse for this, of course, was given by *Luther's* new understanding of the nature of salvation, even though he himself at first continued to use the words *gratiae infusio* (*Works*, Weimar Ed. 1, p. 118), and did not dispute the concept in the conflict that arose over his thesis (*Works*, Weimar Ed. I, p. 450 f.). He soon rejected the Pelagianism of Duns Scotus, Occam and Biel, and maintained the absolute powerlessness of the natural man: 'the best and infallible preparation and sole disposition for grace is the eternal election and predestination of God, from man's side nothing surpasses the grace of grace save a contrary disposition or rebellion' (in the *Disputatio contra scholasticam theologiam* of September 1517). For him *gratia* was virtually identical with *misericordia. Christus . . . est gratia, via, vita et salus* (*Lectures on the Psalms*). He now saw the forgiveness of sins as the whole substance of salvation, the entire content of grace. Influences from Anselm and Bernard of Clairvaux led Luther no longer to distinguish *gratia remissionis* and *gratia justificans* as two separate entities. There can no longer be any question of the inspiration of grace as a substance if the following emphatic statement is true: *verbum, inquam, et solum verbum est vehiculum gratiae* (*Works*, Weimar Ed. II, p. 509; *Commentary on Galatians*, 1519). As in Luther, we later find in *Calvin* (*cf.* Vol. III, *Calvin*, 3*b*.) this personal concept of grace, the *favor gratuitus*, instead of the infused magical substance (*Institutes* II, 17).

In *De servo arbitrio*, 1525, Luther developed his doctrine of grace in a determinist and *predestinarian* sense. He no longer shied away from the idea that God himself caused the Fall. This was the work of the *Deus absconditus*, while 1 Tim. 2.4 is true of the *deus revelatus*. Against Erasmus, who had acknowledged the inability of man, by his own power, to do good, Luther argued that it was impossible for him even to *se applicare ad gratiam* on the basis of the freedom of the natural will.

The Lutheran Church did not adopt his determinist and predestinarian ideas, and he later ceased to give prominence to them himself in his more considered popular teaching, although he did not abandon them. The Formula of Concord, in opposition to the 'Synergism' of the Philippists, which was drawn from the doctrine of human freedom put forward by Melanchthon after 1527, certainly emphasized the fact that God alone was at work to the extent that 'in the nature of man after the fall and before regeneration not a spark of spiritual power is left by which he can prepare himself for grace or grasp grace which is offered or be of and by himself capable of grace or apply or adjust himself to grace or by his own powers do anything for his own conversion whether in whole or a half or the least bit . . .', etc. This rejection could hardly be more explicit. It is further expressly stated that the 'natural free will' was only of effect 'for these things pleasing to God'. At the same time, the Formula of Concord rejects Luther's view, giving a warning 'lest we should try to scrutinize with our own reason the bare and hidden foreknowledge of God, explored and known by no man'; that is, it warns against deriving predestination from the concept of the *Deus absconditus*. It rejects the predestinarian particularism of grace, and clearly takes into account the resistance of man to the grace that is offered him. Thus grace is not regarded as irresistible, nor as incapable of being lost.

The view adopted by the Formula of Concord is inconsistent. Where there is so radical a rejection of the human factor, the acceptance of possible human resistance to grace is out of place: for then the case in which grace was not resisted would imply a 'being capable of grace or adjusting oneself to grace'. But if the irresistibility of grace is asserted, then double predestination is inevitable in view of the fact that many people reject grace. The dilemma can only be avoided by removing the contradiction between grace and freedom. This took place in *German idealism*. Hegel taught that 'what appears as my act, is the act of God, and the reverse is also true' (*Philosophie der Religion* I, p. 157). The formula of K. von Hase implies the same: 'Everything is grace, and everything is freedom' (*Evangelische Dogmatik*, 1870).

4. The Council of Trent
The *Council of Trent* explicitly rejected the Pelagianism and Semi-pelagianism of scholasticism, but in its positive statements left the way open for human co-operation; its characteristic statement is: 'although in them (the

descendants of Adam) the free will was not extinguished, it is weakened and declined'. Again, *iustitia infusa* was still distinguished from the forgiveness of sins, and it anathematizes those who deny that it is possible 'by the exertion of his own will to be prepared and disposed' in order to receive the grace of justification and also those who replace infused grace by the mere *favor Dei* (Sess. VI, can. 9 and 11). But this does not mean that the discussion of the concept of grace was brought to an end among Catholics (*cf.* for example the debate between Banez and L. Molina, and also Jansenism).

KARL ANER

V THE DOGMATIC THEOLOGY OF GRACE

1. The General Significance of the Doctrine of Grace
Grace (gratia, χάρις) is the central concept of the Christian and biblical doctrine of God. It fully expresses the *theocentric* and *theocratic* and also the *existential* and practical themes of faith, doing full justice to the completely positive and exclusive understanding of its own nature which faith possesses. Consequently, it is also the decisive standard by which the Christian understanding of existence is distinguished from any other philosophical or religious view. Because a true and saving relationship to God is understood as grace, the basic principle of the scriptures can be summed up in a single statement: that everything good has its origin in God alone, and especially in his work of revelation and in the redeeming word of God. But this doctrine that all is to be attributed to the action of God is, by contrast to any pantheistic concept of a substance that is the basis of all being, at the same time the highest expression of the absolutely personal origin and character of this divine activity and the relationship it brings into being. Above all, grace means

—both in the usage of modern languages and in Greek
—the highest sovereign act of a ruling will that is bound
by no law. This establishes a third point: that it cannot
be a speculative and theoretical concept in a non-per-
sonal interpretation of the world, but can only describe
a relationship, one moreover which brings the personal
nature of man as such (his freedom) and also his relationship to the world and time, to God and to eternity,
decisively and absolutely within the realm of salvation.

*2. The Doctrine of Grace as a Decisive Factor
in all Christian Doctrine*

This makes it obvious that grace is not an isolated theme
of faith, a single *locus* within the scheme of Christian
doctrine. Instead, it is the decisive factor underlying
every proposition of the Christian faith.

a. The foundation of the Christian understanding of
grace is the recognition of the paradoxical unity of
the divine attributes of *holiness* and *love*. The holiness of
God is the absolute divinity of God, it is what is peculiar
to himself, his own very name, the *incommunicabile*, his
sovereignty, the completely underived nature of his
power and his righteousness, the mystery of the origin and
basis of everything both ideal and real, that beside which
no other being exists independently, the exclusiveness
and majesty of God, his personal freedom, beyond every
law. But Christian faith speaks not only of the holiness
of God, but at the same time of his absolute love. If
God's holiness is his self-sufficiency, his love, on the other
hand, is his equally total 'selflessness', his imparting of
himself. The God of love is one who gives himself to man,
who seeks him, who renounces his absolute royal prerog-
ative for man's oppression as though he were the guilty
one. In the act of giving unconditional grace to the sinner,
to bring him to a perfect communion of love with God,
both the majesty and the love of God are one.

b. Biblical thought conceives of the *creation* itself as an act of divine grace, including in itself the two themes of grace just described. For the creation *ex nihilo* is the expression of a divine will rooted and grounded in itself alone, by contrast to any doctrine of emanation or idea of the world as *mâvâ*, illusion, as in some Hindu thought, any metaphysical dualism. But it is a loving will, a desire on the part of God to impart himself. This is expressed in particular in the creation of *man* as the image of God, by which the participation of the world in the life of God is laid down as its final aim. The being of man, therefore, is an act of grace in a quite different sense from the rest of creation: man can only become what he is created to be by giving himself up completely to receive the divine gift of love. He receives his personality by receiving this gift.

c. Through sin—defiant independence—man loses his original nature by perverting his attitude to God. But it is at this point that we begin to see clearly what is so incomprehensible in the grace of God. It is not simply that God tolerates, through his patience, the ungodly behaviour of man, instead of destroying him, as he would be justified in doing; his grace is revealed above all in the fact that he enters into an eternal *covenant* with disobedient man. The idea of the covenant dominates the self-manifestation of God in the 'special revelation' of scripture. The original meaning of the German word for grace, *Gnade*—a coming near, or coming down— provides a good illustration of what is meant. Condescension, approach on the part of God, a divine bridging of the abyss, are the characteristics of this movement. Even the strictness of the law is based on God's desire to give his grace; this too belongs to the covenant, the near presence of God, and demonstrates the grace by which he chooses and saves men.

d. The innermost meaning of divine grace, however, is

first fully revealed in the express declaration of God's will to bring sinful man as such into communion with himself, that is, in the *forgiveness of sins*. No one can know what forgiveness is who has not recognized the full significance of sin, as a total defiance of God himself, and not as weakness, error, or imperfection, but as a rejection of the divine and sovereign will; and who does not realize the significance of this rejection on the part of a creature, so richly endowed, of the Holy God who desires him unconditionally. Sin is not only the destruction of man's original nature, but the perversion of the relationship of salvation into one that brings evil on him. This is not an illusion of man, coming from the mistaken belief that God is judge, whereas in fact he is a father. The anger of God, from which the threat of judgement comes, is as real as the world itself, over which it is already casting its shadow (*opera aliena*). It is in fact an act of divine grace that he should permit the world to remain for the time being in this ambiguous condition. But the decision, the judgement, the real rejection of all ambiguity, will come eventually. Since sin is not an accidental feature of human life, but the decisive and basic factor in all present historical existence, there is no possibility that man can change his own nature himself. For even the source of all independent activity, the self, is ensnared in sin. Above all, the independent self is incapable of shaking off the past, which in the form of guilt belongs to its present. To 'liquidate one's own debts' in such a way would only be a fresh offence against God to whom the debt is owed. The burden of sin can only be lifted by God himself, by his forgiveness, by the pardoning of man who has come under judgement.

e. This juridical relationship is not a 'persistent survival of Old Testament thinking', but is based on the inviolability of the divine will, which as the result of man's fall from the relationship of grace, has become a commanding, legislative will. Because guilt is an objective reality, and not a subjective misunderstanding, forgiveness must also take place in a real and objective way. A sovereign intervention of the Lord in the historical course of events is necessary if the strict reality of forgiveness is to be preserved. And this intervention must be such that there is an unqualified manifestation both of the sacred validity of the divine legal ordinance, and of the overriding sovereignty of the divine will to forgive. This is why the cross of Christ, as the place of *atonement and reconciliation*, is the point at which forgiveness comes about. This event fulfils at one and the same time the idea present in cultic sacrifice, that forgiveness cannot take place of itself, and that something must happen, and also the moral protest against the sacrificial cult which points out that no external action on the part of man can propitiate God; for the cross is a sacrifice that God himself offers. This is why the cross is the first perfect manifestation of the grace of God (*cf. Christology* III p. 153, above). Although it is true that a juridical interpretation of the idea of atoning sacrifice in the New Testament can easily obscure the fact that the character of the saving act of God is that of an act of grace (though legal analogies are indispensable), yet we must not regard what it really is as identical with this misrepresentation of it, and to ignore the fact of expiation implies an ominous weakening of the idea of atonement. The extent of any damage can only be seen from the cost necessary for repairing it, and similarly the effect of sin can only be gauged from what was necessary to restore the original relationship. And in the same way, the divine love, incomprehensible as it is first, becomes visible in this condescension, in the pursuit of the 'lost sheep' by the 'good shepherd' into the furthest depths into which it has strayed.

f. Atonement is the word of grace, telling of the future act of God's grace. Atonement means *redemption*, the restoration and perfection of the order of creation. Once again, a sovereign act of the grace of God is the only possible basis for such a restoration and perfection. It requires a radical change, bringing to an end historical life with its half measures, its death, and its sin: the redemption through the resurrection of the dead, the creative perfection of what has been begun in the revelation of Christ. Everything else that is called grace in the New Testament is merely a preparation for this true restoration and bringing to perfection through the grace of God the redeemer.

3. Sola Fide

The Pauline and Reformation doctrine of grace (*cf.* III, 2; IV, 3) is the most precise formulation of this essential biblical concept, but adds nothing new to the basic idea. Just as the presupposition of the revelation of the Son of God in the incarnation is a strict monotheism, with an impenetrable barrier between the creature and the creator, so in the same way the Pauline doctrine of grace takes for granted the Old Testament idea of the law in all its sternness. The holy God, a personal will demanding obedience, is contrasted to man. There is no immanent continuity between the human and the divine, to which man can retreat, as it were to the deepest 'ground of his own being', from the fearful commandment of God. The divine image only means the possibility and the demand of self-determination according to the will of God. Thus this doctrine expresses the personal independence of both God and man to a full extent which is not found elsewhere. This is why the demand of God is so unconditional. The objective correlative to the independent activity of man is the divine law. The claim which God makes on man is at the same time the declaration of man's independence and the ennoblement of his being by his creator—and also the cause of his despair.

For man is not equal to the claim God makes upon him. The divine imperative '*you shall*' contains in itself the implication '*you cannot*'; for it expresses the breakdown in the original relationship, man's fall from the relationship with God which God *gave* to the creation. God's answer to man's emancipation is the law, which cannot be fulfilled, precisely because it assumes the false position of man. No act which man makes on his own, no moral or religious achievement, can restore man's original nature. For everything that man now does, he does within a perverted relationship and from a perverted being. It is not so much his works that are at fault as his person. No moral activity can create a new person. 'It is not good works that make a good man, but a good man who does good works' (Luther).

Consequently, all *moral progress* is simply a change taking place within the condition of sinfulness, and to rely on this is a sign that the moral problem is not taken seriously. Moral improvement—the calculation of the degree of moral progress—is what Paul and Luther call 'the righteousness of works'. At heart, it is self-deception, 'hypocrisy'. Only one thing can be of any help: the divine descent to the level of sinful man, the unmerited pardoning of the sinner, 'justification *by faith alone*'. For from the human point of view faith is the complete abandonment of moral self-reliance in the sight of God, through the recognition that in all moral endeavour the subject of the action remains the perverted nature of man. But this abandonment only becomes possible when man can see the possibility of a new kind of life. Either man must carry out the deception of justifying himself, or else God must justify him by the free gift of grace. The thankful and trusting acceptance of this act of divine favour, the ready reception of the unprecedented and unmerited possibility of a new life, is the grace of justification, or faith in justification.

Both of these are one. Faith does not apprehend grace, *it is grace*. Grace consists of God's gift of faith, God's destruction (*mortificatio*) of the pride of man in his alleged moral progress, and his taking away of the despair which inevitably accompanies false pride (*vivificatio*). God, the creator, does this by conquering the heart of the sinner through his condescension and mercy in Christ. It is not the case that man is the subject who apprehends, and the divine word, the object which is apprehended; rather, the reverse is true: *God is the subject who apprehends* and man is the object that is apprehended. Thus the process of the divine revelation of salvation is brought to completion. In the revelation of the scripture it is God who is the subject who acts, who gives, and who creates. He creates faith in the same way —and everything depends upon this. If faith were the act of man, then the decisive action would still have been taken by man himself. But faith *cannot* be man's act. So far as it is an act on the part of man, faith is a half measure, a confused groping. This kind of faith (*credere, fides qua creditur*) is familiar to us. But we are justified by God, and regarded as pleasing to him, over and above this pitiable faith of ours, and we are assured of this through and yet far exceeding our own weak faith (our experience of faith), by the mighty *word* of God, which in so far as it is a voice that speaks within us is called the Holy Spirit. We do not understand how it can come about that the Spirit of God can, as it were, envelop our own self, which has been set down from the place it usurped. All we know is that in this process we are completely passive with regard to God, and completely active with regard to the world. For we were created to be passive with regard to God, to be a 'reflection' of God. But human nature is fulfilled in perfect abandonment to the creative word of God's grace; and in faith a new person is brought into being, a master craftsman who can do good works.

In faith we know that this is true. If we try to *think* about this we are bound to see God and the human self as two similar entities existing side by side and acting upon one another; thus what one gained would be what the other lost. But all this means is that our relationship to God is not a matter for thought, but for existential faith, not a subject for idle speculation, but for serious decision. In faith we understand the mystery that we become independent and free only when we claim and possess no independence in the sight of God. Apart from that, our only freedom is to choose sin, and this means servitude.

4. The Definition of Grace

The term grace is often used outside the Bible and the Christian Church which is based upon it (*cf.* I above). We wish to point out briefly that these usages are in no sense preparatory stages to the Christian faith, nor would they have led to it through a gradual and continuous process of development and assimilation; they are something fundamentally different, involving a categorical distinction which cannot be dismissed as a difference of 'degree'.

a. The concept of grace is common to all *cultic religions*. God, provoked to anger, is made 'gracious' by sacrifices and rites. We have already spoken of the element of truth which is contained in the idea of an expiatory sacrifice in particular. But the error it contains is equally obvious: this is the idea that man can affect divine grace by means of appropriate measures on his own part. This 'primitive' idea is replaced on a 'higher' level by the *ethical* concept that divine 'grace' can be guaranteed by a righteous moral disposition or, as it was later held, by a proper attitude of repentance. We meet this conception at the highest levels of human intellectual life (the Stoics, the Enlightenment, Kant, Lessing), but if anything, it is more directly opposed to Christian thought than the cultic idea.

b. The *mystical concept of grace* (*cf. Mysticism* pp. 355 ff. below) is quite different. It also occurs in two forms. The type of mysticism called personalist is radically opposed to pantheist mysticism. Anything that is good in the sight of God can only be God himself, and not some work, some individual thing, some external. The denial of the value of independent isolated and external actions is often expressed in terms very similar to those of Christian doctrine. But they mean something quite different: the withdrawal of the soul back into its original divine source, which in its most extreme form means the consciousness of the identity of the ultimate self with the godhead. This recognition of identity, compared to which everything that does not share this identity is mere appearance, this consciousness of the unity of the soul with God, which is always present, and has never been, nor can be, disturbed by anything, is referred to as grace. Everything outside it is an involvement in error or even in sin. Thus grace is never forgiveness, and far less atonement, but only the *soul's flight into itself*, which is always, at the same time, a flight to God. Logically, this condition is thought of as being attained by a continuous approach, *per viam negativam*.

A kind of intermediate teaching between this mysticism and the Christian doctrine of grace, is the idea of *gratia infusa*, which dominates the ideas of typical Catholic mysticism, and which A. Osiander sought to introduce into Protestantism, but which was energetically rejected by Lutherans, and especially by Calvin (*cf.* Vol. III, *Calvin* 3*b.*). It is the finest and most sublime expression of *ecstatic mysticism*. In ecstasy, a person feels as a matter of experience, that is, as something which is really happening, that he is lifted up into the divine being, or overwhelmed by spiritual forces or by the 'divine spirit', and, as it were, possessed. In Christian mysticism the directness of this communication of divine power is modified by the central Christian idea of the objective and historical revelation and atonement, by the word of God. Thus what we have here is not in the first instance mysticism, but faith in the word. But the point of this faith is blunted by mysticism; there is ultimately a return to a direct communication of divine power, and sometimes even to a magical infusion of the life of God into the human soul.

Protestant doctrine, and especially that of the Reformed Churches, offers a total resistance to this mystical endeavour. For as Luther always emphasized, its consequence is the assertion of a *direct sanctification*, which is in contradiction to Paul's fundamental insight, that even when we are justified we remain sinners. We receive grace in the *word* and not otherwise; and the form in which we receive it is faith, not mystical experience, not a direct communication or infusion which makes human nature similar to that of God. The acceptance of the word is an *actus forensis*, not an *actus physicus*. This is the only way in which the personal nature of this event can be maintained, and it is always removed by mysticism. A spiritual dialogue and exchange is still maintained, but it is a dialogue which takes place by means of the word, of which the hearer becomes the vessel not in a natural, but in a spiritual way, by the appropriation of the word, by faith. The very fact that our personal activity remains the 'vessel' of the word signifies that this process is not one of *making righteous* but of *declaring righteous*. It is of course a declaring righteous which at the same time is a moral force, and the Holy Spirit is given as a real gift, but both are present in such a way as not to do away with the reality of the sinful personality. The claim to sanctification based on the *infusio gratiae* inevitably leads to hypocrisy and ethical confusion. The doctrine of Osiander recurs at the present day in the form of the 'mysticism of faith'.

The Pauline and Reformation understanding of grace is a paradoxical intermediary between a moralism which isolates the independence and spontaneous activity of man from God, and the mysticism in which this independence is lost in God. The first leads to a deist doctrine of human freedom, and the second to a pantheist naturalism and determinism. The Christian doctrine agrees with moralism in upholding the reality of personal and moral action, but sees it as the act of *God*; it agrees with mysticism in emphasizing that it is God alone who acts, but asserts that he acts *personally*. This is why God acts through the *word*, in which he speaks to the human person and renews him. The fact that human nature is personal depends upon the divine word.

5. *The Dialectic of Grace*

Consequently, the Christian understanding of grace provides a *solution*—but a paradoxical solution, which is worked out within an irreconcilable contradiction— to the opposition between the two principal views of the world: idealism and naturalism, a system of freedom or a system of necessity. It resolves this contradiction by pushing it to extremes. Thus it does not resolve it for speculative thought—if this were possible, it would ultimately be no more than an illusion in any case—but only within and to the satisfaction of existential faith, which recognizes in the maintenance of this contradiction the promise that points to fulfilment.

This is most clearly seen in the development of the Pauline and Lutheran doctrine of grace, in which it apparently touches on the realm of speculation, that is, in the *doctrine of redemption*. It is a central biblical theme, even in the Old Testament, that the grace of God depends entirely upon his free choice. Otherwise it would not be grace, but merit. Free election is an act of God as sovereign Lord, and at the same time an incomprehensible manifestation of his love. This is the subject of the Bible and the faith of the New Testament: that we are chosen in Christ, for all eternity. Here the historical event and the eternal idea are united and one is true only with and in the other. That is why the idea of election is the point at which Christian thought tends towards a speculative synthesis in the manner of pantheism—Augustine and Zwingli did much more than tend towards it!—and at the same time most violently repudiates it. In isolation from the act of revelation, and taken on its own as the theoretical culmination of a system of doctrine—as in Beza and especially, later on, in Schleiermacher—the doctrine of election is a pantheist perversion of faith. But understood in existential and practical terms, as an expression of the truly personal action of God in revelation and faith, it is radically opposed to all speculation, because it bases everything on a personal decision. In its theoretical and false formulation, it means the end of freedom under the iron hand of divine necessity; but in practical and existential terms it is the very basis of the glorious freedom of the children of God, outside which there can be no true freedom at all. In its theoretical misinterpretation it denies the independence of the creature—as in Zwingli's *De providentia*—but understood in faith, it is the guarantee of human independence and dignity, the calling to be 'members of the household of God'.

EMIL BRUNNER

5
Certainty

1. The Problem

Windelband rightly distinguishes between *subjective certainty*, a state of mind which is the object of psychological study, and which varies from person to person according to their previous education and background (more easily, for example, in unphilosophical people, more willing to accept authority, than in a philosopher), and *objective certainty*, which can claim scientific validity. The question is, under what conditions can subjective certainty be regarded as objective? In answering this question we must distinguish *three sources* from which certainties can be derived and which claim to be objective: 1. The 'self-certainty of consciousness' or of 'pure experience', that is, the certainty that I experience what I experience in the way in which I experience it. 2. Logical necessity, or the compelling truth of logical and mathematical principles (axiomatic certainty). 3. Certainty about the supernatural realities which underlie religion and morality (the certainty of faith).

2. The Self-Certainty of Consciousness

The certainty of pure experience is interpreted differently in modern philosophy according to various positions adopted with regard to the theory of knowledge. *a.* According to the thorough-going realism such as is represented by Volkelt, the self-certainty of pure experience contains a certainty about a 'transubjective minimum', that is a certainty about the reality of transubjective existents, existing beyond consciousness independently of whether or not they are perceived, in the form of a numerically identical unity of chemical and physical events. There is a 'practical necessity' for the validity of the account of being which is given by experience. For without it sense impressions would be incoherent nonsense. *b.* According to the view of critical realism, as represented by Külpe and Dürr, the reality of transubjective existents is not exactly demonstrable. It is the object not of knowledge but of belief, that is, 'acceptance as reality of what is logically merely possible', an act of association on the part of the perceiver in which the second member of the association is not given and cannot be given. For there are no inherent characteristics on which to base a distinction between a physical phenomenon and a reality. *c.* According to the anti-realistic or conscientialist outlook, which appears in various forms as positivism, critical empiricism, and conscientialist idealism, there are no existents independent of consciousness. For no object can be thought of without a subject, so that to be conceived of is of the content of any experience (the so-called logical argument of conscientialism, disputed by realists). Consequently, the question of the real existence, beyond consciousness, of what is experienced, loses its meaning. All the certainty that our perception can attain to is the self-certainty of consciousness.

3. Logical Necessity
The second source from which we can obtain objective certainties is that of logical necessity. Axiomatic certainty is expressed in the first instance by the principle of contradiction, and by all so-called analytic statements, which depend upon the principle of contradiction, because their contraries contain a contradiction. But there are also the further fundamental truths which Kant calls synthetic statements *a priori*, which follow necessarily

from the *a priori* basis of the observation of space and time, and are therefore directly convincing (e.g. axioms of geometry such as 'a straight line is the shortest distance between two points'). Philosophers are divided between two divergent views of logical necessity. *a.* According to one view the compelling truth of the axioms is the participation of our finite mind in eternal truths and absolute values which are independent of the relative processes of consciousness. In association with Platonic and medieval tradition the basic principles of logic are still accorded a metaphysical significance by Descartes, Spinoza, Leibniz (*vérités logiques ou métaphysiques*) and Christian Wolff. Ontological metaphysics was a hypostatization of the basic forms of logic. Kant, of course, denied their material significance but retained them as *a priori* basic forms of experience. Windelband distinguishes sharply between the self-certainty which is characteristic of them and causal and psychological necessity. *b.* By contrast, empiricism, psychologism, and fictionalism have denied the absolute character of the fundamental truths of logic and mathematics. They are guiding principles of thought (R. Avenarius) or necessary fictions, which make it easier for us to find our way about the world of experience (Vaihinger). Every civilization has its own logic and mathematics (Spengler). The certainty with which we are convinced by these axioms is therefore not specifically different from the psychological necessity with which inherited habits of thought and involuntary conceptions impose themselves upon our minds.

4. The Certainty of Faith

The third source from which certainties can be derived is that of moral conviction and religious faith. The certainty of faith is certainty about the meaning of the world and of life, of the existence of eternal values and unconditional judgements, of realities beyond the senses, such as God and the immortality of the soul, the redemption and consummation of the world and of the individual soul.

a. THE DEGREES OF THIS KIND OF CERTAINTY. The certainty which faith claims for itself, like the self-certainty of consciousness and the fundamental principles of thought, is asserted to be not merely a subjective certainty, that is, a state of mind which is only of psychological significance, but an *objective certainty*, of which the universal validity must be acknowledged at least as a possibility even by scientific thought.

b. ITS RELATIONSHIP TO THE CERTAINTY OF TRUTH. The relationship between the certainty of faith and the certainty of knowledge depends upon how the certainty of knowledge is evaluated by one's theory of knowledge. If the certainty of knowledge, that is, the self-certainty of pure experience and logical necessity, can be demonstrated in a way that is without dispute absolutely valid, then by contrast with the power of logically compelling demonstrations possessed by knowledge properly so-called, faith has only 'intuitive certainty' (Volkelt). This is based not upon a disinterested perception, but upon a direct feeling. It is possible, with Volkelt, to attribute to these 'intuitive modes of certainty' their own proper right to be regarded as objective truth, and consequently to accept them as a second way to objective certainty, which is just as valid as the logical way and 'complements, confirms and enlivens it'. Or else, with Windelband, one can accord to faith merely a subjective certainty. 'Faith is the subjective certainty which depends upon the psychologically necessary mingling of a theoretical conception with the consciousness of ethical necessity.' In it 'neither the strength of an individual conviction nor the universal empirical applicability of a subjective certainty can be regarded as criteria of objective certainty'. The assertions of faith are postulates of practical reason which do not possess a theoretical universal validity. The relationship between the certainty of faith and logical certainty is different, even though the certainty of knowledge is in the last analysis a form of faith, once we acknowledge that there is a possibility of doubting even the certainty of pure experience and of logical necessity; 'the possibility of this doubt cannot be eliminated by any scientific means'. Even the faith on which our thought is based depends, as recent exponents of the theory of knowledge have shown in various ways (Sigwart, Windelband, Rickert), upon a quite unique and indestructible feeling, the 'feeling of conviction', the 'feeling of assent', the 'feeling of certainty'. Thus the faith which arises from moral need and religious longing is only distinguished from the 'faith on which our thought is based' by its content and the way it arises. But the certainty of both is of equal value.

c. ITS BASIS. The basis of the certainty of faith depends upon what is regarded as the content of faith, or more exactly upon what is distinguished from the inessentials, which may vary, as the absolutely necessary core of moral and religious conviction.

i. There is a kind of faith which does not reach beyond the content of human consciousness and the world of experience. This is the monist faith in the inner unity and harmony of the universe, in the validity of moral ideals and the victory of good in the world. The content of this faith is immanent in the world, and its certainty depends upon the assumption that what is of value is real simply because it is of value. This basis for faith is found as early as the system of Plato, in which the idea of the good, that is the highest value, is also accorded the highest rank in the hierarchy of thought, and it culminates in Kant's doctrine of the primacy of practical reason, to which he accords the right of deriving statements about the nature of things from ethical evaluation.

238

ii. The basis of faith is different when it cannot avoid 'the acceptance of something real beyond the reality to which the world of phenomena points' (Dürr), that is, when it asserts the existence of an absolute and omnipotent personality who stirs our spirit and evokes in us a direct feeling of independence, mystery, and longing (Wobbermin). *The certainty of God* cannot be derived directly, in a single step, from the world of experience (in fact according to Kant a conclusion drawn from relative phenomena can never lead beyond relative causes), nor can it be derived from a single postulate (one cannot conclude from the moral value of an idea the existence of a reality corresponding to it). Rather, the certainty of God rests upon the assumption that the normal human consciousness contains an apprehension of God as a necessary element in itself, in exactly the same way as it contains self-consciousness, that is, that we are as certain of God as we are of our own existence. According to the German mystics the 'little spark' in the depths of the soul is one with God. According to Schleiermacher the consciousness of God is a coefficient of every normal self-consciousness. 'The experience of one's own self', Wobbermin says, 'forms for man the most assured certainty of reality which is possible for him. It is the prerequisite of all belief in the existence of the external world.' But the experience of oneself includes that of the relation of the self to external experience, the apprehension of the limits of the self, and consequently includes within itself a relationship to a transcendent and original reality. Thus faith in God depends (according to Troeltsch) ultimately upon faith in the normality and meaningful organization of our consciousness.

iii. The basis of the certainty of faith becomes even harder to establish when the hard core of the content of faith has to include not merely mystical contact with the transcendental God, but the *redemption* and *atonement* of the world and the individual soul by the *historical Christ*. The question is then how faith can be certain of this matter of historical fact and its redeeming power in the face of historical criticism. An attempt has been made to solve this problem in three ways. The first way is that of the retreat from Christian experience to its immanent and transcendental presuppositions, leading beyond the sensible world, in F. R. Frank's *System of Christian Certainty*. The self, being born again, is certain both of the effect it experiences and also of the factors which have brought this effect into being (*Spektralanalyse*). Frank's method of attaining certainty failed to achieve acceptance because the experience of one who is born again, which in this theory is made to provide the entire certainty as to the content of faith, is never in reality a perfected entity, but is always something growing and struggling towards attainment. By contrast to this subjective approach on the part of Frank, W. Herrmann saw as the basis for the certainty of faith an objective historical reality, which even someone who has no religious experience can still perceive even in the midst of the profoundest doubt, that is, 'the inner life of Jesus'. Anyone who comes through this reality to experience for the first time what the true reality of personal life is, will inevitably cease to ask whether the person of Jesus belongs to true history or to poetry. He will be forced to accept that there must be a power over all things which will not let this Jesus be abandoned in the world. Thus the person of Christ and the reality of God become for him something certain beyond all doubt. This objective basis of certainty proposed by Herrmann has been disputed on the grounds that in fact the first impression produced by the figure of Jesus upon many persons is neither the certainty of God nor certainty concerning the historical reality and redeeming power of Christ, so that this objective entity must be supplemented by a further subjective factor in order to create the certainty of faith. This leads to the solution of Ihmels: certainty arises when God imparts himself to an individual through the Spirit by means of the impression made by the word of Christ. In this 'experience beyond the senses' which must be distinguished from the experience of the senses, but which remains 'a mystery that cannot be passed on', there is also imparted in and within personal salvation the certainty of the transcendental presuppositions of this, the reality of God, and of the saving acts.

5. Conclusion

Philosophical discussions of the certainty of truth, and the theological dispute about the basis of the certainty of faith, have made us conscious of the *problem* which constantly returns in various forms. The struggle for certainty has come to a dead end. So long as we regard the *self* in the traditional way as a spiritual being localized in the human body, and endowed with a limited sphere of consciousness, it is hopelessly confined within the limits of its subjectivity. It can certainly put forward suggestions and draw conclusions about what lies beyond the limits of the consciousness; it can certainly demand, as Volkelt points out, that the 'transubjective minimum' must possess a certain definite constitution if all perception is not to be meaningless. But all these conclusions and postulates cannot attain to the self-certainty of what is directly perceived, which we need in order to speak of certainty. If there is to be any conceivable certainty about anything that is a reality not only for me at this moment, but always and everywhere and to everyone, then the traditional conception of the self must be broken into at the decisive point. As has been clearly shown by Rickert, we must return to a critically examined and purified form of the concept of the self held by German mysticism (*cf. Mysticism* V*b*. pp. 380 ff., below) and German idealism: if we go behind the conventional bodily and psychosomatic meaning of the word 'self' to its ultimate meaning, we are no longer referring to an object of perception, neither to a visible nor an invisible object. We mean by it something which is not of the nature of an object, and which is so immediate, close, and familiar to us, that our perception is quite incapable of considering it in the manner of an object. But if the self lies beyond objective experience, then it also lies beyond the categories and forms of perception of the world of experience. It then becomes possible for the self to break out of the bonds of existence in time and space and to obtain a direct vision through the whole of being. Thus certainty is possible about something which is real not only for myself, but always and everywhere and for everyone. This discovery of the background to the world which *does not exist in the form of objects* reveals a whole world of new relationships to be investigated, that is, the relationships which exist between the unobservable element of the whole of reality, which does not exist in the form of objects, and the observable element consisting of objects. Since the time of Aristotle's 'categories' (set out in the first part of the *Organon*) it has been the more or less evident aim of philosophy to elucidate these primary relationships, that is, the categories in which the world of experience is constructed. The phenomenological school within modern philosophy has once again taken up this task. Although everything is still very fluid, it is possible to affirm the following points as a preliminary *conclusion*. The primary form of experience is time. Within time there takes place a continuous alternation between two conditions of the whole of reality. Everything that exists, exists in the first instance at the present moment in an immediate condition, and not yet in the form of objects. In this condition everything is still alive and undifferentiated. It then passes from this molten condition into the frozen condition of the past. It is only in this second stage that we encounter it as objective experience. It is possible to measure and analyse it. It fits into the structure of causality. It becomes a reality, by contrast with many possibilities which might just as easily have replaced it. It therefore becomes a relative, historical phenomenon. The thorough-going relativism, which draws under its spell everything that enters the consciousness, even logical and mathematical axioms, ethical values, and the truths of faith, and treats them as relative, psychological phenomena, is therefore a necessary expression of the fact that the form of all experience is time. It now becomes clear what is meant by the certainty of faith. The relativism and psychologism which make everything relative and uncertain can only be overcome if there is, outside the condition of temporality, a second non-temporal being. The reality of a supra-temporal being can only be known within the temporal world of the consciousness in one way, that is, when a phenomenon possesses within the world of experience an absolute value of which it is not deprived when it passes into the second stage in which everything becomes relative, that is, into the condition of objectivity. This is why the certainty of God is always imparted by an historical revelation. A person, present in the midst of the temporal context of the world, makes commands and gives forgiveness in the name of God who is beyond time. This claim of Jesus to full moral and religious authority miraculously remains unshaken in the minds of those who are called to be his disciples, when it passes into the condition which makes relative the claim of every other temporal entity to be absolute, that is, when it passes from the condition of a direct experience to be the object of reflection and part of the structure of causality

243

(and of the study of its place in the history of religion). This unshakable conviction cannot rest either on causal or logical necessity. It is the revaluation of a supra-temporal existence within time. It is a self-revelation of God, carried out by the Holy Spirit (*testimonium Spiritus Sancti internum*).

KARL HEIM

6

Philosophy

I THE CONCEPT AND NATURE
OF PHILOSOPHY

1. *The Problem*

The nature of philosophy can only be defined by philosophy itself, for there is nothing beyond it to which a further appeal can be made. It is itself the final court of appeal; consequently any understanding of philosophy is the expression of a philosophical outlook, and it is impossible to talk about the nature of philosophy in general terms. Of course it is equally impossible to give any impression of what philosophy is by listing the numerous definitions of philosophy that have appeared in the course of history; the understanding of a philosophical statement can never be derived from outside philosophy, but only from the philosophical approach, and from the tensions that arise in philosophical work. Consequently, an investigation into the nature of philosophy is necessarily a concrete philosophical study, and its conclusion the expression of a particular philosophical conviction. But the elucidation of one particular element in these assertions is of fundamental importance, and that is the fact that philosophy is its own final court of appeal. For this fact about philosophy means that it has an unlimited possibility of free self-determination. The elucidation of this attribute of philosophy would provide a judgement which transcended the definition of a particular field of philosophical study, and thus would be more than the mere elucidation of someone's own personal philosophical conviction. But this is only true to a limited degree, for this transcendent account would not possess the character of an abstract general statement. Philosophy, which looks to itself as a final court of appeal, can only be described in its own terms. An element is isolated which cannot in itself be regarded as abstract, but is always firmly rooted in the concrete solutions offered to philosophical problems. Thus even the elucidation of this distinctive attribute of philosophy can only be carried out in concrete terms, in the context of a specific philosophical conviction. Even the most general statement about philosophy cannot escape this tension.

2. *Philosophy as a Specifically Human Potentiality*

Philosophy is its own final court of appeal. The first step in philosophy is the rejection of any possible court of appeal outside it. It is the most radical form of inquiry, which on principle assumes nothing beforehand. *Philosophy assumes nothing outside itself; it never begins anywhere except at the beginning.* The possibility of such an attitude is inherent in the nature of man; for it is characteristic of man that he is not limited to what he encounters, but in every encounter is simultaneously able to go beyond it. This means that he is able to have a 'world', that is, he can see what he encounters as part of a whole. Therefore he is able to practise philosophy; that is, he is able to inquire into the whole of what he meets and perceives, into the world. His questioning implies that he is not satisfied with his direct possession of the world, and that he desires to have the world in a new form prescribed by himself; that is, to comprehend it. Comprehension is one way in which man possesses what he encounters, a way in which he distinguishes what he encounters as separate from himself, maintains it as something separate, and then subdivides it; he divides it

246

into what on the one hand he directly encounters, and on the other the true form recognizable in what is separate and distinct from himself. It is this attitude on the part of man to what he encounters which makes him human; it is not yet philosophy, but it is what makes philosophy possible. But this possibility remains latent so long as man's questioning is restricted to the context of his own immediate activity, so long as his intention in distinguishing things from himself is to deal with them aright, that is, to achieve his own purposes in dealing with them. This in itself involves standing apart from what man encounters, and sub-dividing it. But there is not as yet any explicit intention of contrasting and distinguishing between what is true and what is untrue. This is not the issue, but is something that is merely assumed, as for example in the search for the correct form of cult, or the correct technique of performing some task. Philosophy is present at the moment when there is an explicit intention of contemplating what is encountered as a separate entity, and making the above-mentioned distinction with regard to it. This approach can be termed pure 'theory'. But we must warn against a frequent modern misunderstanding: 'theory' should not be understood as a contemplation, sufficient in itself and distinct from 'practice'. In its original sense, theory means rather the attitude of contemplation as the highest form of life. The 'purpose' for the sake of which what is encountered is identified as a separate object, and the distinction made between what is true and untrue in it, is the desire to be one with what is true in itself, with truth itself. There is no intention of 'beginning' some process that will make use of the object of contemplation for something else. The purpose of considering it in this way is rather the understanding of its true being. The whole approach is fulfilled in 'theory'. And in principle there is no intention of seeking any practical result, even though this may in fact come about. This is the original attitude to which philosophy owes its existence and its characteristic approach. Philosophy is the attitude of explicit inquiry, an inquiry that leads to theory and is basically fulfilled in theory. *Philosophy is the attitude in which the specifically human power of inquiry becomes explicit.*

3. The Nature of Philosophy as Historical Reality

This elucidation of the nature of philosophy as a specifically human potentiality is of course in no sense a general definition of philosophy. Such a definition is impossible, since the concrete nature of philosophy depends upon how the attitude of pure theory is related to all possible human attitudes. This can vary greatly. *Not merely philosophical doctrines, but the 'nature' of philosophy itself is historical.*

Philosophy has followed its own historical course, and that is why it is possible for its nature to achieve one *classical* fulfilment, such that all further realizations of it can only lay claim to the name philosophy in a derivative sense. This possibility came about in reality: the original Greek sense of philosophy was never again attained, nor ever can be; for it depends upon the background of Greek existence as a whole. Only on the basis of the world of the Homeric gods, and especially of the Apollinian consciousness, the controlled and serene passion of the Greeks, could 'contemplation', as the perfection of man's being, subordinate to itself and permeate all other attitudes to what is encountered.

The situation alters as early as the ethical and religious schools of later antiquity (the Stoics, Neo-Platonists, and Neo-Pythagoraeans); *pure theory becomes the basis of a rational ethic, or is fulfilled through religious ecstasy.* In Christianity, and later, in a similar way, in Islam, the specifically religious attitude (*cf.* III below) came to be completely dominant. And yet the effect of the Greek inheritance continued to be felt. Contemplation, now admittedly regarded as the vision of the divine in its pure transcendence, remained the goal of religion (*cf. Mysticism* p. 363 below), and—something which was even more important—religious doctrines actually presented themselves as philosophy (*cf. Revelation* pp. 46 ff.) above). Even when they were considered to be derived from revelation, they take the form of answers to radical, that is, to philosophical questions. In these circumstances, philosophy took on a new meaning. Radical inquiry, the return to the absolute beginning, was limited by the assumptions of a religious tradition in question. But it was not ignored. *Philosophy was formalized, turned into a propaedeutic discipline, into an instrument of theology.* Inquiry into what its normal content should be came to an end.

This situation lasted only until the close of the Middle Ages. The formalization of philosophy, as found in scholasticism, could not be maintained. The concept of the two-fold truth, an attempt to avoid the issue, was of value in avoiding a direct conflict but was an impossible theory in practice. Philosophy in the Greek sense seemed to have been reborn with the rest of the ancient world in Renaissance humanism. This was mere appearance. In reality, the destiny of philosophy underwent a change. Its meaning altered. The attitude that became prevalent was not that of the Greeks, that of pure theory, but the active desire of Western man to form a world according to his own wishes. He seized on the tradition of the Greeks in order to adapt it to his own purposes. *Philosophy became an instrument of the radical rationalization of what is encountered, in order to serve man's purpose of ordering the world according to his own desires.* This came about in two ways: philosophy became the theory of a rational science devoted to forming and making use of the world, and it became the theory of a rational view of the world and a rational ethic which accepted that the course of the world was formed by its own immanent laws. In the second application, it came into constant conflict with views of the world based on religion. Sometimes the starting point of this process, the desire to order the world according to a rational plan, seemed to have been abandoned, as in the systems of the romantic period, romanticism, idealism (*cf.* Schelling, Hegel). But here again, this is inaccurate: no romantic philosopher wanted to return to pure contemplation in the Greek sense of 'theory'. The powerful counter-attacks made against romanticism by positivism show what the real meaning of philosophy is in the West.

4. Present and Future Philosophy

A characteristic of present-day philosophy is that it is permeated by the consciousness of its place in historical development. One reason for this is the historicizing of all our thought, not excluding what are alleged to be eternal categories and functions, which are also accorded their place in history. It is also associated with the fundamental attack aimed at philosophy in particular by the sociology that is influenced by Marxism, which attempts to dismiss philosophy as a socially reactionary outlook. Doubt is also cast on philosophy as a possible attitude by modern Protestant dialectical theology. At best, it is accorded the task of defending the limits of what is possible for man against excessive claims based on metaphysics. It is accepted as an anti-metaphysical criticism. Finally, the internal fragmentation of the present philosophical situation has led philosophy to reflect on its own significance at the present day and on its future destiny. It can scarcely be disputed that its significance at the present day is slight. As far as the theory of science is concerned, the lead is taken by individual sciences themselves, and it is a sign of philosophical honesty that in the first instance the philosopher does not attempt to intervene in this process. In its view of the world, and in ethics, philosophy has attained its goal of removing all hindrances to the idea of the formation and development of the world according to its own immanent laws. But it has not provided any positive substitute. It has continually failed to provide an answer to the question of the meaning of the immanent activity by which the world is formed. The answers given by religious tradition, however, are seen to be inadequate to the new situation. In these circumstances, the way has been prepared for a *new stage in the course of philosophical development*, the beginnings of which can perhaps already be seen. The union of the 'philosophy of life' and phenomenology, and the approach of the philosophy of history, which is becoming increasingly prominent, point towards this; for the significance of the philosophy of history is not the creation of a new object for philosophy alongside others, but a new philosophical approach. This is given the name of 'existential philosophy'. The ultimate meaning and the consequences of this complicated concept cannot be seen at the present time. What is certain is that it faces philosophy with a task that is as much different from the aims of previous philosophical work in the West as the latter differs from medieval philosophy. For once the subject of the act of knowing is included in the object of knowledge—this is the meaning of 'existential'—*the straightforward question of the form taken by things and events in the world is replaced by the question of their concrete historical and sociological meaning*. But the answer to this question demands different categories and a different attitude to that of the philosophy which considers the form taken by things and events in the world.

5. *Philosophy and Science*

The relationship of philosophy to other fields of thought itself forms part of the course of philosophy and cannot be defined in general terms. This is particularly true of related subjects; religion on the one hand, and science on the other. They are related to philosophy, in so far as they also ask fundamental questions. But they ask them in a different sense from philosophy. Since the relation of religion to philosophy is dealt with separately (*cf.* III below), we shall only make a few comments here on *the relationship of philosophy to science.* First of all, we must establish that from its very nature philosophy must claim an absolute primacy over science; for philosophical inquiry is radical in a way that scientific study cannot be, because its subject at any time must be given in advance. Consequently, it is inappropriate to speak of 'scientific philosophy'. It is philosophy that defines what science is, and not the reverse. At most, such a phrase can only mean 'strictly argued' or 'methodical' philosophy. But it is not only science which is strictly argued and methodical. Thus the relationship can be defined by saying that scientific inquiry is directed towards concrete types of object laid down in advance, while philosophical inquiry considers the inquiry itself, its character and its object. *Philosophical inquiry is radical*; it goes to the root of the matter, that is, to the point where all inquiry begins, while *science assumes the act of inquiry and its objects.* But this definition has not yet been expressed in concrete terms. It lacks any closer account of the relationship between the two types of inquiry. Once again, such an account cannot be given in general terms. In the oldest Greek philosophy scientific inquiry was still completely identified with philosophy. In the later Greek period it obtained a partial independence. The development from the Renaissance to the nineteenth century is similar. Of course there has never been a complete separation, and there never can be, since the form taken by concrete inquiry is always dependent on the nature of the radical inquiry that underlies it. Every science has an explicit or implicit philosophical basis. Sometimes, the philosophy of a period can most clearly be perceived in the philosophical spirit in which scientific study is carried out. Philosophy is not merely to be sought where philosophical discourse is carried on—this is often the last place to look for it. Consequently, the primacy of philosophy does not mean a temporal and causal precedence of philosophy over science. Rather, it is frequently the case that science comes first, while philosophy later reveals its basic assumptions. This does not affect the nature of the real relationship in principle. The primacy of radical inquiry over questions limited to concrete terms still remains.

6. The Method and Object of Philosophy

The method of philosophy can only be defined by its nature and by philosophy itself. *Its method is its nature.* Phenomenological philosophy is the phenomenological method, and critical philosophy is the critical method. The method and philosophy itself are one, where we are directly concerned with the primary approach; the method of philosophy is to find a method, to mark out a path where no path yet exists. To define the *object* of philosophy is once again the task of philosophy itself. Nevertheless, it is possible to isolate those problems which are of overriding importance. The first results from the fact that the objects of philosophy and of science are largely the same: nature and history, man and his intellectual life, in all their theoretical and practical aspects. Thus the difference cannot lie in their objects at this level. The objects of philosophy cannot be on the same level as other objects; the object of philosophy must be a special quality common to all types of object. *Philosophy is not concerned with particular sets or kinds of object, but with a quality common to them all,* with the quality of being an object at all, the quality of being able to be the object of a radical inquiry, of the inquiry into the nature of all inquiry. In their own way, all objects constitute *the object* of philosophy, in so far as they are concrete representations of the state of being an object, or of the ability to be the object of inquiry. Thus on the one hand, everything can be the object of philosophy, while on the other hand, philosophy has no special object of its own (which is why there is a philosophy of nature, a philosophy of civilization and of history, a philosophy of religion, ethics, etc.). This seems to contradict the fact that certain fields of thought have always shown a tendency to become the particular field of philosophy: logic, the theory of knowledge, and metaphysics. *Psychology* is not included among these. The fact that it is still closely linked to philosophy is evidence of the uncertain state of its own distinctive scientific structure, and also shows how closely the particular questions it asks are related to all inquiry—but this does not justify the evaluation of it as a particular philosophical discipline. With *logic*, the case is different. It is directed towards the *logos*, the rational coherence inherent in every inquiry and in any possible answer. Thus it has a genuinely philosophical quality—that is, so long as it understands its task in these terms, and is not misused by trying to make it a normative doctrine of thought. When this takes place, its philosophical quality disappears. But where it remains an inquiry into the inherent *logos*, the rational coherence of all inquiry, then it is not a special discipline of philosophy, but philosophy itself in its distinctive quality as the absolute beginning of all inquiry.

The situation is similar, although more complicated, in the case of the *theory of knowledge*. The question of the nature of any inquiry directly poses the problem of knowledge. It is not a separate problem, but an aspect of the philosophical problem itself. The theory of knowledge has obtained its special position from a unique conjunction of historical circumstances, the struggle of critical philosophy against a perverse metaphysics. The problem of knowledge is the battle ground on which this conflict is fought. The idea of Kant, that one must first examine the instrument before one uses it, gave the theory of knowledge the rank of the fundamental discipline of philosophy. But this status is as untenable as the idea of Kant which underlies it. Every doctrine of knowledge contains a fundamental answer to the inquiry into the nature of inquiry—as its background and unacknowledged assumption. The 'instrument of knowledge' which is to be examined can only be examined by means of itself, so that it is already assumed beforehand. The problem of knowledge is inherent in the whole philosophical problem, but possesses no primacy or independence with regard to it. Thus metaphysics remains as the most disputed distinctive field of philosophy. *But metaphysics is either philosophy itself, or it is nothing.* The acceptance of a special object which is properly the object of metaphysics is the sign of the perverse metaphysics which critical philosophy destroyed. The transcendence with which all philosophy is concerned is not the false transcendence of a reality beyond the world of experience, but the genuine transcendence of the radical inquiry which looks into inquiry itself. The 'objects' of metaphysics—for this is what metaphysics is—are not separate things, lying beyond experience, but the qualities of the world of experience in which answers to the radical inquiries of philosophy can be found. From this point of view, metaphysics and philosophy are identical, and the questions of philosophical *or* metaphysical inquiry include both logical inquiry and the theory of knowledge, and also the question as to which qualities of all aspects of being are important for philosophy. Thus there is only one philosophy, and no philosophical 'disciplines'. At most, a distinction can be made between fundamental and derivative philosophy. But there are considerations which weigh against even this distinction. The more 'existential' the procedure of philosophy, the less it is able to abstract from the completely concrete limitations laid down by what it encounters in its inquiry. It is in their concrete nature itself that they are of metaphysical significance for a 'historical' philosophy. There is no universal *fundamentum* beyond this concrete existence. Thus even with regard to the distinction between fundamental and derivative philosophy, it is necessary to maintain the unity of philosophy, that is, of radical inquiry, the inquiry into the nature of inquiry itself.

PAUL TILLICH

II*a* PHILOSOPHY AND RELIGION IN HISTORY

1. The Problem

By philosophy we do not merely mean here the theory of knowledge, or a closed system of related ideas about the nature and meaning of the world, but *wisdom about the world* in the fullest sense. This wisdom about the world can include a general world view; it can appear in the form of a theory of rational knowledge, and attempt to control all knowledge; it can also be fragmentary in nature. But in both cases, wisdom is applied to the world, that is to the whole of life, the meaning of which it attempts to elucidate. This is the basis of its essential relationship and, at the same time, of its conflict with religion. For religion also is concerned with the experience of the world in its entirety, and tries to understand the ultimate meaning of life. Furthermore, when religion comes to develop a theology, it can lead to a doctrine of rational knowledge which attempts to regulate all other fields of knowledge; and with the help of this theology it can develop a systematic view of the world. But where religious thought is still elementary, it can make only occasional and incoherent statements about the world as a whole. It can even omit such utterances entirely. But even where this is true, and in fact in every case, all religion brings with it consequences for man's view of the world, and for rational knowledge. Religion also claims to be wisdom; not worldly wisdom but divine wisdom. Both religion and philosophy produce a picture of the world. But philosophy regards the world from below, its starting point being man. Religion looks down upon the world from above. This is why every relationship between the two is possible, from complete identity to mutual contempt and condemnation, depending upon whether the emphasis is on what they seek in common, or on their different starting points. The usual situation, however, is one of mutual mistrust (*cf.* III below).

2. *The Connection between Religion and Philosophy in the History of Religion*

In the *primitive world* our problem does not yet exist. There is a wisdom there which attempts to understand the world. There, too, religion is concerned with a world view. But thought is not yet emancipated; it is still religious *per se*. And the distinction between the world and God, between what is below and what is above, which is decisive for the relationship between philosophy and religion, does not yet exist, or exists only in a rudimentary form. The great distinction on which all religion rests, that of sacred and profane, runs throughout the whole of life, and permeates all thought, in the sense that both exist together. Primitive men do not have the ability to think at one time about God and at another time about the world. The most insignificant 'secular' occasion has a religious meaning; and religious activities are exceedingly practical in nature. Whether thought is concerned with God or with the world, it takes the form of myth (*cf. Myth and Mythology* pp. 342 ff., below), and as such follows its own laws. While later thought, in the form of theology and philosophy, tries to eliminate intuitive apprehension and to replace it by conceptual ideas, and so to replace dependence on the emotions by thought as dispassionate and unprejudiced as possible, mythical thought delights in sensible forms, which are related to one another in accordance with the emotions of the perceiver.

Consequently, we have to look for the beginning of the *relationship between philosophy and religion* in those civilizations which, although they are still extensively affected by mythical thought, have already begun to escape from its total dominance. Philosophical ideas insinuate themselves into religion. If a unified philosophical structure comes into being, it is still strongly marked by religious and mythical views. But there cannot be philosophy unless concern is predominantly directed towards man, his faculties of knowledge and his power to understand the universe. In other words, philosophy gradually separates itself from religion by the means of the theory of knowledge, but adopts religious conceptions in so doing.

A very interesting example of this can be seen from ancient *Egypt*. The so-called Shabako stone, on the left side of which is preserved a very ancient mystery ritual coming from the Old Kingdom, has on its right-hand side a series of theological and philosophical speculations concerning the god Ptah of Memphis. Yet it is not concerned with this god or with the other gods named in the text as such, but with a psychological and epistemological interpretation of the divine forms presented by theology. Ptah is regarded as the 'heart and tongue of the nine-fold divinity, he who created the gods'. Thus the heart and tongue, the organs of knowledge and speech, are made the origin of all things. And because Ptah is this heart and tongue, he therefore becomes the oldest god: following the familiar procedure of theological syncretism he becomes the father and mother of the god Atum, who by that time himself represented an amalgamation of several gods. But here Atum becomes the thought that proceeds from Ptah, that is from the heart and tongue: 'There arose in the heart, there arose on the tongue a thought in the form of Atum'. The heart and tongue acquire power over all the limbs. But what Ptah is at the origin of the world, he is everywhere where knowledge and thought take place: he is 'as the heart in every body, and the tongue in every mouth, of all gods, men, cattle, etc., thinking as the heart and commanding as the tongue all things which he desires'. 'It is the heart which gives rise to every piece of knowledge, it is the tongue which repeats what is thought by the heart. But every word of God comes about through what is thought by the heart and commanded by the tongue.' This is a kind of theory of knowledge, and at the same time a kind of *logos* doctrine. Thought and word, as a unity of two in one, form the principle of the world. The gods, with Ptah at their head, are merely names. In essence, we have here a fragment of ancient philosophy, and only in name a 'memorial of the theology of Memphis', as the text has been called. This philosophy is certainly associated with religion, but is looking for a psychological and epistemological interpretation. That is, it is making an attempt to understand the world from below.

Israelite religion provides an analogous example. Certainly, its nature is quite different from that of any philosophy. The Old Testament religion of Yahweh presents so immediate and passionate an experience of God that there is barely any room even for ethical re-

259

flections. Everything else is directly mythical or prophetic. But once Iranian, Greek, and other influences began to create a religious interest in the human side of events, it was once again a human faculty of knowledge which served to explain the world. *Wisdom* was born at the beginning of time, before the creation of the world (Prov. 8.24); it came forth from the mouth of God (Ecclus. 24.3); it is 'a breath of the power of God, and a pure emanation of the glory of the Almighty' (Wisdom 7.25). Wisdom was a master-workman at the creation (Prov. 8.30), and was sent down to men from the throne of heaven as a revelation of the divine will (Wisdom 9.10). A synthesis of human abilities is exalted above the world and above time, to explain the whole in terms of human understanding. In the same way, the Egyptian Isis became 'wisdom' at the period of syncretism.

Originally, all speculation was also foreign to *Islam*. As philosophical tendencies pressed upon it from every side, and took possession of it, the aim of secular wisdom remained in principle the same as that of religion, but the significance of the latter varied, depending upon whether it was expounded to those who were philosophically enlightened, or to simple people. Philosophers and mystics could reveal the nature of religion, each in his own way, but naïve images were portrayed to the people. This led to numerous disputes. For it was not possible to understand the so-called popular religion as a naïve reflection of sublime philosophical teaching. In *China*, the situation was different again. There philosophical thought was associated with the ancient conception of the 'path of life'. The universe goes upon its eternal way, active and yet without action; man should find and follow this *tao*. A mystical understanding of the nature of the universe is associated here with a primitive belief in fundamental forces, but also with a philosophy which unites man and the world as *one* being. Here again, the starting point of philosophy is human psychology and ethics, although as soon as it becomes mysticism it goes beyond this.

India is the land of the marriage of philosophy and religion. Here again, the great systems, which belong as much to the history of philosophy as to that of religion, proceed from human psychology, incorporating much ancient and primitive material at the same time. Speculation about sacrifice in Vedic religion, etc., was the cause of the important identification of *Brahman* and *Atman*. Brahman is a force like *mana* which operates in the first instance in sacrifice. Atman is the primitive breath or soul. Both become a divine principle, the soul of the world and the soul of man. The highest insight is that of the identity of the two. It is scarcely an accident that the religions in which a mysticism of *infinity* (*cf. Mysticism* pp. 361 ff. below) gradually came to dominate every other aspect, as in Taoism and the religion of the Upanishads, welcomed philosophical endeavour so much more readily than theistic religions such as Israel and Islam. Although the latter are also concerned with an ultimate unity, they do not seek this unity so passionately as the monist and mystical religions. But even where dualism made itself felt in India, philosophy was first of all preoccupied with human psychology, proceeding thence to the world and contemplating God, the world and the soul in one, in an ultimate unity. The Samkhya system faces up to the hard fact of the not-*Atman*, the transitory world of endless variation. The basic substance underlying this world is known by the neuter *avyaktam*, the undeveloped, or by the feminine word *prakrti*. Prakrti has three colours, called *guna*'s: the light or joyful, the moving or painful, and the gloomy or rigid. These three basic categories develop into the infinite variety of phenomena. In contrast to this variety stands the *purusha* (thought of as masculine), the spirit (*Atman*), the one male spirit contrasted with infinite female variety. This is a very ancient pattern, and the *purusha* is originally a kind of Tom Thumb, and so is phallic in nature. These speculations draw on ancient religious conceptions. The *purusha* is restricted by the variety of the *guna*'s; the spirit suffers under this confinement. Thus suffering is the nature of existence. Only asceticism or insight into the nature of suffering can bring redemption, the longing for which means that, in spite of everything, this psychological, ethical and philosophical system still retains the character of a religion.

We meet similar conceptions in *Greek philosophy*. Here too, in Orphic religion, a whole system of the universe is based upon the longing for redemption; here again, matter is regarded as the prison of the spirit; here, too, religious and ethical dualism has turned into a cosmological and speculative dualism. Even today, psychology and philosophy feel themselves hampered by the rigid dualism imposed upon them by this 'Greek experience', according to which the spirit is an independent substance of divine origin, opposed to human life and to the world. This means that even today, in the philosophy influenced by the Greeks, the original religious themes, which aimed at redemption, can still be recognized. But this preoccupation with the human soul and its destiny is only one starting point of Greek philosophy. Another lies in the attempt to experience the infinite variety of the world as a unity, as found in the thought of the so-called hylozoists. Joël has shown the considerable extent to which the search of Thales, Anaximander, and Heraclitus for an $\dot{a}\rho\chi\eta$, an original principle, which at the same time would be an original force, was still based upon mysticism. But once the human spirit, with its divine attributes, becomes the $\dot{a}\rho\chi\eta$, philosophy has become independent.

In *Christianity* and in the western world, influenced by Christianity, attempts to absorb philosophy in religion continually alternate with attempts to make religion part of philosophy. At the same time, there have always been those who have defended a dualism of philosophy and religion. But in general it can be said either that philosophy is a branch of human knowledge which in principle leads on to religion, or else that religion is a pictorial and naïve representation of philosophical truth. Christianity, which as a result of its Jewish origin has an attitude of mistrust to all philosophy, contains in the Incarnation and in the *logos* doctrine associated with it an inexhaustible source of philosophical problems, and on the other hand a ready answer to all philosophical questions.

GERARDUS VAN DER LEEUW

3. *The Origin of the Connection between Philosophy and Religion in Western Philosophy*

Since the end of the ancient world, western philosophy at all its main stages has been powerfully influenced by its relationship to religion, and especially to the view of existence and the doctrines held by *Christianity*. In particular, the great periods during which the constructions of metaphysical systems flourished, from the Patristic age up to Hegel, and on into the nineteenth century, are essentially characterized by the mutual influence of religious and philosophical convictions. And for considerable periods at least in the course of this whole era, the conviction of the necessity of this relationship was held as firmly by religion and theology as by philosophy.

The *earliest origins* of this great historical relationship are to be found in an historical association at a relatively superficial level: in the process of the apologetic and polemical encounter between early Christianity and educated circles in the ancient world, where philosophical reflection and knowledge were very highly regarded at that particular time. A recourse to philosophy seems to have been completely alien to the inner life and thought of this early Christianity (by contrast to other types of religious and mystical life, which sought a way of salvation essentially through degrees of increasing knowledge). After the encounter with the ethical systems of the ancient world, and the further struggle for existence against the newly emergent combinations of philosophy and religion found in gnosticism, in the period that followed the task of forming theological dogma provided the most important motive for the adoption of the conceptual tools, demonstrative arguments, and the whole intellectual assimilation of the experience of existence provided at that time over a wide and comprehensive field by the tradition of ancient philosophy and contemporary philosophical schools. This is why, in a considerable portion of the work of the great Church Fathers, theological and philosophical ideas are inextricably interwoven, and why the inner content of the Christian religion came at this time to be more and more closely associated with the themes and positions adopted by ancient philosophy. Irreconcilable contradictions between philosophy and the Christian faith were confirmed, while at the same time there was an increasing awareness of similar convictions, and surprising possibilities of agreement; in particular, the development of monotheism in ancient philosophy itself, as opposed to the popular pagan religion, made it easier for the new theology to establish a positive link with certain basic doctrines of ancient philosophy. Other points of agreement were found (ideas of immortality, doctrines of creation, ethical aims, etc.), and the need to complement the Christian view of existence by precise conceptions of the nature of reality and the world led to the discussion and adoption of areas of philosophical doctrine which in themselves implied no particular attitude to the inner nature of Christian faith and religion. Thus in the work of the Church Fathers philosophy attained a fixed positive relationship to the religion which gradually came to be expressed in fixed conceptual terms in theology. The conviction of the unity of philosophy, in its search for truth and in certain basic positions attained by the thinkers of the ancient world, with true religion and orthodox belief, became a fundamental certainty for most of the Church Fathers, in spite of numerous violent reactions on the part of faith against the burden imposed on it by the demands made on human knowledge of philosophy. The whole intellectual attitude and work of Augustine is governed by the conviction that the complete blessedness of man, the full development of the gifts bestowed upon him, and the most perfect participation in the divine being is to be obtained by the combination of faith and knowledge, the religious revelation of faith and the philosophical illumination of reason.

The interweaving and mutual interaction of these two intellectual forces brought about, with the passage of time, changes in philosophy itself and in its basic assertions, which were of decisive importance for the later development of the complex of philosophical ideas in the West (not merely in the Middle Ages). The new attitude to existence, to which all philosophical conceptual expressions and the whole philosophical understanding of reality were originally foreign, began to express itself in philosophical terms and to elaborate itself into an intellectual picture of the world. From the conceptual structures and doctrine which it adopted, and which originated in the ancient world (the fundamental outlook of which was ultimately, in certain essential features, contradictory to the new view of life), new patterns of inquiry and conviction began to appear. This is the beginning of the history of *Christian philosophy* (a history by no means concluded even at the present day), which is far from being simply identical with the history of philosophy in the West after the spread and victory of Christianity, but which formed its basic substance for many centuries. The breakthrough of the new attitude to the world, and the new orientation of thought, took place in a decisive fashion, which repeatedly pointed the way forward even at a later period, in Augustine. The emphasis shifted to a completely different area of reality; it passed from the cosmos (the original theme and principal concern of ancient philosophy) to the inner depths of mental and intellectual life, and to the access this provided to the universal reality; all intellectual reality and the sensible world were understood through the personal existence and action of the individual soul, and from the principle of an infinite activity of knowledge and will within the living God. This provided philosophy with completely new assumptions. The way this new outlook prevailed, with its own concepts and descriptions of reality, and its consequences in various fields of philosophical inquiry and understanding, is the subject of the history of philosophy in the Middle Ages and the modern period.

4. The Middle Ages

The whole nature and scope of the philosophy of the Middle Ages, scholasticism, is decided by the relationship with religion and theology which grew up in this way, and became more and more profound. The fundamental convictions of the Christian religion formed, not merely as a matter of fact, but by conscious and explicit purpose, the fixed basis on which all philosophy was carried out. The philosophers of this period were the great theologians. It was only on isolated occasions that philosophical work appeared in the form of purely philosophical writing (for example, in commentaries on ancient works of philosophy); for the most part, philosophy was carried out and expressed in association with theology, in the theological *summae* and works of exposition. Theology needed philosophy to present in rational terms and to demonstrate to the satisfaction of the reason such of the fundamental content of the Christian view of the world and of revealed doctrine as was accessible to it, and to develop in speculation the assertions made by faith; thus philosophy only appears in the framework and context of the aims of theology. For the tasks which made up the content of the philosophy of this period, this meant that philosophy became essentially identical with metaphysics, and with metaphysics not so much in the broader Aristotelian sense of a general doctrine of being, but with specific application to the highest being, the sense in which Aristotle had already described the 'first philosophy' as θεολογική (*theologikē*). The doctrine of God as the absolute foundation of the world and goal of its whole development became the undisputed centre and basic theme of all philosophy; a 'natural theology', that part of theology as a whole which covers the same ground as the philosophical doctrine of being, was developed, becoming increasingly distinct and independent in its procedure from the theology of revelation (*cf. Revelation* V*a*, pp. 46 ff. above). The choice of other problems of being, and the nature of the inquiry into them, was also determined by the themes laid down by theology and religion; philosophical inquiry into the world was more concerned with its divine origin, or with the source of evil and wickedness, than with the demonstrable structures of reality within it. The 'immaterial substances', the human soul in its independent future existence from the body of the senses, and the hierarchy of pure spirits posited by faith, took the central place in the concept of the universe. There was scarcely any development of a distinctive philosophy of nature; nor was there any separate study of the theory of knowledge or of ethics in the narrower sense. The only field of philosophical inquiry at this period which was largely separate from religion and theology was formal logic ('dialectic').

In the hierarchy of theology and philosophy that resulted from this intimate union and association between religion and metaphysics, faith had absolute precedence over knowledge, and theology over philosophy. Their objects were by no means totally identical. The knowledge obtained by philosophical reason was not considered able to reach into the ultimate depths and relationships of the divine being and activity, and in the order of the world laid down thereby; all final and ultimate judgements were matters of revelation and faith as far as their theological evaluation was concerned. Thus medieval philosophy had a place in a system of knowledge in which, although it was itself regarded as the queen of the sciences and the culmination of all knowledge obtained from natural reason, it was accorded a more modest place with regard to theology, as a lower form of participation in ultimate things. The level attained by its inquiries and understanding was on principle below that of the ultimate certainty of the faith. At its own level, however, it had its own acknowledged claim to independence; thus actual philosophical discourse in the Middle Ages in no sense consisted merely of the presentation and confirmation of what was already laid down by theology. The limits of philosophical reason were determined differently by various thinkers and schools; the rationalist tendency, which extended philosophy as far as possible in the direction of the doctrines of faith (even to the specific mysteries of Christianity, the Trinity, and the work of redemption), constantly, and with increasing success, came into conflict with the narrower restrictions and self-limitations placed on the natural reason. The relative separation of philosophy and theology naturally increased with the growing emphasis on the irrational in ultimate things. A particularly intimate union of religion and philosophical and speculative tendencies was displayed by one aspect of *medieval mysticism* (*cf. Mysticism* V*b*. pp. 380 ff. below). In the great mystics of the twelfth and thirteenth centuries, and especially in the German mystics (e.g. Eckhart), the certainty of the inner vision and of unity with the divine was directly transformed into an interpretation of the structure of being and the process of the world, which, in addition to all its mythical and positive dogmatic elements, contained a rich vein of theoretical and philosophical ideas, and thus had a notable historical effect on the philosophy of later periods. In the process of the gradual transformation of the philosophical concepts and views adopted from ancient philosophy, under the influence and in the direction of the basic Christian position, this form of religious philosophical speculation played an important part.

5. *The Modern Period up to the Middle of the Eighteenth Century*

The first success of the philosophy of the modern period was in breaking away from this hierarchical relationship with the theology of the Church; it became independent, and took as its model the free scientific understanding developed since the Renaissance, particularly in the form of modern natural science. The leading philosophers were men of the world, scientists, and politicians, and only rarely clergy. But this by no means signified that this philosophy ceased to be concerned with religion and with the objects and interests of faith. The goal of uniting and reconciling faith and knowledge continued to be of decisive importance among most of the great leaders of modern philosophy, until far into the nineteenth century. God and the human soul, the spiritual kingdom, and the meaningful coherence of the whole course of the world form basic themes in the systems of such philosophers as Descartes, Leibniz, Malebranche, Berkeley, Kant, or Hegel. And most of the leading metaphysicians of the modern period are also dominated by a conscious and explicit tendency to work out a conceptual understanding of the structure of reality in accordance with the basic truths of Christianity. But their starting point has changed from the divine and supra-sensible to the structure of the world as it is given in space and time, and the reality provided by man himself. The new central concern is the structure of nature as it appears to experience; but even this, originally at least, was not a deliberate limitation of attention to the 'secular', in a sense hostile to religion, but is based on the explicit purpose of understanding the 'book of nature' as a revelation of God directly and constantly accessible to us. This is not only true of the Italian nature philosophy of the Renaissance period and of the nature philosophy of Germany at the same period, with its connection with German mysticism, but also of the procedure of the new science and the philosophical evaluation of it. The longing for reality and the cosmic optimism which is so characteristic of almost all the great modern philosophical systems is profoundly rooted in the conviction of the immanence of the divine Spirit and purpose in all things and events. This explains many of the basic features of the new picture of the world (for example, the widespread conviction of the infinity of the universe, both on the macrocosmic and on the microcosmic scale; here again, the profound influence of fundamental religious attitudes on changes in the direction of philosophical inquiry and the formation of concepts is unmistakable). A large proportion of the conceptual themes of modern philosophy can be seen from a close historical examination to be secularized transformations and rearrangements of the material of religious philosophy, which in the Patristic period and in scholasticism had already attained a fully developed form in their application to theology and the transcendent (*cf.* for example the effects of the idea of the kingdom of God on the view of the world and of history held by Leibniz and Berkeley, Kant and Fichte, or Schelling and Hegel, or of the Augustinian and medieval preoccupation with the inner mental processes of man on the subjectivism of modern metaphysics, theory of knowledge and ethics). Many aspects of the Christian attitude to existence are only now receiving their fullest expression, having been set free from the concepts of the ancient world, partly by being carried to their ultimate and logical conclusion.

As philosophy attained its independence and set up a new relationship with autonomous experimental science, there naturally arose the possibility of *conflict with religion* and its doctrines, as well as the possibility of a fundamental *separation from religion*. The new emphasis on the *immanence* of the divine led, almost inevitably, in the first direction. From the very beginning of this movement, important elements of the new understanding of the world came close to pantheism, and both the early champions and leaders of this movement (e.g. Nicholas of Cusa and Bruno), and also many later thinkers (e.g. Malebranche, Berkeley, Fichte, Schelling, Schleiermacher, and Hegel) were involved in serious difficulties of this sort, either in disputes with others or in explicit or concealed problems in their own thinking. The history of pantheist thought in the modern period, and the conflict between the great philosophical systems and the tendencies that unite in pantheism is an important theme in the development of modern philosophy. The full and decisive expression given to pantheism by Spinoza represents a form of modern metaphysics which, in spite of the fact that its basic attitude is determined by religion, nevertheless departs widely from the traditional relationship between philosophy and religion; moreover, its content led to a concept of the world which departed entirely from the Christian attitude to existence. All the later effects of the philosophy of Spinoza in the centuries that followed contain the seeds of conflicts with its assumptions and the positive doctrines of religion. The closed structure of this system has frequently led to this pantheist philosophy being regarded (falsely) as a necessary consequence of the use of reason proceeding in purely philosophical terms, and so to the assumption that on principle philosophy is opposed to religion in its theist form.

The *deism* of the seventeenth and eighteenth centuries represents another departure from living religion in the direction of a philosophical rationalization which nevertheless attempts to maintain religion in principle, and explicitly to put forward in systematic form its most general assertions. Deism is an intellectual movement which was particularly widespread in the English Enlightenment, and then gained an increasing number of adherents in France and Germany. In it, philosophy attempts (in practice taking its starting point from Christian theism) to work out a system of the basic truths of 'natural religion' through the pure, self-evident understandings and demonstrations of reason, and to provide a body of knowledge which was regarded as the single and identical nucleus of all the convictions found in positive religions in so far as they are true at any given time. This philosophical movement, the original and guiding impulse of which was a genuine and serious religious feeling, concealed in itself an essential opposition to positive religion and its supra-rational 'dogmas' (which increasingly came to be rejected as unreasonable). Natural religion was made the standard by which positive religion was judged, and was put forward as a fuller and better substitute for positive religion on the firmer basis, free from denominational dispute, of unvarying human reason and a very limited and systematically arranged selection of the basic principles of positive religion. This was an attempt to make natural religion the whole of theology, and the only theology. In any case, the course of the deist movements led, wherever their influence was felt, to the increasing emptying of the content of religion, and the alienation of philosophy from the true life of religion. This process was strengthened to the extent that the self-confident rationality which provided a constructive and demonstrable foundation for natural theology and religion was itself cast into uncertainty, and in the later Enlightenment was broken down from within (in particular by the penetrating criticism of Hume); the criticism of religion and the basic assertions of religion (together with an historical and genetical 'explanation' of them) moved into the foreground of philosophical discussion. At the same time, however, metaphysics lost its central position in many schools of philosophy (especially in English empiricism and French sensualism), being replaced by a preoccupation with the theory of knowledge, moral philosophy or psychology; and ultimately, the very possibility of metaphysics was disputed. Consequently, where the influence of these schools was felt, the traditional (and partial) identity of content between philosophy and religion gradually disappeared. The principal movements and inquiries within philosophy became indifferent to religion. But certain developments of the Enlightenment and its philosophy also advanced a point of view explicitly hostile to religion. The powerful emphasis laid on the reality of nature and the material structure of the world by the great systems of the seventeenth century has still seen them in the context of the divine infinity and activity, but this association had already been weakened in the constructions of deism (*cf.* the 'dogmatic' meaning of this concept). The reality of nature and the material structure of the world now became the centre of philosophical interest and were completely dissociated from their previous context; with the development of the mechanistic view of the world to an extreme degree, they were considered in complete isolation, and so came to be regarded as the only reality. At this point the opposition between faith and knowledge, religion and philosophical reason, already anticipated in the sceptical observations of Bayle and frequently aggravated since, now became the basic struggle of philosophy, aimed not only against dogmatic theology, but against religion and the religious view of the world as a whole. In the materialism of thinkers such as Lamettrie and Holbach, philosophy approached the position of atheism. Thus in widespread circles in the Enlightenment, philosophy became an intellectual force aiming at alienation from religion, and hostile to it.

6. *German Idealism*

However, the second half of the eighteenth century brought a powerful *reaction against the Enlightenment* as a whole, and especially against the anti-religious tendencies it contained. Rousseau, Hamann, Herder, and Hemsterhuis began to use the weapons of the intellect and of a philosophical criticism more positive in nature, to attack the deism, scepticism, indifferentism, materialism, and atheism of the Enlightenment, on the basis of a new and living religion and a new fullness of life. *F. H. Jacobi* advanced the idea of the truth of the heart, the inner perception of what is beyond the senses, and the direct certainty of reality obtained by faith, against the arrogant claims of the construction of reason, the philosophy of mere reflection, which in the closed world of thought it had chosen to set up was inevitably bound to lead to nihilism and atheism, especially in the form of the identification of the world with God in Spinoza's sense. Such a philosophy, he said, was incapable of revealing true existence; this is based essentially upon the personality of the living God, and expressed in the teleology of the coherence of the universe and in the freedom of human spiritual beings. The highest flowering of spiritual and personal life is religion, which is the true and necessary foundation of a genuinely moral will, and of every full apprehension and truth. In this philosophy of faith, the recognition of an essential and inevitable tension between faith and pure reason leads to a new affirmation of the living forces of religion. *Kant*, again, opposed in his *Critique of Pure Reason* the 'dogmatic' metaphysics of rationalism and deism (united in Germany in the scholastic system of C. Wolff) with its claim to be a demonstrable, closed and self-sufficient system. His 'pulverizing' criticism of reason, with its destruction of the traditional proofs of God and immortality, which threatened all the natural theology and religion of the time, was not aimed, like that of Hume, at the dissolution on principle of the link between philosophy and religion; what he intended to do was to attack and defeat both the dogmatism of the deist rationalist system, and at the same time the opposing positions of the naturalism of Spinoza or of materialist atheism. 'Thus, I had to do away with *knowledge*, in order to find a place for *faith*.' The true aim of this critical destruction of the traditional constructions of philosophical reason was the setting up of a new 'practical and dogmatic metaphysics', that is, the philosophical ordering and establishing of the fundamental truths of God, freedom, and immortality on the basis of the moral conscience, and the 'reasonable faith' based upon it. Within the limits of pure reason, and in inseparable association with the reality of reason and the necessary premises of existential morality, philosophy attained a new positive relationship to religion, and in particular to the fundamental truths of Christianity. At the same time, Kant's later work, *Religion Within the Limits of Pure Reason*, meant the decisive beginning of the development of a 'philosophy of religion' as a special discipline within the framework of the system of philosophy; almost everywhere, the philosophy of religion became a fixed part of the metaphysics and of the systems devoted to the theory of knowledge of the nineteenth century.

The movement of *speculative idealism* which proceeded from Kant set up a new and particularly close and profound union between philosophy and religion. All these great thinkers began as theologians; this is particularly evident in the case of *Hegel*, the outlines of whose system can be clearly seen in the theological writings of his youth. When Fichte sought to describe the importance of Kant in the history of the world, he called him the third leader of mankind after Jesus and Luther. The conviction of the exclusive and absolute truth of Christianity, and the tendency to develop the content of Christian truth in philosophical terms to its full logical conclusion, determined the starting point and the structure of all the systems, every one of which, in fact, saw its final aim and culmination in a philosophy of religion. Once again, and in a different way (by proceeding from the self-perception and self-reflection of human beings), philosophy had become a speculative and systematic metaphysics, at the centre of which was the divine Absolute. It now attempted to see the whole of reality in a new light, that of the Spirit and the supra-temporal life of God (in complete contrast to the naturalistic tendencies of the previous periods); the process of the universe was regarded as the development of the spiritual kingdom on the basis of a self-created nature. The tendency, so characteristic of the modern period and its philosophy, to conceive of the divine as immanent, and to secularize concepts of being which were originally transcendent in their application, was here continued (and once again, the pantheistic theme and the struggle between a basically religious and theist attitude and a philosophical and monist conceptual structure reappears with particular intensity). Yet the structure of reality is not isolated from religion, but is interpreted in every aspect and process as the self-unfolding and manifestation of the divine life of the Spirit. The historical mode of thought displayed by this metaphysics is of particular importance for the philosophical evaluation of the various themes of the world-view held by Christianity; in its truest form, the process of the universe is universal history, seen as the maturing of mankind towards the kingdom of liberty and of the Spirit united with God. Here again, in a new form and a new application, the transferring of reality to the spiritual world, resulting from the Christian religious outlook (and repeatedly and explicitly derived from it), triumphs over the imprisonment of earlier philosophy in the external cosmos. Here, therefore, in this last great flowering of philosophical speculation before the present day, philosophy and religion were once again related to each other in principle and in fact. But by contrast with scholasticism, philosophical reason was no longer restricted to a limited sphere beneath the higher light cast on existence by revelation and faith, but claimed a final and ultimate knowledge. The logic of Hegel claimed to understand the inner nature of the Absolute itself, according to its inner categories; philosophy, as the science of the Absolute, was held to provide a clear and adequate understanding of what religion describes merely in the form of 'images'. Thus in Hegel, as in the other great leaders of the movement, it is ultimately given a higher place than religious emotion, vision, or faith, as a higher, and indeed the highest, level of intellectual life and living certainty.

The idealist movement was continued, in a direction of equal importance for both philosophy and theology, in that of *speculative* theism ('later idealism'), the starting point of which was the philosophy of religion and religious metaphysics of Schelling's later period, and which was then carried on especially by Weisse and the younger Fichte. It was a critical revision of idealist philosophy with regard to the adequacy of its understanding of the personality of God, the personal liberty of the spirit, and the distinctive reality of the actual course of history and the process of revelation. The development of this philosophy (which has not really been justly evaluated until the present day) represents a new form and a new stage of the dialogue between philosophy and religion; in it, religious experience, and especially the experience of the history of religion, was once again accorded an increased significance and independence by contrast to the constructions of philosophy.

7. The Post-Idealist Development

Apart from the numerous schools of thought which continued idealist and theist metaphysics, either in a close or in a looser association with the Christian religion as expressed in the different denominations, which were found in all European countries, the later nineteenth century produced in philosophy, in accordance with the general change in the attitude of the times, a number of tendencies foreign or hostile to religion, which in the course of the century often obtained a dominant influence. The philosophy of *Schopenhauer*, the influence of which was extremely widespread, adopted a very distinctive attitude to religion: while it was completely imbued with the idea of redemption, consequently taking an explicit and positive view of religion, religious mysticism, and asceticism, religious doctrines of evil, sin, and guilt, and of the doctrine that in their natural condition the world and humanity are unsaved, it nevertheless expressed the conviction of the fundamental inadequacy of all actual and positive religion as mere 'popular metaphysics', possessing a purely allegorical link with the truth. Schopenhauer disputed with particular bitterness the tenets of Christian theism and faith in providence (though his real attack was ultimately aimed at the tendency of the rationalism of contemporary philosophy towards a cosmic and historical optimism, and especially against the 'gnosticism' of German idealism). He considered that the truth about the existence and the meaning of the universe was not given by religion, but by philosophical metaphysics alone, which (in this he adopted an Indian view of the world) replaced reconciliation with an imaginary divine spirit by the absorption of temporal and individual being, life and suffering in the all-embracing unity of Nirvana. In Schopenhauer's ambiguous picture of the world, tendencies which were explicitly atheist (and very strongly emphasized by him) and hostile to religion were interwoven with a reaction, indubitably provoked by religious feeling, against contemporary tendencies to exalt man and his reason and to preach an 'infamous' cosmic optimism and a belief in historical progress and fulfilment. In fact, behind this wholly pessimistic existential belief in one absolute and essentially baleful will there lies the assumption, no longer mentioned and only occasionally hinted at in mystic terms, of a principle valuable and blessed in itself. Schopenhauer's philosophy, with its new emphasis on everything that is meaningless and without teleology in the whole reality of nature and of man, gave rise to a new philosophical and religious tendency in the nineteenth century, which was particularly expressed by *E. von Hartmann* (but also by many other thinkers, even up to the present day). The Absolute is regarded as a 'god' divided in himself, suffering and only revealing himself in his saving omnipotence in the course of the evolution of the world. A new pantheism arose, completely hostile to Christian theism, and at the same time completely dissociated from the optimism and secular faith of the modern age (and from the forms of pantheism which had hitherto arisen), representing itself as the true 'religion of the Spirit' and claiming to be the new universal religion of the future. Philosophy here was seeking to draw the powers of all religions, and especially of all mysticism, into itself, to provide itself with the true doctrine of salvation, and to lead man to redemption through the 'euthanasia of religion'.

The philosophy of the nineteenth century came to be *explicitly opposed to religion* in those tendencies which developed the naturalist and materialistic ideas present in the eighteenth-century Enlightenment; these were readily adopted by the powerful upsurge of opinion during this period, which aimed at making the tasks set by the practical and social realities of life, as opposed to any concern with the world to come and 'pie in the sky', the central concern of existence. From the school of Hegel (in its 'left wing') there developed the criticism of religion, turning more and more towards the cosmic pantheism of D. F. Strauss, as well as the thought of L. Feuerbach, with his insistence on sense experience, and his anthropological explanation of religion as the imaginary product of man's desires. The final result, and indeed for the most part the basic motive, of the materialist movement, which aimed at a wide popularity (*cf.* B. L. Büchner), as well as of its offshoots in the 'monism' of the end of the century, with its slight suggestion of pantheism, was a convinced atheism and an emphatic hostility to religion. The positivism and sociological philosophy which captured the minds of educated and scientific circles in the nineteenth century, tried to absorb positive traditional religion into the human religion of social and cultural progress; Comte and others tried to replace the ancient concept of God by the *Grand Être* of humanity. Both religion and philosophical metaphysics were regarded as stages in man's intellectual childhood, superseded by science and civilization; the true philosophy of the present day and the future was to be based purely on the sciences and the world of facts, in isolation from religion and all metaphysics. Other similar schools of thought (e.g. the evolutionism of Spencer) merely limited philosophy to the realm of phenomena comprehensible in scientific terms and the structure of social reality, but conceded the existence of an absolute being behind what is perceptible and accessible to us in practice, as the goal of personal and religious emotion and belief lying beyond all knowledge (even philosophical knowledge). The indifference of the most urgent concerns and central tasks of philosophy towards religion is also a characteristic of the original attitude of the Neo-Kantian school of the last third of the nineteenth century; here, philosophy is fundamentally understood as merely the theory of knowledge and reflection upon the assumptions and methods of science, so that it loses entirely its earlier link with religious statements about reality, a link which inevitably always tended towards the elaboration of an objective metaphysics. However, the scope of this philosophy was extended to include general reflection on the basic principles of all intellectual constructions and cultural products of the human consciousness, and it developed into a universal system of the human intellect. Thus it was led through ethics and aesthetics to discuss the outline and structure of a philosophy of religion, seen as a methodical reflection on the general *a priori* assumptions and fundamental consciousness of religion, to be carried out by the study of positive religion and its ancillary sciences. This view of the relationship between philosophy and religion, therefore, was quite different from that implied in metaphysical systems and in the 'philosophy of religion' developed in the framework and context of such systems. It did not accord to philosophy any direct relationship, on its own account, to the objects and content of religion. Its procedure was limited to working back 'transcendentally' from the forms and manifestations of religious life to its underlying assumptions within the human mind, and it is thus closely related to the psychology of religion (*cf. The Psychology of Religion* pp. 323 ff. below) and to the phenomenology of religious acts which were developing at this period. In the later developments of this Neo-Kantian philosophy of religion, its most important exponents (Cohen, Natorp, Troeltsch) found themselves forced to go beyond this purely reflective approach. But this leads us on beyond the nineteenth century into the twentieth, to the present-day developments, in which the relationship between philosophy and religion has completely changed, by contrast to the nineteenth century.

HEINZ HEIMSOETH

II*b* PHILOSOPHY AND RELIGION AT THE PRESENT DAY*

1. The Crisis in Present-Day Civilization and in its View of the World

The philosophy of the present day is a philosophy of crisis. It is the expression of an age that has lost the foundation it has had hitherto, and has not yet found another. The breakdown of our intellectual culture has

* See also *The Philosophy of Religion*, pp. 310 ff. below.

gone so deep, and has been so extensive, that it can only be compared with the very greatest crisis in the history of the world. We are in the midst of a change in the order of things as great as that experienced by humanity at the end of the ancient world and at the Renaissance. This is the reason for the threat of the decline and collapse of the world which overshadows the present generation, which has been given literary expression not only in the much-disputed work of Spengler, but by many others. It has been strengthened by the Great War, but the shattering effects of the war are not the only explanation; the intellectual catastrophe of humanity was already anticipated and prophesied by *Nietzsche*. Once again, a particular pattern of existence has become exhausted; a way of life has grown old, according to a law to which all life in the world of nature and of the intellect is subject; according to this law, not only do the cells of an organism become worn out, but also the intellectual potency of an age, the intellectual capital of a series of generations must at length be spent. To anyone living in such a transitional period, in which the death of what has gone before and the birth of what is to come cannot yet be clearly distinguished, the catastrophe which he is experiencing appears, according to the particular point of view he adopts, as the upheaval of the social order, the collapse of science, and the decline of morality and religion.

The starting point of the philosophy of the 'modern period', concluding with the end of the last century, was *consciousness*. Its thought proceeded by way of the systematic doubt of Descartes from the conviction of the self to the world and to God. It made constantly renewed attempts to master objective reality. But 'like an animal on a dry heath, led about in a circle by an evil spirit', it remained under the spell of its subjectivism, and every attempt to escape this subjectivism, perhaps with the help of the principle of causality, was necessarily bound to fail through its own inner contradictions. The 'scandal of philosophy and of the universal reason of man, that the existence of things outside us must be accepted through pure faith', lamented by Kant, still remained.

The philosophy of consciousness was confuted by the realization that no operation of the understanding can restore *reality*, once it has been destroyed. The problem is only created by the division of an experience that is a unity into the concept and its object, and this problem necessarily remains insoluble as long as the concept on which one reflects continues to be confused with the fact originally given. But there can be no conception without the activity that conceives of it, and no activity without an act of will, and thus the will is also experienced from the first not as a purely subjective function but incorporated in a much wider context. W. Wundt and Dilthey, in spite of their different scientific approach and the different way in which they formulated their ideas, succeeded in seeing through the *proton pseudos* of three centuries of Cartesian philosophy.

But with the recognition of the relationships of being which precede all reflection, they also asserted the primacy of life over knowledge, and we find ourselves on the way to the *philosophy of life*, of which the most brilliant and perspicacious prophet at the end of the last century was Nietzsche. In the philosophy of life, the irrational takes up arms against the *ratio*. Schopenhauer, who was alone in his own time, prepared the way for this change; Bergson, a generation later, was the most celebrated philosopher of his day. But the blind will described by the one, and the prelogical intuition and the 'life force' of the other are inwardly related.

In order to reconquer reality, the philosopher must stir the waters of Acheron. He touches the very depths of the soul; a blind urge rises up against the intellect, chaos against the cosmos. Everywhere depths of reality are revealed, 'for which idealism was inadequate' (Tillich). At the present day, we have a much more acute insight into the unavoidable rigours and irreconcilable tensions of natural and historical existence, and into the depths of the irrational, which everywhere face the cognitive intellect. This upheaval reaches far into the exact sciences, apparently exalted above every variation brought about by the passage of time: the proud structure of mechanistic science is collapsing; the basic principle *natura non facit saltus* has been refuted, and the most sublime instrument of inquiry, the principle of causality, has become valueless.

Of course it would be an error to see in all this merely a movement within philosophy or within science. Science does not arise in a vacuum, but is the product of the general cultural situation. From this point of view, the intellect, cast down from its dominant position, appears as a mere superstructure built upon what are in fact the violent forces and powers of life and history. Consequently, this process is not merely concerned with a change in the starting point of philosophy, a different solution of the problem of knowledge—which is a matter for academics—but with the rise and fall of the rational view of the world, the world outlook of bourgeois liberalism. Impulses are coming to light which once slumbered behind the protective fence of bourgeois morality, or are just beginning to stir from their concealment. But while the old constraints fall, new ones spring up: man is no longer the atomic soul of Leibniz, the bundle of conceptions of Hume, the abstract rational being of Kant, and is no longer the isolated individual of capitalist society, who can assert his existence only in a brutal struggle for power. He becomes a part and a function of an inclusive general will, a cell of the body social, in which and with which alone he has his being—in the same way as physicists nowadays see material only as a product of a 'field', and modern psychology regards all the constituent parts of the psyche as embedded in a whole emotional structure. From this point of view, of course, the individual now seems to be no more than a function of the mass, which implies an imminent threat to his creative energies.

2. Religion in the Guise of a Philosophy of Life and Existence

Thus since we are in the midst of a general crisis of civilization, not merely a crisis in thought, we must accept that *religion*, like the other driving forces in life, will also be drawn into this crisis. Christian socialism regards the position that has come about in the following way: Bourgeois society is penetrated by a worldly spirit. Completely at the mercy of the forces of science, economics, and technology, the bourgeois world has lost sight of the eternal. But the war and upheaval which are threatening to drag the whole cultural heritage of European man into the abyss have made the questionable nature of the products of its civilization terrifyingly obvious, and thus have prepared the way for a new awakening to the eternal.

Of course it cannot be said that the experience of the war led those who came home from the trenches back to God; quite the contrary: the senseless self-destruction of the Christian nations dealt an enormous blow to belief in a just and loving ruler of the world. Nor does the demand of the proletariat for power in itself signify a renewed turning to religion. Rather, it inclines workers to see in the Church and in religion merely devices used by the bourgeois state and capitalist society to exercise authority and control. But if religion is 'the reaching out of the conditional to the Absolute' (Tillich), then it does seem in essence to be in plain contradiction to a bourgeois civilization based on the self-sufficiency of the finite world. If it is said in answer to this that the aims of the proletarian struggle are themselves wholly within the world, it must not be forgotten that the will and the hope to create a new earth and a new humanity contain the essential features of a powerful faith transcending reality. Whether such a faith can still be called religious ultimately depends upon the definition of the word religion. A philosopher should not define it in too narrow a sense; wherever something infinite is opposed to what is finite, something absolute to what is relative, and something ideal to what is empirical, one can rightly speak of religion. In this sense, even Nietzsche's faith in the future superman may be called religious.

From what we have said, it follows that the apparent turning away from religion at the present time in fact merely means a break with the organizational Church and with ecclesiastical doctrine. This path is still very difficult to perceive at the present day, because the working-class movement has not yet cast off the intellectual bonds of the naturalistic bourgeois enlightenment of the second half of the last century, because religion has not yet learned to put aside the veil or the dogma which concealed it.

The rediscovery and revival of religion is in fact taking place in the form of *mysticism* (*cf. Mysticism* pp. 355 ff. below). This is the form of religious activity which appears to be most closely linked in its feeling, and most in accordance in its ideas, with the philosophy of life of the present time. The strength of the present-day inclination towards mysticism can be seen from the flourishing of occultism, and the attraction exercised on people's minds by theosophy and anthroposophy.

Now, both ancient and modern religious mysticism has always had a powerful tendency towards pantheism, and in fact the mysticism of the present day seems to be leading back to the pantheist religious feeling of German idealism. But the mysticism of the philosophy of life is in no sense similar to that of idealism; above all, it lacks its boundless optimism. *Nietzsche* affirms existence, in spite of the depths of his suffering and, in spite of the shattering fact of the cyclical recurrence of all things, struggles forward to a heroic belief in the present. *Bergson* sees the divine life force carrying matter to a new level, as it were refined by a Heraclitan conflagration. This development must not be understood in mechanistic terms; rather, as a ceaseless new creation, it is irreconcilably opposed to all mechanistic thinking. But it is not a teleological process, directed towards fixed goals already laid down. It is a creative struggle and a constant self-purification. And Bergson's concept of God is not purely pantheist: God is a freely creative will, and his form of consciousness is similar to that of personality; but on the other hand, he is not a 'closed and completed being' and contains in himself more tendencies than have in fact attained to development in the world. Consequently, Bergson's vision of the world contains a certain dualism, in which a pessimistic element is not entirely lacking. If one bears in mind in addition to this the irrationalist theory of knowledge, which rejects the intellect in favour of intuition, and regards it as incapable of understanding reality, one can see at once the deep gulf that separates the modern mysticism of life from the monist idealism of the German classical period.

Heidegger agrees on the one hand with the philosophy of life, and on the other with socialism, in the idea that man is to be regarded in the first place not as *homo sapiens* but as *homo faber*. But while the philosophy of life, resting content with the affirmation of this fact, has for the most part returned at once to the familiar problems of the theory of knowledge and metaphysics, the central question for Heidegger has been the status of man in existence. Just as Socrates once brought down philosophy from heaven to earth, so Heidegger has made the primary question not that of cosmology, but that of anthropology. What he has created is a philosophical anthropology on a fundamentally religious basis. For man as Heidegger sees him, existence is not something 'laid on for him', but something 'there to be taken if he will'. His relationship to his environment is that of 'taking care of it', to his fellow man that of 'caring for him', and indeed man's fundamental attitude to himself is that of 'care'. But it is when he really turns towards himself that he has his first realization of 'anxiety' (*Angst*). This anxiety lifts him out of his absorption in his environment, brings him back to himself, and fills him with the consciousness of the 'unfriendliness of the world', in which he had imagined himself to be at home, and teaches him to understand his own being as a 'being directed towards death'. But it is this 'being in anticipation' which distinguishes man for what he is, and gives him the consciousness of his limited existence as a creature, and so brings to life the possibilities inherent in him as a unique existence. This is the voice of conscience, the hidden divinity, which calls upon man and leads his own self, through his consciousness of guilt, to liberty and truth. According to Heidegger, this call of eternity reveals the deepest significance of human existence. The extent to which this philosophy finds religious and even specifically Christian categories indispensable for the understanding of the world is significant. But again, it is also notable how strong the irrational and pessimistic element is in it. Human life only obtains its significance from the certainty of annihilation.

Heidegger is very strongly influenced by *Kierkegaard* who saw the world as torn between irreconcilable contradictions, and in whose life and thought anxiety played a decisive part. The concept of 'existence' in the profound and meaningful sense of the form of existence of an individual comes from Kierkegaard; it is a concept which in Heidegger has replaced that of life as the term that typifies his view of the world. Within Protestantism the threads of Kierkegaard's philosophy have been taken up again by 'dialectical' theology, which widens the contradiction between the absolute and the finite to an extreme degree, and places the believer, in his relationship to God, in a situation of permanent crisis.

3. *Religion in the Light of Phenomenology*

Although such an historian as Heinemann believes that existentialist philosophy can be seen as having overcome in a dialectical conflict both rationalism and the philosophy of life, yet the dominant form of thought in the years immediately preceding the present time, and even, at least in part, today, is that of phenomenology. This was in fact Heidegger's starting point. As a philosophical approach which seeks to rise above the concrete phenomena which 'happen to be the case' to the 'vision' of their true and eternal being, it displays in its basic tendency a relationship to religion. Furthermore, the position taken by phenomenology to the theory of knowledge gives it a special access to the realm of transcendence: its contemporary character is typified by the fact that it goes beyond the philosophy of consciousness, that is, of Cartesianism in the broadest sense. Its links with the past go further back than that, to Catholic scholasticism. It is true that the starting point of phenomenology is the content of consciousness, but it allows the fact of consciousness to be exceeded by acts of 'intention'. When we conceive and think of the world, we are consequently 'intending' not the fact of which we are conscious itself, but the object represented in it. Of course, here phenomenology brings back a dualism into the starting point of the process of cognition, and so falls back into the error of Cartesianism. But this is not the place for a detailed criticism of this approach.

We must, however, place in this context the comprehensive application of the phenomenological point of view to the problem of religious knowledge that has been carried out by *Scheler*. Among the philosophers of the present day and the recent past, it is Scheler who has perhaps submitted the problem of religion to its most thorough examination. According to him, if certain purposes of the human mind are to be distinguished as religious, it is not sufficient to characterize them in purely immanent terms. Rather, the fact that in themselves they possess a relationship to God is 'the first essential mark of their unity', and to this extent 'they already necessarily presuppose the idea of God'. At this point, Scheler inevitably comes into conflict with *Schleiermacher*, and the confrontation between the two is perhaps the best way of understanding the thought of Scheler himself. He regards as Schleiermacher's principal error the view that the dogmas of religion are nothing more than the subsequent description of the mental attitudes of religious devotion. He reproaches Schleiermacher for reducing the object of religion to emotion, 'not in a purposive, cognitive relationship, but in a purely causal relationship'. He regards as a false premiss in this the idea that reason can only come to indirect conclusions, and cannot directly 'contemplate reality'. This criticism of Schleiermacher, admittedly, seems to miss the point; it is not true that he was led to suppose, by the view that religious dogma is a subsequent conclusion based on religious emotions, that this is the source on which it is entirely dependent; in fact he explicitly stated that in religious emotion the whole experience comes to us as the revelation of God, and that in it God enters into our lives. But when Scheler affirms that the love of God, reverence, holy awe, etc., are not aroused by the idea of God, but are mental acts in which something divine and holy is apprehended, he is in exact agreement with Schleiermacher. And when he goes on to say that Schleiermacher does not give a proper place to the rational idea of an infinite being, he forgets that the infinite can never be directly accessible to us except in feeling, for the consciousness that no limit attained by thought is ever the last is something of which we are always only assured by our feelings. But from Scheler's point of view, not only Schleiermacher's starting point, but also the conclusion of his philosophy of religion appears unsatisfactory. For Schleiermacher hopes to restore, with the help of his philosophy, not merely the impersonal universal being of the infinite of philosophical discourse, but the personal God of Christianity. And this is something which he regards as only possible by way of the direct 'vision of being through reason', in which the object of the cognitive act is as much distinct from an emotional experience, which is always purely subjective, as it is from the rational argument from causality. Scheler does not imply the rejection of the proofs of God in rational theology; but he regards their fundamental error as everywhere the same: 'A conclusion is alleged, the content of which is already provided by a quite different source of knowledge. The conclusion is drawn within the world of religious contemplation, and rightly so, and yet it is supposed that the material of this conclusion can be drawn from facts that lie outside religion.' This is an error, similar to the false opinion that a real external world can be logically deduced from the mere content of consciousness. The famous argument from causality in natural theology Scheler regards as fully justified if it has a previous basis on two 'indeducible and intuitive conditions of being which are necessarily assumed in every religious view of the world'—the awareness on the one hand of the presence of absolute

being in every apprehension of a contingent phenomenon of nature or the mind, and on the other hand of the
character of being a product or creature possessed by
every object in nature. 'This character of being a product
is not something that can itself be deduced, but is an
intuitive element in it in the sense that—to look at the
matter in non-religious terms—I do not recognize this
table as the work of a man as the result of a logical
deduction, but see by looking at it that it is an artifact'.
He does not, of course, ignore the question whether we
would recognize it as an artifact without previous experience in this field. Why, for example, it is so difficult
to decide whether the stones called eoliths are natural
products or are formed by a human hand. Ultimately,
according to Scheler, the foundation of all Christian
belief is what was made known to Christ concerning God
and concerning himself—not in the form of faith, but in
the form of vision. But for Scheler this does not signify
the separation of religion from metaphysics—a procedure
which in fact he reproaches in A. Ritschl. He regards
the distinctive statements of metaphysics as being exclusively hypothetical in their significance. However,
by being traced back to the 'original phenomena' that
gave rise to them, they can be made indirectly 'visible'.
In order to bring to light in this way the power of conviction of the individual proofs of the existence of God,
modern man also requires the conscious practice of
religion. On the other hand, he regards it as a 'certain
insight of reason' that the world, which owes its existence
to a free spiritual cause, has subsequently declined into
a fundamentally different condition. 'The world that
we know in reality is much worse than its basis leads us to
expect.' Consequently, the evil of the world forces us to
seek its origin in a 'concentrated power of evil', and
therefore, since evil can only be the essential attribute
of a person, in a wicked person. This philosophical re-

habilitation of the devil reveals the pessimistic side of
Scheler's speculation, which he shares with the contemporary philosophical systems mentioned above.

*4. Other Modern Thinkers and their Attitude to
the Religious Problem*

In order to complete our picture of modern philosophy
concerned with religion, we shall mention a few other
matters, in addition to those we have already discussed,
although we are conscious that to some extent we are
leaving the area in which the religious problem is dealt
with in distinctively modern terms. Nevertheless, what
Simmel had to say about the religious situation even
before the war is still of sufficient significance for the
present day to merit a summary here—especially since
Simmel also had close connections with the philosophy of
life. It was his view that up to the present time religion
had always survived religions, 'as a tree survives the
repeated picking of its fruit'. But the immense and serious
problem of the present situation lay in the fact that it is
not particular dogmas, but the transcendental content
of faith as such which is being accused on principle
of being illusory. This is what leads to the situation, so
deeply provoking for modern man, in which his intellectual conscience will not permit him to make statements, the content of which he 'sees asserted by minds
of the highest rank and superior intellectual capacity as
indubitable realities'. Thus he must necessarily have the
uneasy feeling that he completely lacks any sense of a
certain kind of reality. In this dilemma, faced with having
to abandon faith in his own reason, or in the leading
intellects of the past, the only ultimate certainty which
remains to him is of the religious need which is indubitably present. However, according to Simmel, this
religious need is not necessarily and furthermore,
not exclusively, satisfied in the relationship man sets up

with a transcendental being. The alternative of the Enlightenment: either there is something divine outside man, or, if 'science' no longer permits this to be asserted, then faith in such a divinity is an illusion to be explained in purely psychological terms, is an alternative which Simmel claims is false. For there is a third alternative. It is possible for religious faith, as a psychic fact, to be itself a metaphysical reality. Just as the concept of space does not demand as a prerequisite, or require the conclusion, that there is a spatial world which transcends consciousness, but in Kant's sense the concept of space already contains in itself the whole of spatial reality, so subjective religious feeling does not in any sense guarantee the presence of a transcendental object or value, but itself directly signifies all the metaphysical profundity, all the wide comprehension and sublime holiness that seemed to have been lost along with the objects of religious belief.

It can be seen how close Simmel is here to Scheler. Both agree in asserting the direct religious experience of reality. But while Simmel, in spite of everything he does to avoid it, is constantly threatened by the charge that he reduces the substance of religion to nothing, by transforming it into a purely inward relationship of the soul to itself, Scheler has always to face the question whether the phenomenological 'intuitive vision of reason' really goes any further than the arguments based on reason in rational theology.

A third well-known attempt at a solution, which may be discussed here, has been put forward by *Troeltsch*: trying to develop certain ideas of Kant, he seeks to demonstrate a religious *a priori*. That this idea is irreconcilable with Kant's genuine doctrine of *a priori* categories, has already been adequately demonstrated by his critics.

On the other hand, if one begins with the fact earlier

established, that Cartesianism has in any case failed to provide a solution to the problem of the external world, and if, in contrast to rationalism, one clings to the directly experienced reality of a reciprocal relationship between God and man, the one possible solution of the problem seems to lie in the field of pantheism. But, as Simmel again makes clear, pantheism does not satisfy the religious need that demands a personal relationship between God and the believer. Yet there is no reason to reject faith in a personal God as anthropomorphic. Rather, the idea of personality is only fulfilled when the intellectual processes within personality form a completely closed system, absolutely self-sufficient and self-dependent. It follows from this that the content of the word 'personality' is not an experience but an idea, that is, it signifies a category which is not satisfied by any single empirical being. Thus the idea of personality is first completely realized in the idea of God. Simmel, of course, clearly recognizes that traditional theism, regarded both from the philosophical and from the religious point of view, still remains unsatisfactory. Any independence of other things with regard to God removes his absoluteness. 'But perhaps this state of being driven from one conclusion to another is the only adequate expression of our relationship to the infinite, which we may not hope to identify with an unambiguous formula.'

What Simmel suggests is nothing new in itself. Within the Protestant dogmatic theology of the previous century, R. A. Lipsius, for example, put forward with particular emphasis the idea that only absolute personality could be personality in the full sense of the word. But in our present context, the ideas of Simmel are important because they show that some of the more prominent representatives of the philosophy of the present day and the recent past are once again tending towards a theist solution of the problem of God. Apart from Scheler and Simmel, we would mention here only *Eucken* and *J. Volkelt*.

By contrast, *Driesch*, while not asserting pantheism in dogmatic terms, suggests that it is the most probable solution of the problem of God. However, if one examines his thought more closely, it can be seen that he does not intend to signify by pantheism 'the concept of the whole sum of reality'. Such a doctrine would really be atheism, in spite of the use of the word God. God is more than the sum of every individual existence; he is the unity of the world and the wholeness of the past and the future. According to Driesch's definition, the theist regards God as perfect being. But since the future is not yet perfect, God cannot be perfect. Thus true pantheism recognizes only one God, who as *causa sui* freely creates himself, and who does not possess his nature but 'becomes' his nature. Consequently, God is fundamentally unknowable even to the pantheist. If one adds to this the dualist tendency displayed by Driesch's philosophy, it becomes clear that he too could not avoid paying the tribute exacted by modern irrationalism and pessimism. Nevertheless, Driesch is close to rationalism; but he admits that he cannot know whether reality is rational. This is even more the case with *T. Ziehen*, who calls his point of view 'nomotheism'. To him, as formerly to Fichte, God is identical with the ordering of the universe according to fixed laws.

F. R. LIPSIUS

III THE FUNDAMENTAL RELATIONSHIP BETWEEN PHILOSOPHY AND RELIGION

1. The Apparent Contradiction
In order to define the nature of philosophy (*cf.* I above) it is necessary to work out a philosophy in concrete terms,

and in order to define the nature of religion it is similarly necessary to work out a philosophy of religion in concrete terms. But since neither of these tasks is to be undertaken here, it is only possible to give preliminary and tentative definitions, and only such as are of significance for the relationship between the two. Philosophy is the attitude of radical inquiry, an inquiry into the nature of inquiry itself and into all objects, in so far as they are able to provide concrete answers to this radical question. Religion is simply to be apprehended by the Absolute, by what is beyond being, by what gives being to being and meaning to meaning. Thus religion is a possession although it takes the form of 'being possessed'. Philosophy, on the other hand, is the exact negative of possession, the very first step, a first step taken without possessing anything, without any previous assumption. Thus the relation between philosophy and religion is that between not possessing and possessing, between questioning and having the answer. They seem to be *completely opposed*. Philosophy seems to begin where the substance and certainty of religion break off, and religion to begin where philosophy comes to an end, where radical inquiry ceases. A number of formulations of the opposition between religion and philosophy go back to this circumstance. Religion believes it can dispense with philosophy, since it possesses the truth and therefore has no need of inquiry, while philosophy believes that it must avoid religion, since by its assumption of the truth religion hinders radical inquiry. Thus we seem to have two attitudes which are mutually exclusive, since they both claim to be absolute. Religion can no more deny that the state of being simply apprehended (in faith) is absolute, than philosophy can deny the absolute exclusiveness of its pure inquiry. This conflict cannot be avoided by distinguishing between two types of person (on psychological and sociological grounds), the religious and the philosophical. For religion lays claim to every person, and would be abandoning its task if it did not do so. And while philosophy does not demand that everyone should be a philosopher, it does demand the recognition of radical inquiry as the method by which a decision is made between true and false. Thus it too cannot be regarded as one type of thought of relative value. But the opposition cannot be allowed to persist. For if it persisted, and if at the same time both religion and philosophy were the expression of an *ultimate* human potentiality, this would mean a hopeless division in man; and it would be impossible for him even to decide in favour of one or the other. For in order to make a decision it is necessary to be in full control of oneself, to possess personal unity. The contradiction can only be understood and ultimately overcome by a deeper analysis of what is meant on both sides.

2. *Their Ultimate Identity*

Religion was characterized as *the state of being purely and simply apprehended*. By 'purely and simply' we mean being apprehended not by something conditional, but by the unconditional and absolute, by pure transcendence; this implies that religion contains within itself an element of criticism of any concrete form of being apprehended, of any concrete 'faith'. Such a form of being apprehended always comes under the suspicion of being not yet 'pure' or of being 'defiled', that is, to be an apprehension not *only* by the Absolute, but *also*, and perhaps primarily, by something conditional. Where this suspicion is justified, religion becomes 'demonic'. Within religion, there is a contrast between the demonic and the critical, which is the radical demand for 'purity', that is for a purity in being apprehended by God in truth, the absolute, and transcendent. Thus religion also contains an element of radical inquiry, by which every one of its own presuppositions is brought into question. Of course in the case of concrete religions, this criticism is not the dominant element. It is one element, which makes it possible for religion to surpass itself. The claim of religion to be absolute sets up within true religion an irreconcilable tension between the absolute and concrete reality.

Philosophy was characterized as an attitude of *radical inquiry*. But the existential form of radical inquiry is concrete questioning, and concrete questioning is inquiry into a concrete situation. This situation can, for example, be that of the pure and yet concrete state of being apprehended, the religious situation described above. Thus radical inquiry takes on an existential form in the concrete application of its questions, which may be determined by a particular concrete state being apprehended in religion. Philosophy cannot avoid this 'existential condition'. Its characteristic of always taking the first step without presupposition means that it has the nature of pure and unlimited possibility, and this possibility is retained in its concrete reality. At any moment philosophy can be called into question together with the situation in which it exists. But this can only take place under the pressure of a different concrete situation. Thus its unlimited possibility means that in its application it is not limited to the concrete elements to which it is being applied. Yet this unlimited nature can only be maintained as a matter of fact in a concrete situation. It is in this state of radicality, full of tension, in the unity of absolute and the concrete, that philosophy and religion are alike.

But the further contrast still seems to be present in the fact that religion must always assume that it is religion, that it is the state of being unconditionally apprehended, while philosophy can question even this assumption. This raises the central problem of the philosophy of religion (*cf. The Philosophy of Religion* pp. 310 ff. below), on the solving of which the ultimate definition of the relationship between religion and philosophy depends. It is the question of the sense in which religion must continue to assume itself. If the state of being purely and simply apprehended is identified with one particular religion, distinguished from other forms of religion or from irreligion, so that it becomes one particular attitude parallel or opposed to others, then it is possible or even necessary for philosophy to go beyond religion and to question it like everything else. But the critical principle within religion forbids the limiting of religion to any existing form of religious devotion; it can, in the name of religion, take arms against religion as it is actually practised, it can lead to profanation, to doubt, and to protest, without removing the situation of being purely and simply apprehended, for this situation is indestructible. It is identical with human existence, with man's position with regard to the Absolute. Philosophy and any given pattern of religious devotion must be understood as realizations (along with others) of the *one* human possibility, described by philosophy as radical inquiry, and from the point of view of religion as the state of being unconditionally apprehended. The abstract formulation of this radically unconditional state distinguishes the element which is common to both religion and philosophy, and which is nothing less than the possibility which constitutes man as what he is. But this can also be shown from the point of view of philosophy: to carry out the radical inquiry means to inquire into the very roots of the matter. But the image of 'roots' implies the negation of everything that grows up out of the roots, that is, of everything given, in the concrete form in which it appears. The tension that characterizes this approach is ecstatic in character. Every great philosophy is ecstatic in character, ecstatic here meaning lifted out of every association with phenomena as they are given. The radicality of philosophy is essentially ecstatic, as is the religious state of being unconditionally apprehended. Both point to a demand and a fulfilment outside the context of what is given. Philosophical inquiry deals with the same 'ultimate' which is apprehended in the religious state of being apprehended. Of its nature, philosophical inquiry is itself a religious state of being apprehended—however firmly this may be concealed in the act of carrying on philosophy. Thus there is an *ultimate identity with religion and philosophy*, in which religion radically understood is a superior expression, and as understood in concrete terms is an expression on the same level of what is superior to them both.

3. *Structural Differences*

This identity of religion and philosophy does not exclude *tensions* in its practical realization, but gives rise to them. It is because they are essentially so close that in fact contradictions arise between them. Their structure is different. The unconditional nature of religion affects man as a whole. While it is false to say that religion is 'a practical affair of the human intellect'—it is not restricted either to practical matters nor to the intellect —it is nevertheless true that the idea of 'pure theory or contemplation' (*cf.* I above) is in no way the ideal of any actual religion that exists. The task of forming and changing reality, even in the limited form of a change in one's own soul, as in pietism, cannot be separated from religion. On the other hand, in philosophy the totality of human life is explicitly placed in the background. The conduct of its radical inquiry is not concerned with the 'salvation of the soul' of the inquirer, or the well-being of the group to which he belongs. Consequently, philosophy can be understood in a 'non-existential' sense, that is, in the sense that the inquirer stands outside his inquiry, and adopts the point of view of 'pure knowledge' outside an existential situation. But this is only true of the purpose of the inquiry, which for philosophy must be radical, and not for the application of the inquiry as an expression of the situation of the inquirer. The inquirer becomes part of the inquiry through the way in which it is conducted. The difference, therefore, is that in philosophy the existential situation is the background, whereas in religion it is the foreground, what is actually aimed at. The second structural difference is associated with this: as a radical inquiry, philosophy is directed towards knowledge. But knowledge is bound up with the forms of knowledge, and these are linked to certain historical, social, and psychic conditions. They are not available to every person, or to every group of persons, at every time. They are esoteric. The case is quite different with religion. It does not presuppose the possession of any formal basis of understanding. Its claim is upon everyone in every group and every period. Its symbols and actions are directly accessible. It is universal in its claim. It is exoteric, even if it develops an esoteric side. This esoteric side—for example the *fides implicita* of Catholicism—is its philosophical aspect, the aspect of pure inquiry, of theology. In the structure of theology the distinction between religion and philosophy is particularly clear. In intention theology is existential like religion; but in the way it is carried out it is esoteric, dependent upon certain formal prerequisites in the same way as philosophy. At one and the same time it is explicitly existential, concerned like religion with the whole man, and esoteric, accessible like philosophy to only a few. The fact of theology is the proof of the ultimate identity of religion and philosophy, and also of the difference in their structure. Theology, in fact, contains a structural element drawn from both. Consequently, it can approach either to one or to the other, as in their turn philosophy and religion can approach theology—

and so approach each other. The more the existential background of philosophy comes to the fore—this is part of the programme of modern 'existential' philosophy —the more it approaches theology and through it religion. And the more philosophical elements religion takes into its immediate consciousness—the present-day situation makes this unavoidable for large groups of religious people—the more it takes on a theological and therefore a philosophical character. And the same is true from the point of view of theology: the more formal and radical its questions become, the more they are philosophical, and bring religion close to philosophy; the more it remains prophetic, the more it takes on the character of religion. This complex interrelationship and movement is due to the distinction between religion and philosophy on the basis of their ultimate identity.

4. Typical Views of the Relationship between the Two
The history of the relationship between religion and philosophy is identical with the history of theology. We are only able here to give *typical* outlines of this relationship, in a systematic interpretation. From the standpoint both of religion and philosophy, three typical forms taken by this relationship can be distinguished. These can be characterized as relationships of assimilation, co-ordination, and sub-ordination.

From the *point of view of religion*, the following possibilities exist:

a. Religion recognizes its ultimate identity with philosophy and consequently claims philosophy for itself. However, it rejects certain philosophies, because it recognizes them as the expression of a different existential situation. At the same time, it transposes the esoteric form of philosophy into the esoteric form of religion. This is basically the attitude of the early Christian apologists. It gave rise to the dogma of the early Church with its

distinctive synthetic structure, in which the philosophical element was soon no longer understood, and
exalted into the sphere of inviolate mystery. An attempt
in this direction can also be seen in Schleiermacher and
the *Vermittlungstheologie* of his time. The negative evaluation which is made of this approach at the present time
is due—apart from fortuitous aspects of the present-day
situation—to the failure of this theology to be sufficiently
radical; it has led to compromise rather than to genuine
meditation in the sense of assimilation. The aims of this
theology, which it shares with the early Church, are
bound to be sought, once the common identity and
different structure of religion and philosophy are recognized.

b. This identity is rejected, and philosophy limited to
formal and empirical considerations. Religion is regarded as possessing even the truth which is the goal of
philosophy. The form of philosophical inquiry is separated from the normal application of that inquiry, and
philosophy is also deprived even of the existential character of its background. It becomes the tool of empirical
science. This is the attitude of early scholasticism,
nominalism, particularly that of the English Franciscans,
and also the attitude of English religion, both conservative and positivist in its outlook. It is the attempt to
remove the tension by depriving philosophical inquiry
of its force; or, to use historical and sociological terms,
it is the theory of a practical pattern of life, for which the
inquiry into the nature of inquiry has no reality.

c. The existential character of philosophy is recognized. But it is demoted to the level of a preparatory
stage of religion. This can take place in two ways, a
positive and a negative. In the positive conception,
philosophy can be accorded the ability of reaching a
certain level in the sphere of religious truth, that is, as
far as natural revelation reaches. In the negative view,

philosophy is denied this possibility. Instead, it is given the task, as critical philosophy, of preventing itself from going beyond its own proper limits, and so of preparing for revelation in a negative sense. The positive view is characteristic of Thomism, while the negative view is found in certain tendencies of Protestant theology (e.g. in the dialectical theology of the present day). This solution turns the difference in structure between religion and philosophy into a difference of level and value. It does not formalize philosophy, but attempts, in the name of religion, to impose fixed limits upon it. Consequently, it destroys the radicality of its inquiry. The existential background which philosophy always possesses is transformed into a concrete heteronomous prerequisite of philosophy—something other than philosophy which must be present before it can begin its task. Consequently, this solution produces more conflicts than any other, and satisfies no one. The struggle against it was one of the causes of the collapse of the Middle Ages, it created the alienation between Catholicism and modern philosophy, and it threatens Protestantism with the same isolation and rigidity.

From the *philosophical side* the same positions arise, though they display the opposite symptoms.

a. Religion is accepted in its true sense and criticized in its concrete content. Philosophy takes over the task of the critical principle within religion itself. (One has only to compare the criticism of religion on the part of the Greek philosophers with that of the Jewish prophets.) The identification of the highest principle of philosophy with the highest God of religion expresses the identity of the radical inquiry of philosophy with the absolute nature of the state of being purely and simply apprehended in religion. The structural differences are assimilated, in the direction of philosophy. Myth (*cf. Myth and Mythology*, pp. 342 ff. below) is understood in metaphysical terms. As a result, metaphysics comes to possess a religious force, which in the formalized state of philosophy is often no longer perceptible, although it remains latent. While in dogma the philosophical element is transformed into mystery, here, in the formalization of philosophy, the religious element becomes a philosophical category, but does not disappear. Most of the great metaphysicians define their relationship to religion in this way, both among the Greeks and in the West. Thus, the Greek philosophers can be called θεολόγοι (*theologoi*), and Cartesians such as Spinoza and Malebranche can turn with religious ecstasy to their ultimate metaphysical principle, and the German idealists can see themselves as the champions of a new theology, or indeed of a new religion.

b. Religion is excluded from the sphere of radical inquiry. It is exiled into the sphere of mental subjectivity, where it is given a scope as unlimited as that of philosophy in the sphere of the objective understanding. Its claim to truth is ignored or transformed. This is the solution sought by nominalism and critical philosophy. At this point it has much in common with the corresponding attempts at a solution from the side of religion. But the manifestations are different. Whereas in the opposite approach philosophy is deprived of its force by being limited to formal and empirical questions, so religion now loses its force by being excluded from the sphere of objective truth. With this solution, everything depends upon the attitude adopted, and this varies according to whether it is from the side of religion or that of philosophy that the co-ordination of the two is sought. It is always difficult, as can be seen from the fact that a leader of positivism such as Comte let his philosophy develop into something like the foundation of a positivist religion, so that he in fact returned to the type of assimilation.

c. The claim of religion to objective truth is recognized, but it is turned into a preliminary state of philosophical truth. This can take place in two ways. Either religion becomes an historical preparation for philosophy, as was supposed especially by the rationalism of the Enlightenment; or else it can be regarded as a dialectical preparation for philosophy, and so be maintained. This is what Hegel does. According to him, religion presents in imaginative terms what is seen in pure conceptual terms by philosophy. This definition is as intolerable to religion as the reverse for philosophy. The radical inquiry of philosophy cannot on principle exceed the absolute claim of religion. Thus the struggle against rationalism and the Hegelian 'left wing' was a struggle for existence on the part of religion.

Naturally, this series of typical conceptions by no means exhausts the forms taken in practice by the relationship between religion and philosophy. But it provides a sure starting point for the understanding of the numerous historical manifestations of this relationship.

5. *The Problem at the Present Day*

Bearing in mind the different typical attitudes and the fundamental definitions given above, we can go on to give some indication of the situation at the present day. Since the *subordination* either of philosophy to religion, or of religion to philosophy, inevitably involves a direct struggle between the two, it does not do justice to the real relationship between religion and philosophy. Even the task which 'dialectical theology' gives to philosophy, of preparing for it by a negative criticism of the claims of philosophy, is unacceptable to philosophy. This task may be carried out in the name of philosophy, in which case it is a discussion within philosophy about the possibility of a philosophy free from metaphysics, which can only be decided in philosophical and in fact in metaphysical terms. Or else it is a claim for the overriding authority of theology, and then philosophy is bound to make a radical inquiry into the basis of such an overriding authority; that is, it must reject any decision imposed in advance about the meaning of its inquiry. In practice, it is the type of *co-ordination* which is predominant, and the philosophical inquiry is not posed in the radical manner which gives it its meaning and its ecstatic character, so that it is not really philosophy, but science or logic. Thus the solution must be based on the first type, that of *assimilation*. Powerful tendencies in this direction can be observed at the present day, and this article itself is the expression of such tendencies. Theological radicalism in Protestantism, of which the most representative manifestation is 'dialectical theology', has distinguished the critical principle within religion as its authoritative standard. Even religion exists in the critical, borderline situation, and has to face an ultimate radical inquiry. In its turn, philosophy seeks to involve the inquirer in the inquiry itself. It attempts an 'existential' procedure. Its background must somehow be brought to the fore. How this is to be done is not yet clear. But as soon as the inquirer is included within the inquiry, he is drawn into the critical, borderline situation in the same way as in religion (Heidegger speaks of an 'annihilating nothing' from which the inquirer rebounds). At any rate, there can be no doubt that philosophical inquiry in this form cannot merely exist *alongside* religion, but either replaces it or is taken up into it. We cannot yet see how these ideas will develop. They are also decisive for the solution of the problem of religion and philosophy.

PAUL TILLICH

7
The Philosophy of Religion

1. The Philosophical Approach to Ultimate Questions
   within Historical Religion.

Almost every positive *religion*, even primitive religion, shows tendencies fowards the formation of a philosophy of religion. Myth (*cf. Myth and Mythology*, pp. 342 ff. below) often turns into a philosophy of religion. And wherever theoretical convictions coalesce to form a coherent and systematic *doctrine*, the starting point for the development of a philosophy of religion is present. Wherever the ultimate refinement of doctrine, *dogmatic theology*, comes into being, as in Christianity, Judaism, Islam, and Buddhism, philosophical reflection is concerned in the first instance with building up and establishing dogma, and then with criticizing it, and even with opposing and destroying it, both from within and from outside. It is sometimes difficult to tell whether a particular manifestation should be regarded as theology or philosophy of religion (*cf. Philosophy* IIa. pp. 256 ff., above). Even where the religions of higher civilizations have failed for various reasons to develop a fully elaborated philosophy of religion, we can still see reflections of this nature manifesting themselves on isolated occasions, as in Egyptian, Babylonian, Iranian, Japanese, and Mexican religion.

The strictly philosophical elements are in the first place systematization—a feature which in itself can develop entirely within the framework of a 'systematic' dogmatic theology, but goes beyond it at certain points— and secondly, the use of rational arguments and methods. Characteristic difficulties arise from this. A tendency to autonomy and exclusiveness inherent in reason constantly leads to *conflicts* with the source and norm of the apprehension of faith, which is revelation. Thus in Christian, Jewish, Islamic, and Indian philosophy of religion we see a conflict between reason (philosophy) and faith (revelation), which only in the first case led to a real emancipation of philosophy (*cf.* below), going beyond what was achieved in Greek thought. Wherever within a religion a revealed doctrine was given dogmatic form and defended as a dogma, the *criticism* mentioned above, undertaken from the point of view of the philosophy of religion and rationalist in its approach, often had one foot in the camp of heterodoxy and heresy, and sometimes went over to it altogether. The degree of tolerance shown to it by orthodoxy varied, according to the principles and individuals involved. Frequently philosophy was only required to have some link, however loose (perhaps an exegetical connection), with the religious norm, as was usually the case in the oriental philosophy of religion, which chiefly regarded itself as an interpretation of the sacred writings; *cf.* the orthodox and heterodox Indian systems.

What we have said is not only true of the *rational* or rationalist philosophy of religion, which has developed in every civilization in which thought has attained to such a degree of independence, beginning with the Mu'tazilites in Judaism, and Islam, and with the Ionian nature philosophy in Greek thought, and developing in India during the period of the composition of the *Brahmanas* (800–500 B.C.). It is also true of the second type of philosophy of religion deriving from positive religion (theology), that of *mysticism*. Mysticism (*cf. Mysticism* pp. 355 ff. below) developed in China, India, and Greece, as well as in Christianity, Judaism, and Islam; a mystically orientated philosophy of religion grew up from a religious devotion mystical in tendency. Where mysticism does not appear as the root or heart of the religion in question, it derives directly from it, so that in many cases it was not until later, or scarcely at all, that there was a breach and division between 'orthodox' and mystical devotion and thought. In a mystically orientated philosophy of religion, a distinctive *attitude to life*, associated with a characteristic view of God, the world, nature, and man, is more clearly evident than in rational philosophy of religion. If it does not go beyond a certain limit in the quantitative and qualitative sense, it is possible for it to be satisfied within a given positive religion; but it repeatedly transcends it, and this gives rise to the great conflicts between mystics and the religious body to which they belong, such as can be found in the history of Christianity, Judaism, and Islam. These conflicts can lead all the more easily to catastrophe, in that the mythical philosophy of religion, by contrast to that which remains within the realm of rational thought, usually has a direct practical effect upon the conduct of life. In spite of the mystics' mistrust of reason on principle, those whose tendency is towards philosophy usually make use of its methods, and mystical doctrine develops, paradoxically, into an explicit philosophy of religion. Mystics such as Eckhart, Ibn al-Ar'abi, Shankara and Ramanuja are among the most outstanding thinkers of the whole of history. There is naturally not a strict distinction between the two different approaches to the philosophy of religion; but just as the philosophy of religion which is primarily mystical in its orientation frequently betrays the influence of rational philosophy, so many representatives of the latter are clearly affected by mysticism. Examples of this are Thomas Aquinas, Ghazzali, and Nagaryuna. But every kind of philosophy of religion, whatever its attitude to positive religion (interpretative, critical, or hostile), has its effect upon the latter, from which in a sense it is derived.

Thus the philosophy of religion, as we have regarded it so far, seeks in general, with variations which depend upon the outlook and means available at a given time, to *establish and develop the truth contained in revelation*, which in no sense excludes criticism and opposition to the 'dogmatic' expression of it. On the one hand its task is to lay the basis and give an exposition and analysis of religious apprehension, and then to set out the view of nature and history contained in revelation, and to formulate the view of man and his nature and purpose, all of which provides the starting point for philosophical discussion. As long as philosophical reflection upon religion is limited to the study, elucidation, and elaboration of dogma in the narrower sense, it is no more than the continuation of the task of dogmatic theology with other (philosophicial) tools. But where the 'elaboration' we have mentioned goes as far as the outline of a systematically developed view of the world (based upon revelation), criticism, debate, and opposition arises; this stage was reached in Christianity, Judaism, Islam, Zoroastrianism, Buddhism, Hinduism, and in China. This leads to the necessity of polemics and apologetics, which consequently become an important task of the philosophy of religion; and where the philosophy of religion, rooted in revelation takes up a defensive position (*cf.* 2 below), this task becomes of decisive importance.

2. Philosophy in Isolation from Positive Religion

The emancipation of philosophical reflection from positive religion or from the view of the world derived from it, took place in the strict sense and on a large scale only within the development of Western thought (*cf. Philosophy* II*a*. pp. 256 ff., above). Of course we also find 'autonomous' thought in East Asia, where in general knowledge seems to have been less restricted in its scope than elsewhere in the East; and even in *India* individual schools and personalities succeeded in emancipating themselves from traditional speculation. In *Judaism* and *Islam* even the Greek influence failed to bring about any fundamental separation of religion and philosophy (apart from isolated phenomena such as the 'materialism' of certain thinkers). On the other hand, in the West, the construction of a distinctive 'theoretical' and later of a 'scientific' philosophy, differing widely from traditional belief, first took place in *Greece*. It was concerned both with the defence, deepening and enlightenment, as well as with the interpretation of religious thought, and also with criticism and opposition to it. The closing centuries of antiquity produced not only a philosophy of religion profoundly orientated towards revealed faith (of Greek and oriental origin), but also an *autonomy* in philosophical speculation which can scarcely be said to have been achieved anywhere in the East, even if one takes into account the fact that much work, especially in Islamic countries, was carried out in a concealed and disguised form, because political requirements demanded an outward conformity. The *Christian Middle Ages* once again brought the construction on a vast scale of a unified and specifically Christian philosophy; only towards the end of this period do we encounter thinkers who are beginning to abandon this common ground. Finally, as Dilthey in particular has shown, the *recent intellectual history* of the European nations has manifested a gradual retreat from the specifically Christian view of the world, accompanied by the consistent application of the principles of thought proper to natural science, and especially of mechanistic ideas, and the ignoring of the teleological point of view. The attitude to life characteristic of the Renaissance led to a philosophical conception which it was difficult to harmonize with the fundamental Christian outlook. Nevertheless, Christian impulses and themes were still a powerful influence in the tumultuous philosophy of religion of the Renaissance period. The Reformation was the greatest of numerous attempts to renew the doctrine of the gospel. Consequently, it provided in its turn, at a later period, the impulse for the development of a Protestant philosophy of religion.

At first, the guiding theme of philosophical discussion was the specifically *humanist* impulses of the *Renaissance* movement. A kind of fundamental basis for the new outlook was provided by the so-called '*natural system* of the intellectual sciences'—though alongside this, and within it, philosophy continued to be carried out on the basis of Christianity. Thus the attempts to set up a natural religion—undertaken in many cases in conscious imitation of tendencies of late antiquity, such as Stoicism —represented a characteristic new departure in the history of the philosophy of religion. They reached their culmination in Lord Herbert of Cherbury and Spinoza, and especially in Hume. The *Enlightenment* then continued these tendencies on a wide scale in the main European countries. From the very first, two possible lines of development presented themselves: either that of expounding the opposition or contradiction between positive and natural religion, pitting the one against the other, or that of overcoming or concealing the opposition by means of a harmonization which was often achieved at the expense of historical religion. While the first path was frequently followed by French philosophy, German philosophy of religion at the time of the Enlightenment— and it was followed in this by the transcendental philosophy of German *idealism*—endeavoured to reconcile the religion of reason and the religion of revelation; the philosophy of religion of Herder, Lessing, Kant, Fichte, Schleiermacher, Schelling, and Hegel represents the highest achievements of these endeavours. It is natural that 'rational' religion varied greatly, according to the different thinkers who concerned themselves with it, and was more or less close to Christianity in each case, and that the harmonization achieved constantly varied in its detail. The thought of German idealism united themes from the Enlightenment and from Christian philosophy (in its Protestant form). Meanwhile, the aims of the Protestant philosophy of religion were advanced in a more radical form than by the philosophers mentioned above, by such thinkers as Hamann and F. H. Jacobi. With the *decline of classical speculative philosophy of religion* the criticism of Christianity, and attacks upon it, grew sharper (D. F. Strauss). This involved a materialism which was irrelevant to the philosophy of religion (as in the French Enlightenment); furthermore, other thinkers, such as Feuerbach and Nietzsche, endeavoured to set up a non-Christian philosophy (hostile to Christianity or indifferent to it) in terms of immanence or 'humanism', etc. Here the emancipation of philosophical thought from traditional religion attained a new level. In the second half of the century existing schools of philosophy frequently followed their traditional course, and a philosophy of religion which showed little originality prolonged its existence on the sidelines. The late idealist tradition in the philosophy of religion was maintained (Krause, Weisse, Lotze, Fechner); the influence of Kant and Hegel continued, or was renewed (Neo-Kantianism). But the thought of many people was increasingly determined by the primitive 'philosophy' of naturalism in all its forms (Darwinism, monism, evolutionism, the economic view of history, etc). Towards the turn of the century, it became clear that the dominant theories of the closing decades of the century, *positivism* and *naturalism*, which with its dogma of evolution and its theory of illusion was opposed to all religion, were incapable of an ultimate victory. Under the influence of the powerful rise of the scientific and historical study of religion, the attempt was made to widen the basis of the philosophy of religion (Vatke, Pfleiderer, Wundt). Neo-Kantianism led to the development of a philosophy of values (Windelband and Rickert). The theory of knowledge and psychology of religion played an increasingly important part in religion (Simmel, Troeltsch, James). There were no major original achievements in the field of the philosophy of religion. Recently, phenomenology and dialectical philosophy have also affected the philosophy of religion (Heidegger; *cf. Philosophy* II*b*, 2, 3; III, 5; pp. 286 and 308 above). As modern views of the world and interpretations of life become increasingly anarchical, and contemporary philosophy, divided as it is into numerous schools of thought without any wide authority (*cf. Philosophy* II*b*. pp. 282 ff. above), becomes increasingly incapable of creating a dominating and normative system of thought, it has increasingly to give way in consequence to individual branches of study the more the philosophy of religion simply becomes philosophy *about* religion (*cf.* 3 below).

For the *autonomous philosophy of religion* (the distinction between this and philosophy rooted in a positive religion is sometimes slight) the decisive issue is the attempt to establish ultimate truths independently of all revelation. In this process, full reliance is placed upon the capacity of human knowledge, to which faculty the ability to understand and perceive the truth is always accorded. This optimism with respect to man's capacity for knowledge is accompanied by a similar optimism with regard to the structure of his being, and its development, and with regard to the purpose of man. Even where, as in the 'pessimistic' philosophy of religion (Schopenhauer, von Hartmann), it accepts that man is finite and imperfect, it always affirms, if not a thorough-going self-redemption, at least a significant co-operation of man in his own salvation through the knowledge he obtains and the actions he carries out. The conviction of the dignity and

317

greatness of man, which was a characteristic foundation both of the 'humanist' philosophy of religion, and also, to a considerable extent, of the idealist philosophy of religion, often leads in the context of an autonomous philosophy of religion to a basic anthropocentric orientation, which opposes to the ideal of redemption that of perfection, and can even appear to be taken to the extreme of a 'Promethean' outlook.

The autonomous philosophy of religion makes a more or less positive evaluation of man's endowment with regard to his cognitive faculty, and on this basis considers him able successfully to *elucidate ultimate questions by his own efforts*. The metaphysics which in the situation described above (*cf.* 1 above) served to confirm and interpret the knowledge given by revelation, now becomes a substitute for religion. Where religion is still regarded as valid and not as superseded or refuted, it is considered to be either a lower preparatory level, an esoteric form of philosophical knowledge, or the expression of the same truth in other terms and by other means. In other respects, the autonomous philosophy of religion constructs a more or less systematic complex of knowledge, in which cosmology, the philosophy of nature and history, anthropology, and ethics are usually derived from a self-sufficient and self-consistent body of principles. We can distinguish between certain types of basic viewpoint, which vary according to their understanding of the concept of the Absolute and its relation with the finite, their understanding of man and their evaluation of his action, and according to their attitude to human development, to the world and to life. How far a philosophy which in this sense undertakes to provide an answer to ultimate questions can be called a philosophy of religion may be disputed; in any case, there are forms of metaphysics which are scarcely to be distinguished from religion, just as on the other hand many 'philosophies of religion' are scarcely concerned with the answer to ultimate and decisive questions. In general, looking at the matter from an historical and systematic point of view, one can say that the autonomous philosophy of religion only exists in tentative forms, and one can affirm that it seeks to establish a relationship, often very close, with religion (and tradition). Apart from this, it is not easy to find a common denominator for the immense number of different schools of thought and doctrines which tend in this direction; at the present day (*cf.* 3 below) we are experiencing, under the influence of a new outlook in the Protestant philosophy of religion, the beginning of a fundamental conflict in this field.

3. The Philosophical Consideration of Religion as an Objective Phenomenon with regard to its Nature and Forms

It is possible to consider and make an intensive study of religion as an objective phenomenon with regard to its nature and forms, from both the points of view described above. To reflect objectively upon religion as such, however, has only become possible since the concept of natural religion (*cf.* 2 above) was developed. Previously, a naïve tendency to regard one's own religion as absolute was dominant, and this must have made it seem impossible or superfluous to seek or to find 'religion' anywhere else; so far as it was possible to speak at all of religion in general (apart from one's own) it was always measured and judged by the standard of one's own. The new orientation with regard to *principles*, which the conception of natural religion gave to all philosophy concerned with religion, was followed by a profounder understanding of its historical forms, which, inspired by study, travel, archaeological discoveries, the rediscovery of antiquity, and the division of the Church, and even earlier by the Crusades and by pilgrimages, came into its own at the beginning of the modern period and was expressed in historical, linguistic and ethnic studies. This process again was accompanied by a deeper realization of the psychological laws governing the nature of religion (*cf. The Psychology of Religion* pp. 323 ff. below). It was in the eighteenth century that the first significant attempts at a philosophy of religion in this sense took place, making use of ideas and outlines drawn from a period when the system of natural religion was in vogue. The forerunners of this attempt were *Hume* and *Herder*. The two real founders of a systematic philosophy of religion (the first being more historical, and the second more psychological in approach) were *Schleiermacher* and *Hegel*. Both the *Discourses* of Schleiermacher and the philosophy of religion of Hegel exercised a powerful influence upon the period that followed. It was through this influence more than anything else that the philosophy of religion of the nineteenth century which, moreover, faced a severe struggle against the opponents who disputed its very right to exist, became a philosophy about religion. This posed numerous important problems, such as the question of the development of religion and the laws it follows, its structure (the analysis of the religious act), its types and the form they take, and ultimately that of the relationship between religion and the other phenomena of human intellectual life, as it is expressed in history and civilization; and the task of the philosophical ordering, judging, characterization, and evaluation of the forms taken by religion. The approach to these tasks can be made in very different ways: that followed by the philosophy of religion of Hegel is an attempt, carried out with marvellous speculative power, but in a somewhat one-sided way, to set up a unified philosophical construction of the whole history of religion. From the theological side it was followed by the patterns elucidated by *Vatke* and *Pfleiderer*, neither of which are imaginable without Hegel; the latter in particular attempted to make use of the results of the historical study of religion, though he continued to retain the idealist construction, which saw the history of religion as a single coherent development. The great project undertaken by *Wundt* (the study of national psychology in myth and religion) also showed a great increase in the quantity of empirical material subjected to study, while in addition the whole material was subdivided into psychological categories, albeit only a few. *Spengler's* philosophy of the history of religion was developed within the context of a pluralist philosophy of civilization and metaphysics. Once again, the *problem of appropriate standards* came to a head: the construction of *one* set of values (monism) or *several* (pluralism) can only take place if certain basic norms are laid down. This can be done either by a positive religion (*cf.* 1 above) or an autonomous philosophy (*cf.* 2 above). Thus at the present day, for example, we can see a contrast between attempts to give a Christian interpretation of the history of religion (a theology of the philosophy of religion), and other attempts, from the point of view of a 'religion of the future'. The more profound the understanding of the infinite variety and distinctive nature of the forms of religion on the part of the philosophy of religion, the more it will hesitate to make hasty absolute judgements, and the more it will be ready to adopt a typological point of view which does justice to the ultimate differences and distinctions which are manifested in the nature and forms taken by various religions. Of course, in so far as there will always be an appreciation not only of the necessity of doing justice to individual manifestations —and only a philosophy of religion which is convinced of this necessity has any right to be taken seriously— but also of the need for a more or less unified comprehensive understanding of the world of religion, in its nature and development, the attempt to provide such an overall view of the great variety of religious phenomena, and to give a coherent description of their development, will constantly be taken up anew.

JOACHIM WACH

8

The Psychology of Religion

*1. Two Principal Methods of Study in
the Psychology of Religion*

The problems raised by modern psychology of religion
can best be described with reference to Schleiermacher.
It was thinkers of his school who in fact used the concept
in the technical sense for the first time, meaning by it a
concern with the psychological structure of the religious
consciousness, and especially for the distinction between
its thought forms, either naïve and popular or dogmatic
and conceptual, and the specific content of faith, the
object of religious conviction. Consequently, the decisive
task both of all scientific study of religion, and also of all
specifically theological study, came to be regarded as
that of attaining to the specific content of faith by way
of its thought forms. Thus this approach to the problem
of the psychology of religion is entirely orientated towards the *objective side* of religious faith. It presents a
far-reaching analogy to the so-called *phenomenological*
mode of thought of modern philosophy, such as is particularly evident in the existential phenomenology of
Heidegger. For Schleiermacher's approach to the psychology of religion is concerned both with its notional
content and its existential manifestations. But other
thinkers at the present day regard the effect of the psychology of religion of Schleiermacher as having diverted
attention from the objective side of the conviction of
faith exclusively to the *subjective side*. This judgement does
not do justice to Schleiermacher's intentions, but is
justified to the extent that the intentions of Schleier-

macher were diverted by some of his followers in this direction. In fact, important problems also exist from this point of view.

Both on historical and truly practical grounds, therefore, we must make a fundamental distinction between the *two principal methods of study in the psychology of religion*. The first, in which the preliminary work was done by Schleiermacher, and which consequently looks to him as its inspiration, attempts to carry out in pure and strict terms his basic intention, which in its turn was determined by the Reformation, and by Luther in particular. Consequently, its real work is concerned with systematic theology, and as a conscious means to its end it subjects itself to the guiding principles of this study. The other main method describes itself as the empirical psychology of religious life. It brings the methods of empirical psychology in general into its own special field. Its value from the theological point of view is principally to be found in dealing with the problems of practical theology.

The understanding of the different nature of these two principal forms is necessary for a proper judgement on the whole modern movement in the psychology of religion. Confusion and obscurity have frequently been caused by ignoring them, and this is particularly evident in the judgement of the so-called dialectical theology. Nevertheless, the links between both must not be overlooked. They are both based upon the common intention of penetrating from the outward manifestations of religious or Christian faith to its innermost depths. Thus from an historical point of view, the efforts of both have flourished simultaneously since the end of the last century.

2. *The Empirical Psychology of Religion*

Nevertheless, in the first instance, and up to World War I, it was the work of the empirical psychology of religion which attracted the main interest. Its origin lay in *North America*. In particular, the disciples of Stanley Hall began from 1890 to concern themselves specifically with the religious phenomena of the age of puberty (conversion, rebirth, profession of faith)—and to study them more closely. The first scholar who must be mentioned is E. D. Starbuck (*The Psychology of Religion*, 1899), and with him J. H. Leuba ('The Psychology of Religious Phenomena', *American Journal of Psychology*, 1897). The work of both was taken into account by W. James in his *Varieties of Religious Experience* (1902), a work which had an enormous effect. However, a double note of caution must be sounded in including this work among the products of the empirical psychology of religion: two different tendencies are at work in it simultaneously, one along the lines of the second main approach in the psychology of religion, mentioned above, and another based upon the so-called pragmatism of American philosophy (the latter element was to a considerable degree eliminated in the German version of the work).

The typical major work of the school of Stanley Hall is that of Starbuck. His method was the *use of questionnaires*, with the statistical examination of answers given to specifically formulated questions. In this way he sought to discover the nature and significance of the phenomena of conversion which bring about a decisive break in a person's religious development. Among the sources of error in this procedure, the most disturbing are the lack of direct evidence, since the answers are based upon conscious reflection, and the suggestive influence of many of the questions. But in both respects considerable improvement can be obtained by appropriate measures. James proceeded from the distinction between *institutional religion* and *personal religion*. He intentionally left out of account institutional religion with its objective and historical patterns of the organization of religious life in cultic institutions and systems of Church doctrine. He limited himself to the examination of individual, subjective, and personal religion, that is, the inner religious life of religious personalities. As source material he used in the first instance autobiographies, diaries, testimonies, and books of prayers. James made his selection from this material on the methodological *principle of extreme cases*. In this way he attempted to identify and distinguish from one another different types of religious feeling, by the process of relating the attitudes of the religious consciousness with general basic tendencies of human mental life, especially with the optimistic and pessimistic tendencies. Thus he found the principal types of religion to be the healthy-minded and the morbid-minded, that of the 'once-born' and that of the 'twice-born'. However much the distinction laid down by James between institutional and personal religion may be not only justified in itself, but also of methodological importance, it was nevertheless over-emphasized by him to the point of forcibly separating these two entities. But in fact both are constantly related and mutually influence each other. James's misunderstanding of this state of affairs led to his principle of extreme cases going beyond the methodologically justified point of view of 'distinctive' cases to the point where the decisive standard was the eccentric, another concealed sense of the word 'extreme'. A middle way between the approach of Hall and Starbuck and that of James was followed by T. Flournoy. He expanded what he called the *méthode d'expérimentation* of Hall and Starbuck by his own *méthode d'observation*. Here he analyses written accounts of religious experiences and religious developments, taken either from sources written for other purposes, or composed at the request of the investigator.

Explicitly opposed to James is the *genetic psychology of*

religion, based on national psychology, which W. Wundt makes part of his 'national psychology'. The most marked expression of this opposition is found in the thesis that religion is from the very first a question not of individual psychology but of national psychology. This belief is in its turn one-sided, but in the opposite sense to that of James. And its one-sidedness is increased by the fact that the genetic inquiry is almost exclusively concerned with the religion of primitive man, without taking any serious account of contemporary religion.

The *psycho-analysis* founded by Freud is formally analogous to the work of the psychology of religion, in so far as it also seeks to penetrate into the innermost depths of mental life. However, the theory of religion advanced by Freud himself and his immediate disciples, which derives both the origin and the present state of religion from repressed sexual urges, is a forced construction. It is based not upon this tendency as such but on a limited and one-sided version of it assumed as a *petitio principii* at the beginning of the argument. In so far as 'psycho-analysts' are able to overcome this limitation, they can make fruitful use of this approach in the psychology of religion, both in theoretical study and in practical pastoral care. For example, the work of Oskar Pfister lies in this direction.

The attempt to make use of *experiment* in the strict scientific sense of the word in the empirical psychology of religion arose in the school of the psychologist O. Külpe, who was followed by W. Stählin (1914), then by Girgensohn, and more recently by W. Gruehn. Religious texts are placed before a group; their statements concerning the religious feelings, conceptions, and movements of the will which arise in them are noted down, and serve as material for the study. Girgensohn is particularly concerned with the synthetic character of religious experience, in so far as it represents the combination of ideas and of the function of the self in an indissoluble unity. Gruehn tries to obtain the greatest possible accuracy in his experimental procedure, on the pattern of natural science, by a better choice of appropriate texts, suitable persons for the experiment, the shortening of the period during which the reaction is formed, the taking down of the record by shorthand, a more exact analysis of every individual detail, and a concern even for quantitative considerations. At the moment there is some dispute as to whether this is really an experimental procedure in the strict sense of natural science, or whether the results obtained—whether as a whole, or in substance—are in fact differently derived and only clothed in the form of an experiment, as is stated in the criticism of E. Spranger. The journal *Archiv für Religionspsychologie (und Seelenführung)*, founded by W. Stählin (Vol. I, 1914, II f., 1921), is devoted to this experimental psychology of religion, and since 1929 has been edited by W. Gruehn under the longer title. The *Zeitschrift für Religionspsychologie (Beiträge für religiöse Seelenforschung und Seelenführung)* edited by K. Beth, from 1926, with articles by Beth, F. Niebergall, A. Römer, etc., is more comprehensive in nature. The *Zeitschrift für Religionspsychologie*, founded by J. Bresler and G. Vorbrodt, ceased publication in 1912, and the *American Journal of Religious Psychology (and Education)* in 1916.

3. The Psychology of Religion with Specific Reference to Theology

The other main approach seeks to use the ideas of the psychology of religion for the central task of theology (dogmatics, ethics, and the philosophy of religion). The danger of a transformation of systematic theology into empirical psychology, with the resultant setting aside of the idea of revelation (*cf. Revelation* pp. 29 ff. above) which is fundamental to theology, is excluded from the first, and on principle, by this approach to the problem. So too is the danger of the violent misuse of the investigations of the empirical psychology of religion, against which those who have carried them out, for example Stählin and Gruehn, have rightly uttered a warning. However, on both sides, the relation between the two fields of study is accepted, since the intention of penetrating to the profoundest levels of religious or Christian belief is recognized as common to both.

The first steps in such a *systematic psychology of religion* were made in the period immediately preceding World War I by theologians who followed Schleiermacher more closely than was then usual, and in part at least went back beyond him to Luther; especially W. Herrmann, J. Kaftan, E. Troeltsch, and L. Ihmels. The first three belong to the school of A. Ritschl. There is an understanding of the psychology of religion at the heart of his theory of value judgements, but it is distorted by the theory itself, and presented in a perverse form. His three disciples, each in his own way, have sought to correct his theory, and at least indirectly have advanced the understanding of the psychology of religion which underlies it, by recognizing the character of the conviction of faith as a *personal and existential decision*.

The systematic elaboration of this insight is carried out most fully by J. Kaftan. Yet even in his work, as in that of the two others, the historicism which is the basic premiss of Ritschl's position prevents his argument from being developed consistently. This is all the more the case, in that these thinkers, as a result of the same circumstances, are unable clearly to affirm their own approach to the psychology of religion by contrast with the psychologism which is all too easily associated with any kind of historicism; thus in part (Herrmann and Kaftan) they had to deny it both to themselves and to their readers, and in part (Troeltsch) distorted it into its opposite by a rationalist 'supplement', so tending to a rationalization of religious belief. R. Otto is also very similar to Troeltsch, in so far as his concept of the 'holy' not only contains a profound analysis of the psychology of religion, but also implies a philosophical and rationalist reapplication of J. F. Fries's attempt to give a psychological basis to the critical theory of Kant.

Ihmels is a disciple of the Erlangen theology (F. H. R. Frank), which distorted Schleiermacher's approach to the psychology of religion in the direction of psychologism. Ihmels's theology of the 'psychology of faith' is aimed against this distortion, by applying the principle of the dependence of the fundamental Christian experience upon the holy scripture. This entirely appropriate corrective work, however, is prevented from attaining its true effect by its inclination towards a biblicist dogmatism. The work of M. Köhler, A. Schlatter, and R. Seeberg is similar in content; but their posing of the problem, and therefore their attitude to it, is less accurate than that of Ihmels, who with his method of the 'psychology of faith' has touched on the essential point.

Thus the most important demand made by post-war systematic theology is that of the *liberation of the methods of the psychology of religion or the psychology of faith from the spell of historicism and psychologism. Dialectical theology* on the one hand, and the so-called theology of 'the psychology of religion' in the narrower sense on the other, have devoted themselves to this point. Dialectical theology has succeeded in throwing out the baby with the bath water by rejecting not only false historicism and psychologism, but also historical and psychological thought itself. The theology of the psychology of religion has attempted a fruitful application of the fundamental purpose of the psychology of religion, that of penetrating to the profoundest level of religious or Christian faith, to the task of theology as a whole. Moreover, the most recent tendency of the Ecumenical Movement (at the conferences of Stockholm and Lausanne; *cf.* Vol. III, *Movement for Christian Unity* III) is also working in this direction. Consequently, the Scandinavian theology which has been influenced by Søderblom can be linked with it (especially that of T. Bohlin, also that of G. Aulén, E. Berggrav, A. Nygren, and A. Runestam). The interest recently shown in Søren Kierkegaard also points in the same direction. For the latter's most important insights he owes to his category of 'inwardness', which is unquestionably a category of the psychology of religion.

To carry out the aim mentioned above, the first necessity is a more exact definition of the psychological structure of the religious consciousness. For the distinction made by Schleiermacher, between only two levels, is inadequate, as has been established by the investigations of the empirical and experimental school of the psychology of religion (Stählin, Girgensohn, Gruehn). One must distinguish between four, or more precisely five, levels. The fundamental religious conviction is rooted in an existential experience of faith unique to each person; it is expressed on the one hand in the form of intellectual apprehension and, beyond this, in conceptual forms of a primary and secondary nature.

Furthermore, the examination of the psychical structure of the religious consciousness also requires that a systematic consideration should include the examination of its *logical structure*. The disputed question, whether it is the concern of religion for life (according to Pfennigsdorf, etc.) or its concern for truth which is decisive in forming the logical structure of the religious consciousness, ought properly to be decided in the latter sense. This necessarily means that account must be taken of the concern of religion for truth, as a fundamental methodological principle. This, of course, must not lead to an attempt to find, far less to assume, a rational solution to the problem of truth. To do so is a misunderstanding, with no basis in fact, made by many exponents of the empirical and experimental psychology of religion (Stählin, Gruehn). The true purposes of this study should be to work out the *psychological content of religious faith* according to the standard of a specific personal or general Christian understanding of faith, with the deliberate exclusion of all themes, ideas, and conceptions drawn from other sources. This is only possible if the closest regard is paid to the personal conviction of faith and the experience of the individual. From the point of view of the philosophy of science, this understanding of the task can be legitimately called a transcendental psychological approach, and in fact the whole mode of investigation of what is called phenomenology is the same. Nevertheless, this terminology is always subject to misunderstanding (although it is not contradictory in itself, as is asserted by Brunner, etc).

The methodological approach of the systematic psychology of religion must consequently take care that justice is done both to the objective and the subjective sides of the situation of faith (*fides quae creditur* and *fides qua creditur*). This can be done if the fundamental connection between the two poles of the religious condition, the objective and the subjective, is worked out according to the principle of their *mutual relationship within the psychology of religion*.

The objective pole (God), however, is not directly accessible to scientific and methodological study. Consequently, the attention of the latter is limited to the objective basis of religious conviction, and thus must seek to establish the constant interrelationship between this objective historical basis and subjective religious conviction, dependent upon one's own personal experience.

So far, this is true of all religious convictions. A further consideration, however, in the case of Christianity, is that for Christianity the objective historical basis of the conviction of faith is primarily to be found in the holy scripture, as the historical record of the revelation of God which culminated in Jesus Christ, in his life and teaching, his suffering, death, and resurrection. Consequently, the form taken by this principle in Christianity is that of an *interrelationship within the psychology of religion between the holy scripture and the personal experience of faith of the individual.* Within this fundamental mutual relationship between the scripture and the experience of faith, the systematic psychology of religion must nevertheless recognize the scripture as primary, since the Christian experience of faith does not exist except under the influence—either direct or indirect—of the scripture. This judgement on the relationship between these two elements, and the consequent evaluation of the scripture as the *sole source* of evangelical doctrine, is not contradictory to the approach of the psychology of religion, as has been falsely asserted, but can be seen in the light of it to be both appropriate and necessary.

GEORG WOBBERMIN

9
Religious Principle

1. The Meaning of this Concept in the History of Philosophy

The expression 'principle' is only found in modern scientific religious thought, because it originates wholly in the more sophisticated modern historical psychology and in the historical thinking to which it has given rise. Thus its precise meaning is the recognition of the fundamental impulse and force lying behind all individual psychological phenomena and facts, a force which can only be recognized by intuition and divination, but forms a clearly perceptible unity. It is the derivation of an interrelated body of psychological phenomena from a unified, and for the most part purely instinctive, basic force which as it develops follows a tendency intrinsic to it; it manifests its full content only in the course of the adaptation and conflict to which its underlying tendency gives rise, but it is also subject to all kinds of outside influences and deformations. It is a concept of historical psychology, which must be applied to every totality brought into being by any specific movement, and can signify the analysis of the character of an individual person, or that of a whole people, in so far as they form separate and distinct segments or factors of a culture. Thus one often hears of the 'spirit of a nation' or the 'spirit' of an age or a Church; or of the 'nature' or 'fundamental idea' or simply the 'idea' of something, or of the 'civilization' of the Renaissance or the 'civilization' of the ancient world. In the sphere of religion, Schleiermacher speaks of the 'coherent pattern of life', and R. A.

Lipsius of a 'basic religious attitude'. Hegel derives every religion from its own underlying principle; Biedermann describes the Christian principle as the redeeming power of Christianity which can only be seen personally in Jesus (*cf. Christology* III, p. 138 above); D. F. Strauss saw idea and principle as embodied in purely mystical terms in the biblical account of the beginnings of history. It is always a general concept of a specifically historical nature, which both formulates the content of a totality of ideas and events in general terms, for the purpose of describing and representing it, and also sees in this general idea a formula which characterizes the real and actual driving force of the development of the totality. The teaching of Hegel was an attempt to derive the Christian principle ultimately from the development of a universal first principle, the development of a world idea, regarded as an impelling, developing and logically unfolding universal principle, thus making the Christian 'principle' merely a subsidiary element of 'the universal principle'. This, however, takes us outside the realm of human forces, and we must be content in the first instance to seek in the case of every group of phenomena the principle which it has always possessed, so long as it has had any inner unity at all. We must also bear in mind that any such formulation of a 'principle' or impelling force is affected by the point of view of any given observer, by the extent to which its effects are perceived, and by the future development that is expected of it, so that it always contains a powerful subjective element. Nevertheless, a subtle and profound understanding of this point can also provide a valuable insight into the objective totality of the group of phenomena under discussion, and can also correct a too narrow or one-sided view, due to the fortuitous point of view and interests of the observer. Every new formulation of a principle in this way brings with it a renewed submersion and absorption into the fullness, breadth, and continuity of the actual historical facts, but also a new revelation of their consequences, an adaptation to the present and the future, and the simplification and rejuvenation of religious thought. By this formulation biblical and historical theology are transformed into systematic theology.

2. *The Meaning of this Concept in the History of Doctrine*

The use of the expression 'principle' implies *the application of historical and psychological methods to religion in the place of dogmatic methods*, which have regarded religion merely as a number of revealed doctrinal statements, cultic institutions and ecclesiastical ordinances. Even the attempt to derive these revelations (*cf. Revelation* Va, pp. 46 ff. above) as an intellectual unity from a single fundamental doctrine, and so to give them the character of a principle, would be no more than the drawing together into a unity of fixed doctrinal statements, or an outward adaptation to the modern concept of 'principle'. But what this concept means for religion is the view of the totality of a religion as something which can be psychologically explained and derived from a single fundamental tendency, in which its beginning and basis is an original and embryonic form of the principle, still not revealed in its whole fullness, which works itself out in its subsequent history in innumerable assimilations and conflicts, as long as its content is not exhausted and not overcome by a stronger religious principle. The psychological view of religion does not regard it as fixed revealed statements, but as a fundamental attitude of the mind and soul, the basic relationship between God, the world, and man, which later gives rise to individual doctrinal statements and images, through a largely instinctive and half-conscious process of deduction. This attitude determines the unity and continuity of a development unlimited in extent, producing a fullness of adaptations, assimilations, new ideas and rejuvenations, varying according to the richness and profundity of the religious and ethical thought of any particular religion. Thus the principle signifies the point of unity, usually subconscious, on the basis of which individual ideas and historical developments can be understood as coherent. This is an understanding of religion based on the analogy of the psychology of the great cultural themes, which have developed in a continuous fashion. Only from this point of view is there a possibility of understanding religion in terms of its historical development, through an analysis going back to its ultimate roots and determining its further development through the understanding so obtained. This brings us to a new concept of revelation, which shows revelation as the fundamental point of breakthrough of the unified spiritual force of the principle. Outstanding and fundamental persons and periods are so important, because they possess a creative and intuitive insight into the new principle which becomes distinct from the circumstances that have hitherto obtained, though at the same time they are altogether incapable of exhausting the whole profundity of the new principle which is being revealed in them. This also leads to the view of religious doctrine and institutions as a more or less accurate symbolic expression of their underlying principle, making use of the means of description and visualisation available at the time. Again, it leads to the distinction between the conceptual expression of a religion and the principle or idea that lies behind it, which only scientific study is concerned to formulate in abstract terms. It is this idea, moreover, which first allows us to assert the continuity and spiritual unity that exists even where there is a change in symbolic conceptual expression and in worship, as a result of reformations and transformations arising from the development of rational thought; they all continue the same underlying principle and perhaps even make it clearer, even though they give up much of the earlier symbolism. Thus to consider Christianity as a principle, in association with the understanding of the great ecclesiastical and historical forms it has taken as principles in themselves, implies the whole modern mode of thought, with its concept of the history of religion.

3. *Religious Principles and Religion*
This, of course, may lead to the misunderstanding that the principle is the religion itself; that the principle, as a concept summing up the ideas which determine and characterize a religious force, is the redeeming power, the actual effective element in what takes place in religion. But this would be an intellectualist error, of the sort frequently found in the theology of the school of Hegel. The principle is only the inner unity of everything that takes place within the religion, conceived and recognized by us as an intellectual process, and the presentation of all these elements with the help of this one dominant concept, making it possible to present them all as a unity, with the help of the ideas concerning God, the world, and man, in which a religious attitude to life is expressed and on which all its practical manifestations depend. But the actual processes of religion do not simply consist of thinking these thoughts, but of a religious upheaval and fundamental transformation carried out by means of these ideas, but not limited merely to the acceptance and thinking of them. Thus it would be as false to understand by the principle the religious doctrine, rather than the totality of process making up the religion, understood as an intellectual and impelling unity, as it would be to suppose that the processes of the religion consisted of no more than the working out, developing, and progress of the funda-

338

mental principle. Rather, it is only a matter of a totality of ideas, an abstraction expressing the unity of an irrational experience and the forces at work on it. It is not the principle that is at work in the ideas, but God; but these effects produced by God can be comprehensively represented in a unified intellectual principle, and manifest themselves in the realization of this principle. Here, therefore, we exclude the interpretation of religious principle given to it in the rationalism of Hegelian theology, which regarded the principle as an autonomous idea unfolding in its intellectual content the life of God himself, and as the timeless substance of universal and autonomous reason, a view in which it was impossible for any historical or positive element in the religious principle to have any real significance. In fact, a religious principle may quite well include an historical dependence upon fundamental historical facts which provide the guarantee and certainty of the religion, and this may be its most characteristic feature. For what is at issue is not the intellectual acceptance of the principle as a logical proposition, but a certainty about God in association with certain ideas concerning the will and nature of God; and this certainty is ultimately always the act of God himself in the souls of men, any ideas having merely a mediatory function. The principle does not redeem man and make him blessed, but the processes by which he is redeemed and made blessed can be represented as the principle. And since, according to the Protestant view, these processes take place in ideas and apprehensions of God, the principle is a driving force and complex, capable of development, of unified religious ideas, and of the religious and ethical forces which proceed from them.

4. The Consequences of the Concept of Principle for Doctrine

From the historical and psychological view of faith implied in the concept of religious principle, there follows for *doctrine* the important basic tenet, that its task is the representation and unfolding of this principle, together with that of expressing in conceptual terms the symbolism, appropriate to any given period, of individual doctrines, which, of course, includes not only the adaptation of them, but also the correction and combating of ideas which are religiously intolerable. Revelation is the breakthrough of the religious principle, and the whole history of Christianity (*cf.* Vol. III, *Christianity* II) is the unfolding and development of the principle, which must be isolated by a critical examination of the actual historical processes that take place. Thus the principle or the nature of Christianity, seen in the light of its whole historical development up to the time in which a theologian is writing, is the substance and basis of doctrine. The Bible contains the classical and original expression of this principle; the various great denominations show its further development, and the various syntheses it has formed with our present-day intellectual world provide its most vital contemporary task. In this contemporary task, a real universal, which it is possible to abstract from the facts, an historical and psychological reality, is transformed into a valid truth. But this means that something valid is isolated from the actual facts, by a distinct act of perception, and this valid truth is given a contemporary form of its own by being placed in the context of the tasks and problems posed by the contemporary situation. Thus the religious principle is the source of doctrine in this sense. All doctrinal concepts must be presented in the way in which they have been derived, formulated, and worked out individually from the basis of this fundamental principle. And like the *matter* of doctrine, the basis of the *subdivision* of doctrine must also lie in the religious principle. Every religious principle signifies a practical fundamental relationship between God, the world, and man, in which man, by the relationship he seeks to win with the divine in his religion, is in some sense overcoming the world. Thus the presentation of the Christian religious principle can be subdivided into the description of the Christian concept of God, the Christian concept of the world, the Christian concept of the soul, and the Christian concept of redemption. And since this fundamental relationship is everywhere associated with a religious society and the expectation of the ultimate consummation, each of these headings covers the same material, but in each case looks at it from a different point of view, so that taken together they provide a full and complete account of the principle of the Christian religion for the present day. But in so far as there was a historical background to the power and living force of this principle, in which it took its original concrete form and from which it developed as a powerful and convincing impulse, the presentation of the principle of Christianity must be preceded by that of its historical basis and of the religious value and significance of that basis. And not only is the principle as a whole related to this historical basis, which gives the historical facts their religious value, but so also are all its subordinate elements. Thus doctrine can be divided into historical religious statements and contemporary religious statements, both groups of statements proceeding from the principle of faith itself, and having a close mutual relationship with each other.

ERNST TROELTSCH

Myth and Mythology: The Concept and the Religious Psychology of Myth

1. The Definition of the Word and the Method of Study

Myth is the history of the gods. This is a definition of the word which must never be forgotten, but can only be given content by a series of definitions in practical terms. This definition assumes two things: first, that the concept assumes the existence of the world and of the gods, and secondly that the gods are thought of as carrying out activity and undergoing experience in time and space. Both these elements are not always present: the state of consciousness in which there is still no concept of the gods, but in which elements are present which can give rise to such a concept, can be termed *pre-mythical*. The state of consciousness in which the conception of the gods exists, but which is such that the gods, or god, are no longer regarded as acting and suffering in space and time, can be called post-mythical. The nature of myth may be deduced not merely from the period of its fullest and most integrated development, but also from the preceding period during which it was coming into being and the subsequent period during which it is *breaking up*. Only when these three stages are examined together is it possible to obtain an understanding of the inner nature of myth from within. At the same time, we have to ask

342

whether a wholly *non-mythical* consciousness is possible, what it consists of, and where there have been tendencies for such a consciousness to come into being. But all these questions can be answered only by looking at the same time at the actual historical manifestations and at the structure of the human intellect which creates myth.

2. *Negative Theories of Myth*

From the earliest period of Greek philosophy, right up to the present day, philosophical thought has attempted to understand myth. A number of theories of myth have been put forward, which, depending upon their purpose, can be divided into negative and positive theories. The negative theories deny that myth has any independent intellectual content. They explain it by deriving it from something else, and consequently remove its own independent significance. For example, *allegorical* theories of myth were used by many Greek natural philosophers to defend the truth of the Homeric poems, which were regarded as sacred. They explained myth as natural science concealed in allegory, a view which was derided by Plato, who by contrast made use of myth in his philosophy. The *psychological* theories of myth attempt to explain it on the basis of certain psychical tendencies and laws. A typical example is the apperception theory of Wundel. According to this, myth arises from the objectification of human mental processes, through the apperception of objects in a personified form, as in animism. Naturally, the theory does not accept this objectification as factually correct. The *psychoanalytical* theory of myth attempts to explain mythical figures as the symbols of unconscious desires, especially those which are erotic in nature. It points to facts which are of very great importance for the nature of the content of myth, but cannot explain the nature of myth itself. The psychoanalytical approach to myth has never got beyond the level of a negative theory, although it possesses the capacity to do so.

3. Positive Theories of Myth

Positive theories of myth accord an independent and real significance to mythical creations. This can be done either in metaphysical terms, or in terms of a theory of knowledge. The most important *metaphysical* theory of myth is that put forward by Schelling. In his final period in particular, his whole thought turned upon the question of myth. He saw it as the expression of a genuine theogonic process, that is, a process in which the principles united in God are worked out in contradictory terms in the human consciousness. At the present day, the theory of myth which sees it in terms of a *theory of knowledge* is represented by Ernst Cassirer. He ascribes to myth its own genuine inner content, which is expressed in the coherent structure of the mythical world in accordance with its own laws. Like science, art, and language, myth is an essential element of intellectual life. Its reality does not consist, any more than the reality of these other realms of thought, in being a correct representation of a reality in itself, but in the creation of an intellectual world that is meaningful in itself. The *symbolic-realistic* theory of myth which is put forward by the author of this article in his philosophy of religion, attempts to overcome the opposition between the metaphysical view of myth and that which sees it in terms of the theory of knowledge. Here myth is seen as a symbol, built up from elements of reality, for the Absolute, the being beyond beings, which is the object of the religious act. Myth possesses reality; for it is directed towards what is absolutely real. This is the element of truth in the metaphysical view. But it does not possess the reality of a direct representation, for it is composed of symbols, the choice of which is not of course arbitrary, but is subject to laws which depend upon the particular concept of the absolute, and to general laws which apply in every case. This is the element of truth in the view which regards myth from the standpoint of the theory of knowledge. We now pass from the general theory of myth to a question of the relationship between myth and religion.

4. *Myth and Religion*

The particularly close connection between myth and religion has always been recognized, although widely differing views of the nature of this connection have been held, while tendencies have been observed either to deny the connection or to equate myth and religion entirely. Both these attempts, however, have been without success. For the relationship between myth and religion involves a distinctive dialectic of its own which is very difficult to understand. The *intellectualist* view of religion tends to regard myth as an essential of religion. The history of religion is treated as though it were the history of myth. A religion is regarded as being understood when its mythology is known. By contrast, the *emotional* view of religion tends to regard myth as valueless. It points to the scientific and artistic elements in myth, which have nothing to do with religion. It seeks the essential features of a religion in its cult and devotion, and regards myth as an entirely secondary formation. Both views are one-sided and inadequate. More accurate is the *theory of correlation*. It asserts that every religious act is related to a religious object, and that a religious object is only what is aimed at by a religious act. There can be no cult and no act of devotion without a mythical content; on the other hand, no myth is religious unless it is a living force in cult and devotion.

This would be a satisfactory definition of the relationship between myth and religion, if a *protest against myth* had not developed within religion itself. The objectification of the divine in time and space and in anthropomorphic conceptions, which takes place in myth, is disputed by prophetic religion, regarded as inadequate by mysticism and dismissed as unworthy and absurd by philosophical religion. The correlation between act and object, between cult and myth, appears to have been no more successful in doing away with myth than its attacks upon the cult have been successful in doing away with cult. Both have persisted, and their correlation has persisted too. Even in anti-mythical religion use is still made of mythical material, although it is a different use. The divine is regarded as the Absolute, beyond being; it does not enter into time and space. But it can only be perceived in symbols, which have a temporal and spatial character. Such religion has passed beyond myth, but the substance of myth has remained. This is the case with the prophecy of the Old Testament, with Christian dogma, and in mysticism and religious metaphysics (*cf.* 7 below). Myth is replaced by statements about the nature of God and his relationship to nature and history. In place of an unbroken myth, we have a *fragmentary myth*, broken up by the consciousness of the absolute transcendence of the divine. With regard to the unbroken structure of myth, religion is bound to protest against myth. With regard to fragmentary mysticism, the mythical is an element of all religion: *myth is a religious category*.

5. *The Objects of Myth*

The truth of both these statements can be seen from a glance at the objects of myth.

Histories of the gods which describe the origin and the nature of the gods are called *theogonies*. Stories of the gods which explain the origin and form of the universe by a conflict between two divine beings or by the actions of a god are called *cosmogonies*. Stories of the gods which are intended to explain certain processes in the world can be called *cosmological myths*, and in so far as they are concerned with men, *anthropological myths*. In so far as the myths contain representations of the end of the world, they are *eschatological myths* (*cf.* Vol. I, *Eschatology* I). The different fundamental pictures which the religious consciousness has of the relationship between being and what is beyond being correspond to the different directions taken by the mythical imagination. Inevitably, then, Christian dogmatics, and also religious metaphysics, have the same objects; there is no difference in the themes with which they are concerned. The difference lies in the manner in which their discourse is conducted. In all its symbols, this later fragmentary mysticism is trying to preserve the pure transcendence, the absoluteness of the divine, in spite of its use of pictorial symbols, while all the statements of the earlier, fully integrated myth deny this transcendence, and involve the divine in the contradictions and variations of the conditional.

6. Myth and Science

In all myth, the picture presented of the gods is associated with a particular picture of the world. In fact, in the earlier unbroken form of myth, which brings the gods down into the world of being, this distinction does not even exist. But this means that there is an inseparable connection not only between myth and religion, but also between myth and science. In fact the scientific study of myth has predominantly emphasized this connection. Even at the present day, the most frequent view of myth is as a primitive, imaginative, and subjective explanation of nature. There are many facts which support this view. Some myths are expressly meant to provide an explanation of certain processes, the *aetiological* myths. Inner relationships are represented

347

through *totemistic* myths, handed down from the pre-mythical stage of intellectual development. Not only astrology, but also astronomy developed from *astral myths*. Greek natural philosophy arose from the *cosmogonic* myths, such as are found in *Hesiod*. The mythology of the periods of world history developed into the science of history. Finally, the division of the world into earth, what is above the earth and what is below the earth in the *myths of the heavens and the underworld*, provided the basis for the view of the world held in antiquity. These facts clearly show that myth conceals a particular understanding of the world, and that in fully integrated myth the concept of God and the view of the world are inseparable. But this does not prove that they are both the same. Rather, it is true to say that just as the consciousness of transcendence destroys myth from the religious point of view, so the consciousness of immanence destroys it from the scientific point of view. And just as in the contemplation of the transcendent the substance of myth continues to be used, the same is true in the study and contemplation of the immanent. There is a difference between a view of God and a view of the world; but a link persists, though it is often hidden, in the surviving substance of myth. For in all scientific understanding a background of fragmented myth still persists. The more science comes to depend upon its own intrinsic means of expression, and the more it objectifies and rationalizes the world, the more the mythical element withdraws into the background. The aim of science is a non-mythical view of the world. In order to achieve this aim it takes away from material objects not only their divinity, but also their life, their individuality, and their quality. It breaks them up into functions that can be defined in quantitative terms. But there is an absolute limit to the activity of science; everything contains an element of 'being', something indestructible and fundamental, a profundity

348

which is evident even in the most thorough-going rationalization, which reveals the mythical background to scientific understanding and makes possible a link with the mythical element of religion.

7. Myth and Metaphysics and Dogma

This mythical background then becomes the explicit object of metaphysics, and so returns to the foreground. Myth and metaphysics are very closely linked. For metaphysics is myth conducted in the terms and by the methods of science. The distinctive tension of metaphysics is that it creates myth by rational means. It is this tension which explains the fate of metaphysics, that as a whole, and with regard to every construction it creates, it can always be rationally rejected, and in every period is so rejected, and yet it survives all scientific understanding. The force of metaphysics lies in the myth it contains. Its weakness is its rational form, which is unavoidable in the context of the post-mythical development of the intellect, that of myth fragmented by science. Metaphysics can be used to bring to light the secret mythical link between religion and science. This takes place in dogma. Myth and dogma are not identical; dogma is not simply Christian mythology, but is myth in the context of the post-mythical intellectual situation; it is myth fragmented by religion and science, and is the form in which the unbreakable mythical link between science and religion becomes manifest. Dogma is the combination of direct religious language, with its fragmented mythical symbols, and rational metaphysical language with its fragmented mythical concepts. Dogma reunites what has been torn asunder in the post-mythical consciousness, that is, God and the concept of being, though this, of course, takes place under the dominant impulse of the concept of God, while in metaphysics the criterion is the concept of being. But both metaphysics and dogma can only be understood on the basis of the fragmented myth which is at work within them.

8. Myth and Poetry

The important part played by the imagination in the formation of myth leads to the question of the relationship between myth and poetry, and so to that of the *form of myth.*

We must first distinguish between the mythical theme, the individual myth, and mythology in the sense of a systematically constructed complex of myths (the word mythology can also be used in the sense of the scientific study of myth). The genuinely mythopoetic force lies in the *mythical theme*; here there is no distinction between description and concept, imagination and thought, poetry and science. These separate functions have not yet taken on an independent form. Consequently, the mythical theme is properly the main object of the comparative study of myth. The same themes constantly recur in numerous forms; for they are the direct expression of the mythical consciousness. The psycho-analytical theory has shown itself to be a very fruitful source of understanding of mythical themes, and this will be even more the case when the subconscious tendencies represented in mythical themes come to be seen not merely as subjective but also as objective, real and meaningful processes. A mythical theme is expressed in an *individual myth*. This is not merely a product of the mythical impulse of the human mind, for within it the poetic and scientific elements take the first step towards their own separate development. The purely mythical impulse is even less directly at work in the process of combining myths into a *mythology*. Here the desire to bestow a poetic form on the material has relatively free rein, and it is accompanied by the logical urge towards systematization and comprehensive compilation, often without any real relation to the original mythical impulse. Nevertheless, in all these forms, the poetic element is still ultimately linked to the mythical. This is also attested by the fact that the earliest poetry, like primitive language as a whole, derives its power from the mythical consciousness. On the other hand, the derivation of myth from language is impossible, although naturally the linguistic sources available can have an effect on the form taken by individual myths.

However, as soon as the mythical consciousness has been broken down, the poetic and lateral so the scientific elements can become independent. The mythical content of the stories can be transformed into a poetic content. This transformation can already be seen, for example, in Homer. In the later stages of the development, the ancient mythical themes lose their force and become allegories without reality. But the mythical consciousness remains in the background of poetic creation; it continues to ensure the powerful effect of the poetic word, and maintains the hidden relationship between poetry and religion. The mythical element becomes explicit in metaphysical poems such as Dante's *Divine Comedy*, Goethe's *Faust*, and Nietzsche's *Zarathustra*, where the hidden myths of each period are given a distinctive form separate from that of dogma and metaphysics, and the original unity is restored between religion, poetry, and science in the post-mythical situation.

9. *Myth and History*

The relationship between myth and history is not simply a function of the problem of myth and science. For the study of history is always a participation in the task of creating a meaning for history. But the meaning of history points towards the transcendent and thus, where it is manifested, it is mythical in character. This explains the close connection between myth and history, in the fact that the form of myth is historical, and the way historical characters and events so easily take on mythical significance. The less the mythical consciousness has been broken down, the more strongly it affects the historical picture, extending even to the account of Christ. The more it is fragmented, the more the facts assert themselves against the myth. But even in the history which is most completely scientific in form, myth is not excluded. So little has it been excluded, that at the present day the myth of the 'pattern' (*Gestalt*) has been created as an historical ideal. The form of history which is most strongly influenced by myth is naturally *religious history*. Of course, in the context of the post-mythical intellect, the mythical element falls more into the background, and only becomes clearly visible at certain points (e.g. in the gospels). A human event takes up the foreground, being turned by the religious outlook into legend, but also attracting elements from folk tales and sagas, the ultimate roots of which are similarly to be found in myth. *The interpretation of history as a whole* necessarily contains mythical features. It makes manifest the mythical background even to rational history writing. Typical historical myths in a metaphysical disguise are the dialectic of history in Hegel and Marx, the idea of progress, and historical pessimism. In them there is manifest the original unity between the historical outlook and religion in myth, something that is still at work, though it is often hidden.

10. Myth and Ethics

Since myth is an expression of man's approach to the Absolute and transcendental which is the object of the religious act, and since, however, the Absolute is not merely an object of contemplation between myth and ethics, in every mythical outlook there is an element which determines human action, and no outlook which is originally mythical is possible without an act of moral self-determination. The only time this is not so is when the scientific or poetic element has been given free rein, and has made possible a view which in part at least is morally indifferent. Thus, for example, whenever the element of myth is manifested in a metaphysical form, it has an ethic underlying it and it contains in itself an ethical implication. An example of this is the way Spinoza calls his metaphysics 'ethics', and another is the passion for social ethics and the immeasurable social and ethical effects of the Marxist myth of history. A natural result of the strict correlation between myth and ethics is that the *transformation of ethics and myth takes place simultaneously.* The earlier myth was full of daemonic and vital forces, which were the points at which the criticism of myth in later periods was directed. This can be seen in the criticism of Homer by Greek philosophers such as Plato. The destruction of myth by prophecy was carried out in the name of righteousness. Yahweh, as the righteous God, was exalted to pure transcendence, and so recognized as the only true God. The direct mythical consciousness was destroyed in the name of religion by an absolute moral demand which made any confusion between God and the world impossible. Absolute transcendence and moral holiness went hand in hand, and forced into being the post-mythical intellectual outlook. From the post-mythical point of view, the whole of the fully mythical world, with its spirits, devils, and angels, was daemonic in character. Even the gods which are regarded in the myth as overcoming demons are themselves demons, in so far as they lack transcendence and an absolute ethical sanctity.

11. The Intellectual History of Myth

A summary of this series of individual analyses forms an intellectual history of myth. Its first task is to delineate the characteristic nature of the *pre-mythical* age. In general, this consists of the belief that the divine power (*mana*) is not thought of as personal but as neutral, only in such a way that this neutral force is not opposed to the personal, but is one with it: personality as such is not yet distinguished from the world of things; consequently, neither personality nor things exist separately. The *genuinely mythical* period develops when the significance of the category of the personal comes to exceed that of the material element, and the divine energy in material things is summed up in a number of individual divine personalities. The post-mythical period begins with the destruction of the mythical world of the gods, by the different forces we have described, the final and decisive blow being dealt by the exclusive monotheism of the Jewish and Christian evolution. The myth has broken down and has been forced into the background, but it has not disappeared. There is no such thing as a truly non-mythical intellectual outlook. And in every new creation of religion or culture, even at the present day, the hidden myth is manifested. It may grow constantly less symbolical, more realistic and closer to reality. But it remains a myth, and this is inevitable; for it expresses the fundamental basis of all human intellectual life and of being, its inseparable link with the Absolute, with what is beyond being.

PAUL TILLICH

Mysticism

I THE CONCEPT OF MYSTICISM

1. A Formal Definition of the Term

The *concept* of mysticism is a product of the Greek language and religious outlook. In Greek usage the word μύειν means 'to close the eyes' (Plato *Soph.* 239 E; *Theaet.* 164 A). In relation to the mysteries it signifies the exclusion of all apprehensions to the sense, in order to receive 'the divine illuminations' in their place (Suidas s.v. Μύησις· εἴρηται δὲ παρὰ τὸ τὰ μυστήρια καὶ ἀπόρρητα τελεῖσθαι ἢ διὰ τοὺς μύοντας τὰς αἰσθήσεις καὶ ἐπέκεινα σωματικῆς φαντασίας γενομένους τὰς θείας εἰσδέχεσθαι ἐλλάμψεις: 'The term arises from the act of initiation into the mystic and unspeakable, or because those who seal (=shut) their senses and go beyond bodily sensation receive divine illumination.'). It also means 'to close the mouth' in order not to betray the mysteries to the uninitiated (Scolion on Aristophanes, *Frogs* 459; μυστήριον δὲ ἐκλήθη παρὰ τὸ τοὺς ἀκούοντας μύειν τὸ στόμα καὶ μηδενὶ ἐξηγεῖσθαι. μύειν δὲ ἐστι κλεῖν τὸ στόμα: 'A mystery is so called because those who hear it seal (*muein*) their lips and reveal it to no one. "*Muein*" is to lock one's lips.'). The verb μυεῖν means to 'initiate' and is directly associated by Plato with ἐποπτεύειν 'to look at'—(*Epist.* 333 E; *Phaedrus* 250 C): in general, it means to 'carry out mysteries' (Heraclitus in Diels 12B 14: τὰ γὰρ νομιζόμενα κατ'ἀνθρώπους μυστήρια ἀνιερωστί μυεῦνται: 'The secret rites practised among men are celebrated in an untidy manner.'). τὰ μυστικά are in the first instance the mysteries themselves (Thucydides VI, 60). Similarly, the adjective μυστικός is applied to everything which is connected with the mysteries. Further, μυστικός is applied to what must not be uttered, and so especially to everything that is to be understood in a symbolic and allegorical sense (thus in the *Praeparatio Evangelica* III, 1, 1 Eusebius speaks of a mystical symbolical theology and in III, 5, 4 of the mystical theosophy of the Egyptians). Further material on the history of the word 'mysticism' has been collected by H. Leisegang in *Philologische Wochenschrift* 44, 1924 p. 138 ff.

If we look at the significance of all the various words which denote mysticism, we can say that mysticism is a method of making contact with the divine, coming under its influence and obtaining knowledge of its secrets, through *cultic actions* which not everyone can understand and which are kept secret, in order to protect them from profanation (*disciplina arcani*), and through *physical experiences* which are associated with these cultic actions (though later also separated from them), and which not everyone can enjoy. This definition is wide enough to include all mystical phenomena, from magical and cultic practices, the eating and drinking of divine substances, the sacred marriage, ecstasy brought about by means of stimulation and intoxication or by music, dancing and asceticism, and even the psychical techniques of meditation, concentration, and contemplation, as well as the mystical and philosophical speculation (*cf.* II–V below), which is still only concerned with the mental process of mystical knowledge, intellectualizes it and provides a way to it by a special technique of thought with distinctive structure.

2. *The Original Experience*
The numerous manifestations of mysticism can be traced

back to a single original experience which underlies them all; man, who is distinct from the things that surround him, perceives and takes possession of them, removes the distinction between subject and object and experiences himself in other things, and these things in himself. He discovers an identity of being between what is within himself and what lies outside; 'Nothing is within, nothing is without; for what is within is without.' Thus mysticism is a consciousness of a unity between the self and what is not the self. Not only do man and the world, the microcosm and the macrocosm, correspond; man *is* the world. The opposition between I and you disappears. '*Tat twam asi*' (you are that) is what the mystics say to everything. Meister Eckhart explains: 'The eye in which I see God is the same eye in which God sees me. My eye and God's eye is *one* eye, and *one* countenance and *one* knowledge and *one* love.' Here all distinction between God and the world disappears. God is in all things, and all things are in God. Thus man too is in God, and God in him. But God himself, who is everything, also becomes, as a direct consequence of the fact that all recognizable distinctions are done away in him, and that he is the highest concept comprehending all others, a concept utterly empty of meaning, to which one can only ascend by a series of total negations, leading to complete nothingness. Thus Eckhart, following Dionysius the Areopagite, who for Christianity is the creator of this apophatic mystical theology, says, 'God is a being exalted above all others, and a nothingness above all being.' Spatial and temporal distinctions, by means of which man orientates himself in the world of objects, are removed as subjective limitations: 'I am as great as God, he is as small as I: he cannot be above me, nor I beneath him' (Angelus Silesius), and the Indians say: 'The least thing in my soul is wider than the width of heaven, the place that lies a thousand miles beyond the sea is as near to me as the place on which I stand; the riches of God have a length and a width that is neither long nor wide.' Again, Jakob Böhme says of time: 'He to whom time is like eternity and eternity like time, is free from all struggle.' The following description by Suso gives a clear understanding of the nature of mysticism: 'Thus take the first word, which is *I* or *self*, and consider what it means! Then you will recognize that every man has a five-fold self. The first self he has in common with the stones, and that is existence or being; another he shares with the plants, and that is growing; the third he shares with the animals, and that is feeling; the fourth he shares with all men, that is, he has a universal human nature, in which all other human beings are one with him; but the fifth, which is properly his own, is his personal manhood, both the sublime side, the spirit, and the fortuitous side, the body. Now, what is it which leads man astray and robs him of his blessedness? It is the last self alone; for this causes man not to make his way back into God, as he should, but instead to lose his proper self towards what is outside, and to build up a self of his own from chance, that is, he appropriates to himself through his blindness what belongs to God, or at least tries to do this, and in the course of time fades away into weakness. But anyone who would truly abandon this self should consider three things in his soul. In the first place he should contemplate the nothingness of his own self, and thus fall away from himself, and recognize that this self, and the self of all things, is a nothing which has emanated and is excluded from the Something which is the only effective power. Secondly, he must not forget that in the highest degree of resignation, when all its turmoil has come to an end, his own self still constantly remains in its distinctive and effective essentiality, and is not totally annihilated. Thirdly, and lastly, man must go into himself and utterly abandon his own selfish desire in all things to which this has previously extended, in the creatureliness which makes itself of importance, in servile distraction, in shutting out the divine truth, in joy or sorrow, in activity or inactivity. In this way man will be richly endowed, and will be lost to himself, undistracted by earthly multiplicity, will leave himself irrevocably and become one with Christ in eternity.'

Let us imagine the bond of life that links all creatures with each other and with God as an electric current going out from a power station, providing power to millions of lights, and then completing the circuit back to the power station. As long as each individual source of light believes that the light that it is giving is its own, that the world outside consists of what its own light has made visible, and that there is nothing else except what appears to it, because it is illuminated by its own light and that of the others, there is no mysticism. But as soon as it considers and traces back what is happening to its source, as soon as the individual recognizes that 'it is not I who am giving the light, but the light is shining through me; it is not I who think, but someone who is thinking in me; it is not I who live, but my life is another's,' then the decisive step towards mysticism has been taken. This analogy provides an explanation of sayings important for the understanding of mysticism, such as that of Scheffler, 'I know that without me God cannot live for an instant, and that if I became nothing, he must necessarily expire,' or that of Eckhart: 'If I did not exist, God would not exist'; for in the instant that one of the bulbs is taken out of the circuit, the current ceases to travel from one terminal to another and every light goes out. Thus God needs man and man needs God for each to live his own true life.

3. *The Mystic View of the World*
Wherever mysticism has been exalted to the level of a

distinctive view of the world, it turns into a *doctrine of the unity of all things* (Monism). The world appears as an organism complete in itself, in which the divine light flows out from the One to the All, and returns once again to the One. Schelling once summed the picture up in these terms: 'This original, necessary and enduring life thus ascends from the lowest to the highest, but on reaching the highest point it returns directly to the beginning, in order to ascend once again; and only then do we have a complete conception of that primary nature, that is, that it is a life which eternally returns into itself, a kind of circle running from the lowest to the highest being, and from the highest back again to the lowest.' This view of the world also finds an expression in the language of all mystical philosophers, in the construction of the sentences in which they formulate their basic ideas. Mystical statements do not consist of the linking of subjects with the predicate that describes their properties (e.g. man is a mortal creature), such as we find in the statements of rational logic; but they bring contradictories together in a chain of concepts which lead back to their origin, the first concept: 'One is all, and all is one' (Heraclitus), or in a more elaborate form: '*The continuous circle* is *constant and unvarying*. What is constant and unvarying is the eternal symmetry of becoming. The symmetry of becoming is the nature of life. Knowledge of the nature of life is peaceful clarity of vision; ignorance of the nature of life is confused darkness of vision. Knowledge of the nature of life leads to individual existence. Individual existence leads to higher existence. Higher existence leads to mastery. Mastery leads to sublimity. Sublimity leads on to the way. The way leads to the universal All, *which is constant and unvarying*.' Mysticism has its own form of thought and its own logic, the laws of which were first formulated by Leisegang.

4. The Ethics of Mysticism

The mystical view of the world, the basic principles of which are expressed with remarkable agreement by the most widely varying thinkers from all ages and countries, leads on to mystical practice and ethics. The mystic's insight into the nature of process of the universe demands that he should not resist this process, but find his own proper place in it and let himself be carried on by it, so co-operating in its consummation. Since all creatures must return to God, from whom they have come forth, the mystic returns directly to God, fulfilling in himself a part of the process of the universe. According to the scope that is accorded to his own creative activity in this, it is possible to distinguish between an *active*, a *contemplative*, and a *quietist* mysticism.

HANS LEISEGANG

II MYSTICISM IN THE HISTORY OF RELIGION

Among almost all *primitive* peoples there exist mystical practices, cults, and often systematic and elaborate speculation on man's relationship to the universe and the gods, which draw much of their force from the fact that primitive thought does not recognize the distinction between subject and object in the same way as civilized thought, particularly that of the West.

1. China

In Chinese civilization mysticism occurs in the form of Taoism. Lao-tse says of the *tao*: 'Something exists which is incomprehensible and perfect, and which existed before heaven and earth. It is still and formless; it is the only thing that exists inviolate without change and variation; it is present in every place. One can call it the

mother of all things. I do not know its name but I call it
tao.' Here the mystic strives to purify his mind of everything with which selfish desire has filled it, and so to make
room in it for *tao*, the silent force which now fills the
whole of man, so that he himself becomes *tao*.

2. India

In India, a highly developed mysticism exists in the
Vedanta philosophy of the Upanishads of Vedic and
Brahman religion. The Brahmans derived their many
gods from one whom they called Atman or Brahman.
Brahman is described as an impersonal spiritual being:
'He sees without eyes and hears without ears, he does not
speak in words, in fact, he does not think with thoughts,
and he breathes without breath.' Brahman-Atman himself is the breath, the light of the world, from whom
everything is derived, and to whom everything returns,
the sole being free from decay and unvarying in all
change. Everything that we see with our own eyes is
mere illusion. Man too is an emanation of Brahman, and
so the great life of the All lives in him as well. But the
task of man is to return into the life of the All; he is like a
spark sprung from the fire of the deity, which has to fall
back again into the flame, a drop from the sea of the
deity, which has to be lost again. Redemption from this
life and from all the lives to come, through which the soul
passes in its pilgrimage, has as its goal only disappearance
into Brahman, known as Nirvana ('Extinction'). This
condition can only be reached through asceticism by
Yoga, a series of systematic and elaborate exercises in
concentration, in which the ascetic sits 'with his legs
crossed, holding his breath, his senses under control, his
thoughts directly towards Brahman, his eyes firmly
fixed on the contemplation of being, his self reposing
in the Self (Atman).'

3. Greece

In Greece there developed from the mysteries of Orphism and the religion of Dionysius (*cf.* I, *1* above) a speculative mysticism which was first systematically worked out in the doctrine of the unity of all things held by the pre-Socratics, which was linked by Plato with his doctrine of the ideas, and by the Stoics with their pantheistic *logos* theology, and which was elaborated in numerous directions in Neo-Platonism and in the theology of the mysteries. Above all, the Greeks gave mysticism a *philosophical* expression. They created the picture of the world which was typical of Western mysticism, that of the cosmos, a self-contained entity in which matter (earth and water), the soul (air), and spirit (fire or light) are all present together and interpenetrate one another, so that it is possible for man, who as a microcosm contains in himself the elements of the world, to reject and set himself free from the earthly elements, and to work his way up from the material world to the world's soul and thence to the spirit; this sets up a *scala mystica*, an ascent of the soul in stages from the body to the spirit, which at the same time means a progressive descent into oneself. They elaborated in philosophical terms the doctrine that the cosmos came into being from a primitive material, which formed itself into the world, and which relapses into the original element at the end of its development, and so laid the basis of a thorough-going monism and pantheism, with which the doctrine of the journey of the soul and the eternal and cyclical return of all things is organically related. Similarly, the idea of the mutual sympathy of all parts of the cosmos, and especially of the soul with the heavenly bodies, which is an important idea for mysticism, also comes from Greek philosophy, where it was particularly developed by Poseidonius.

With the mystical idea of the development of the

cosmos taking place cyclically and constantly returning to its beginning—the One becomes the All, and the All returns to the One—the Greeks associated a corresponding mystical metaphysic of history, which regarded the historical process as a circle, beginning with the Golden Age, following a descending course to a period of depravity, and then reversed by an act of redemption to an upward course, until mankind is once again restored to his original condition, and a new aeon begins with a new Golden Age. Furthermore, the Greek philosophers systematically developed the sciences of alchemy and astrology, which correspond to the mystical view of the world, and are only possible in terms of it; they adapted many oriental elements. They partly invented and partly systematized and turned into philosophical methods the techniques of allegory and numerological and alphabetical speculations. Above all, they intellectualized the conceptions, which originally existed in quite concrete terms, of the *unio mystica*, which in the Greek mysteries was obtained by eating and drinking food and drink that was filled with divine power, and by sexual intercourse with the divinity; they reinterpreted this as an ascent of the soul into God and its endowment with divine thoughts in an ecstasy obtained by profound philosophical contemplation. Almost the whole of the imagery of Western mysticism, from Eckhart's idea of the soul as a little spark, to that of the bridegroom of the soul in pietist thinking, was created by the Greeks. As a result of Philo's reinterpretation of the Old Testament in terms of almost the whole range of Greek mysticism, it found a place in *hellenistic* Judaism, from whence it was easy for it to come into close contact with *Christianity*. Thus themes from Greek mysticism were soon to be found in Christianity, and grew in profusion in gnosticism, and their number was constantly increased by the elaboration of Christian theology with the aid of the

Greek philosophy, powerfully influenced by mysticism, by Clement of Alexandria and others up to Augustine. From Augustine, who united the system of Plotinus with *Christian* theology, and from Dionysius the Areopagite, who introduced that of Proclus, there is a continuous development leading to the Eastern and Western mysticism of the Middle Ages (*cf.* V*a.*, V*b.* below) and also to *Jewish* (*cf.* III below) and *Islamic* mysticism.

HANS LEISEGANG

III JEWISH MYSTICISM

1. The *distinctive nature of Jewish mysticism* is due to that of Judaism as a whole. In so far as Judaism makes the fulfilment of the commandments the task of human life, piety is restricted to certain earthly limits. Mysticism attempts to go beyond these limits by penetrating through speculation, asceticism or prayer into what is conceived of as a spiritual cosmos, to the point of a direct contact with God and his creative power; it attempts to widen an ethical piety until it becomes a cosmic piety. The doctrine of the *first man* and the cosmic *Messiah*, and also that of the *Shekinah*, the dwelling of god among men, provide the starting point for this development. A characteristic of it is that piety is not detached from its earthly sphere; the significance of the commandment remains, and is even heightened, since it now becomes cosmic in its application and effect. Thus the intention of this mysticism is neither redemption from the will or from the self, nor is it pantheist; its emphasis is upon man and his decision, and upon the personal God, the one God of righteousness and love. Consequently, it retains the messianic concept of history, which in fact receives in this mysticism its most powerful, cosmic emphasis. This mysticism had a powerful effect in two

directions; in the spiritualization of the Sabbath, which it turned into a mystical day, and in a profounder interpretation of worship as the true *unio mystica*. On the other hand, it had a narrowing influence through all kinds of magical 'cabbalistic' activity.

2. Evidence of a mysticism of an ecstatic and visionary nature, similar to that of the ancient Apocalypses and Ascensions, are found in the Talmud. Related in nature are the ancient mystical writings, the books of the 'Heavenly Halls' (*hechalot*), which belong to the beginning of the *Middle Ages*. The '*Book of the Creation*' (*Sepher Jezira*) comes from approximately the same period, and shows the influence of the philosophy and terminology of Proclus. It became influential principally through its doctrine of the ten *sephirot* (spheres), which as the highest principles, together with the twenty-two basic letters of the alphabet, demonstrate the ways in which God works, and consequently provide the devout with an access to the creative power of God.

The conceptions found in these works are united and developed in the *second period* of mysticism, that of the true *Cabbala* (tradition), which had its origin in Provence, and is largely associated in its development with the personality of Isaac the Blind (*ca.* 1200). Its earliest stage is represented by the book *Bahir* which links the idea of a *pleroma* (an intelligible primitive material; *mālē'*) with that of the powers of creation, and also includes in its mystical system the doctrine of the journey of the soul, which from then on remained characteristic of mysticism. After this, more and more emphasis was laid upon the ancient doctrine of the spheres, as they were now usually named in accordance with 1 Chron. 29.11, the spiritual and moral cosmic forces which provide the ways between God and the creation; later on, they are regarded as being opposed by the elementary forces of the evil one, the 'shells' (*keliphot*), whose conversion and reconciliation is brought about by man. Among those who spread and elaborated this mysticism, particular mention should be made of the Talmudic scholar Moses ben Nahman of Gerona (1195–1270) and the enthusiast Abraham Abulafia of Saragossa (1240–*ca.* 1291). The consummation of this period of mysticism was reached in the book *Zohar*, composed by Moses ben Shemtob of Leon (1250–1305), with the use of older sources and traditions, in the form of a midrash on the Pentateuch attributed to the Tannaite Simon ben Yohai and written in Aramaic. It rapidly became the canonical book of mysticism. Besides this Southern mysticism, there was also a German School, which sometimes influenced it. Its leading personalities were Samuel the pious of Speyer, his son Jehude the Pious (who lived about 1200 in Ratisbon), and Eleazer ben Jehuda of Worms (1160–1237): here, the speculative element is of less importance than the concentration of the mind upon adoration and its absorption in the love of God.

The *third period* is that of *Saphed* in Palestine, which became the centre of a renewal of mysticism. The systematic speculations of Moses Cordovero (1522–70), who developed in particular the idea of the 'self-limitation of God,' (*zimzum*), are a dominant influence. Isaac Luria (1533–71) from Germany, through his personality, his joyful and devout asceticism and his mysterious sayings, became the saint of this group; his apostle was Chaim Vital Calabrese (1543–1620); the devotional book of Isaiah Horwitz describes his personality and work in the form of popular sermons. Luria provided mysticism with its 'law', making it a mysticism of customs, practices, and prayers, intended to prepare for the time of redemption. He is the dominating influence on the period that followed; Hasidism draws its inspiration from his ideas.

LEO BAECK

IV MYSTICISM IN THE NEW TESTAMENT

1. The *faith in God* and the *devotion* of the New Testament are not mystical. Certainly, the view that man in the state in which he is here and now is not what he truly intends and ought to be, is common to the New Testament and to mysticism, as to all religions; so also is the conception that God is above and beyond everything that exists here and now. But the view of the New Testament concerning the relationship of the world and man to God who is above them is different from that of mysticism (*cf.* I, 2 above); for the New Testament follows the Old in believing in God as the creator of this world and the ruler of history. Thus the world and history are regarded neither in the sense of a dualistic mysticism as evil, or as strictly speaking non-existent, by contrast to God, who alone possesses true being; nor are they regarded, in the sense of the pantheistic mysticism, as a symbol or manifestation of the deity, who is everything that exists. The New Testament does not speak of God with regard to the nature of his eternal being beyond this world, but in respect of his action within this world. Yet his action is not seen as a universal process governed by eternal laws, and accessible to speculative thought, but as the concrete acts of the Lord which man encounters as the claim and the word of God. And man is not regarded in the light of his condition as a cosmic being, who has to attain to his own true reality, to communion with God, by laying aside the condition he has in this world through a method of asceticism or speculation or in ecstatic experiences. Instead, he is considered from the point of view of the intentions and actions which are exercised between one man and another (between me and my 'neighbour'). Here, man is called by God not in order to receive a higher cosmic form of existence, but

to obey God and to honour him by doing God's will and loving his neighbour. By 'saving' and redeeming man, God is giving him hope of a future existence in heavenly glory. But this 'salvation' has already taken place, not by God's lifting man out of this present world, but by his forgiveness of man's sin. Thus it is true that he redeems him from himself, but this means that he redeems him from his perverted will. And God does not redeem man by letting him contemplate his eternal being or by giving man psychical experiences of union with God, but by an historical act, the sending of Jesus Christ, and the word which proclaims this sending. Man apprehends this redemption not in speculation or in ecstasy, but in 'faith', that is, in obedient recognition of the saving act of God, through which the world is judged and forgiveness brought to the believer as a gift. The act of God has brought the old world to an end and set up a new creation, a new humanity; thus it is the 'eschatological' act of God. The New Testament is distinguished from mysticism by its eschatology (*cf.* Vol. I, *Eschatology* III).

2. The expressions of the idea of faith found in the different writings of the New Testament and the forms of piety they contain vary greatly, and many of them contain *mystical elements*.

a. Mysticism in any form is completely remote from the *synoptic gospels* and the tradition of the *preaching of Jesus* (*cf.* Vol. I, *Jesus Christ*) which they contain; they are closest to the language and piety of the Old Testament and Judaism. There is a 'mystical', or better, perhaps, a 'mysterious', note in the saying Matt. 11.27= Luke 10.22. It is in fact a saying drawn from the hellenistic belief in revelation that grew out of the mystery religions, which has been attributed to Jesus; it does not reflect a true mysticism.

b. Hellenistic Christianity, which grew up in an environment where the religion of the mysteries and mysticism were active forces, was influenced by them, as Philo had been to an even greater degree. We cannot deal here with the influence of the mystery religions on the view of worship and the sacraments that is found in Paul (*cf.* Vol. I, *Paul*). In the opinion of Bousset, Paul developed a genuinely mystical piety on the basis of his mystical view of the Christian community. Certainly his language is sometimes influenced by mystical terms describing union with the deity, for example Gal. 2.20; Phil. 3.7-14; but in both passages the context shows that for Paul man's relationship to God is laid down by Christ's act of salvation and by faith. A genuinely mystical feeling is only manifested by Paul in 2 Cor. 12.1-4, where he tells of an ecstasy which represented for him a climax in his whole life. But that he does not mean to imply that man first partakes of the new life in such experiences is shown not only by Phil 3.7-14, but also for example by 2 Cor. 4.7-18, where he makes clear that the certainty of the risen life of Jesus is found in his historical activity here and now. Whereas a high value was placed in the local churches on ecstatic experiences, Paul placed a limited value on ecstasy, though without condemning it (1 Cor. 14). For he too regarded it as supernatural, and consequently, when it occurred in church, as a sign of the working of the Spirit of God; but it was no more than a sign for which one could be glad and which was a source of consolation (Rom. 8.15,26; Gal. 4.6); it was not characteristic of what it really meant to be a believer. For while the condition of faith was brought about by the 'Spirit', this meant being without fear before the judgement of God (Rom. 8.15) and was exercised in ethical activity, and above all in love (Rom. 8.13; Gal. 5.13-25). For while, like everyone in the ancient world, Paul certainly regarded the 'Spirit' as something marvellous acting upon man and in him, he does not really mean to signify by 'Spirit' the endowing of man with a new divine nature, but a new attitude made possible by 'justification', and in accordance with the will of God. Similarly, 'flesh' does not mean man's being in this world, in the sense of his nature, but the perverted and sinful attitude of his will. Consequently, when Paul discusses the fundamentals of salvation in Romans and Galatians, he terms it 'righteousness,' while 'faith' means for him obedience (as for example in Rom. 1.5; 10.3). But 'righteousness' is a part of the eschatological salvation which God has brought about through his saving act in Christ (Rom. 3.21-26). Consequently, Paul can describe the relationship to God set up by faith as being 'in Christ' (*cf. Christology* I, 3*b*. p. 80, above). Though the formula 'in Christ' is similar to a mystical or mysterious formula 'in the Spirit', which originally referred to ecstasy, for Paul it had no mystical sense, but signified a belonging to Christ and to the new creation (2 Cor. 5.17), and therefore had an eschatological meaning, and could also be used to describe the Christian's new way of life.

c. Thus the Pauline contrast between 'flesh' and 'Spirit' cannot be taken in a mystical and dualistic sense, nor can the opposition between the world and God in *John*. For in John 'the world' does not mean man's existence in this world, transitory and subject to fate, but the essence of everything that men desire and do because they have turned away from the will of God, and which presses, in the form of historical forces, upon each individual man from the first. Freedom from the world in this sense is not obtained by speculation or psychical experience, but by the saving act of God, the sending of Jesus and faith in him. John too sees the sending of Jesus into the world as an eschatological event, which also signifies the judgement of the world (3.19; 5.21-27). The guarantee of the new life of the believer is that he can freely pray to God and walk in love (14.13; 15.7; 16.24,26; 13.34 f.; 15.9-12), as one who is not taken out of the world, but preserved within it (17.14-18). But John emphasizes more strongly than other New Testament writers that salvation and life are already present, and he is consciously making use of mystic formulae to describe this presence, when he speaks of the knowledge and the sight of God, or of God being in Jesus and Jesus in the believer (14.7-9; 17.23; *cf.* 14.23, etc.). But there is a complete absence of descriptions of God which describe him as being without attributes and qualities, of any interest in a method to regulate the approach of the soul to God, or of any suggestion of mystical experiences; in addition, Jesus' revelation does not contain speculation on the nature of God, and 'to see God' does not mean to gaze upon his eternal being. According to John, God can only be seen in him who reveals him, or more precisely, God can only be received in listening to the word of proclamation which demands that man shall give up his own will and do the will of God (7.17). But man cannot do this at any time he pleases, but only in his encounter with the revelation contained in the sending of Jesus and in his preaching.

d. In Paul and John it is strongly emphasized that the new life does not consist of the soaring of the soul above the present world, but is exercised in faith in the preaching of the Gospel and in walking in love here and now, and is based upon the saving act of God, which is an historical event constantly made present as it is proclaimed in the course of history (and in the sacraments). Similarly, the later *New Testament writings* share the view that Christianity is constituted by the Church and by doctrine as historical entities which make salvation available, and that this means that God's saving act was carried out and is now carried out within history, so that the visible Church represents the eschatological work of

God and the culmination of the history of salvation. Thus there can be no possibility of mysticism here.

RUDOLF BULTMANN

Va EARLY CHRISTIAN AND BYZANTINE MYSTICISM

1. Introduction: Leading Mystics

The roots of the mysticism of the Eastern Church go back to the primitive Christian preaching. The vision of the glory of the incarnate *logos* in John, and in primitive Christianity as a whole (*cf. Christology* I, 5*b.* p. 86 above), and the feeling, to which Jesus's disciples bear witness, of an all-powerful and transcendent presence of God in Christ, which seizes hold of them, and which is at the same time a concrete and bodily presence, has impressed itself upon the innermost nature of this mysticism, and the language it uses is found both in Paul and in John (*cf.* IV, 2*b. c.*): 'We have *seen his glory*'. They too are the source of the Eastern Church's account of the continued working of the exalted Lord in the heart of the believer: 'It is no longer I who live, but Christ who lives in me'; 'We will come to him and make our home with him'; 'He must increase, but I must decrease.' At the same time, an invariable characteristic of this mysticism is that it is concentrated upon the historical figure of Jesus; it is christocentric, both realistic and concrete, and at the same time transcendent. It looks upon the glory of Christ and is nourished by it. This aspect is expressed both in the cultic mysticism of the community and in personal mysticism.

The Johannine mystical element is manifested with particular force by Ignatius of Antioch. (He writes to the Ephesians: 'He who truly possesses the word of Jesus is also able to listen to his silence, and so to become perfect'). Clement of Alexandria and Origen (who put forward a more speculative mysticism, in some respects strongly influenced by ancient philosophy; *cf.* I, 3 above) are important figures in the further development of early Christian mysticism. In the fourth century, mention must be made of Gregory of Nyssa, whose language much enriched the forms of expression available to Christian mysticism, and who also seems to have been the first to describe the mystical experience as in fact the ἀπόλαυσις θεοῦ, the enjoyment of God; Macarius the Great, whose writings have been a continual and important influence in the mysticism of the Eastern Church, is also important as the earliest representative of Christian monastic mysticism; his concepts of the 'imprisonment' of the soul (αἰχμαλωτισθῆναι),and of its becoming the throne of the Spirit of God, are strongly mystical in form. Nilus of Sinai belonged to the fifth century, as did Diadochus of Photice and Hesychius of Jerusalem, both of whom described the inner life in terms that were a model for later writers; the sixth century produced Barsanuthius and his disciple John, and also the writer known as Dionysius the Areopagite, who was most powerfully influenced by Neo-Platonism, and whose writings came to be of fundamental importance not only to the systematic thought of Christian cultic mysticism, but also to Christian mystical speculation (particularly in the West). The Christian mysticism of the East probably reached its climax in Isaac of Nineveh (seventh century). These mystics were followed by such figures as the Abbot Dorotheus, Maximus the Confessor, Philotheus of Sinai, and Symeon the 'New Theologian', whose doctrine of the contemplation of the divine light is one of the sources of the enthusiastic and mystical movement of the Hesychasts. Later, there came Palamas, Nicholas Cabasilas and a long series of others whose writings were taken up into the great mystical and asceti-

cal compilation known as the *Philocalia*, which covers
the period from the fourth to the fourteenth centuries,
and was drawn up in the eighteenth century by the
ascetic and mystic Nicodemus of Athos.

2. *The Characteristics of the Cultic and Personal Mysticism of the Eastern Church*

The cultic mysticism of the Eastern Orthodox Church
is a contemplation of the glory of the incarnate Word
shining towards us from the incarnation, suffering, death,
and resurrection of Christ: 'Oh how marvellous! How
could the life of the universe taste death! Only because
he desired to send his light upon the world.' It is a
loving adoration, a humble prostration, an astonishment
and joy and trembling: 'Oh life, how can you die? How
can you make your dwelling place in the grave? But you
destroy the kingdom of death, and show the dead the
way up from the abyss of hell.' The climax of this cultic
community mysticism is the celebration of the Eucharist.
The Lord comes and gives himself to the soul as its
nourishment, and becomes the principle of eternal life—
the life of the future resurrection—even for our bodies:
'Today the heavenly hosts share our worship; see, the
king of glory is coming; see, the mysterious sacrifice is
carried out. Let us approach with faith and love, that
we may partake of eternal life. Alleluia' (from the Liturgy of the Presanctified). 'I am not worthy, O my Lord
and ruler, that you should enter under the roof of my
soul; but since you, who are merciful, wish to live in me,
so I take courage and approach . . .' (Liturgy of St.
John Chrysostom, prayer before communion). 'Come,
my physician, and heal my wounds. Come, divine fire,
parch the thorns of my sins and melt my heart with the
flames of your love. Come, my king, sit upon the throne
of my heart and rule within it. For you alone are my
king and Lord' (Demetrius of Rostov, *ca.* 1700).

The Eucharist, which is cultic mysticism, community mysticism, and personal mysticism at one and the same time, leads us back to the question of *personal* mysticism. Again the basic content of this mysticism is the idea of being apprehended by Jesus Christ. 'It is an unceasing prayer to Jesus, a sweet stillness of the spirit without fanaticism, and a certain marvellous condition that comes from being united with Jesus' (Hesychius of Jerusalem). Its dominant atmosphere is that of the highest spiritual exertion, the utmost activity, and at the same time of the highest degree of quiet and repose. This condition is called the 'silence' but also the 'vigilance' of the heart (according to the verse of the Song of Songs which these Fathers loved to quote; 'I slept, but my heart was awake'), or the 'guarding of the heart' or 'spiritual sobriety' or 'sobriety and prayer' (as a concept summing up the whole of the spiritual life). The heart of man must be purified and kept pure. This does not merely refer to outward virtue: 'Purity of heart, that is perfection' (Macarius). The deepest and most hidden roots of evil thoughts must be extirpated from the depths of the heart. Man is besieged by an army of sinful thoughts; he must fight against them with his whole power (μάχη ἀόρατος—the 'invisible battle'). What can he do? 'The human spirit cannot overcome the illusions of the demons by its own power; nor ought it ever to dare to try . . . but if you call upon the name of Jesus, they will not be able to resist for a moment or undertake anything against you' (Hesychius of Jerusalem). Consequently, the inward and spiritual life consists of a constant 'inner ascent' to the Lord, a constant inner calling and crying out to the Lord, a constant knocking at the door of his grace. This leads to humility and humble trust, the union of extreme exertion and utter peace. 'The heart becomes like a little child, and when one begins to pray, tears pour down' (Isaac of Nineveh).

'An unceasing calling upon Jesus with an intense longing has the effect of filling the air of the heart, as the result of this profound recollection, with a silence full of consolation. But the cause of the purification of the heart is Jesus Christ, the Son of God, and God himself, the source of all good and the creator. For he says himself: "I am the Lord who makes peace."' (Hesychius.) Man is spiritualized and already lives another life—the life of the Spirit; or rather, the Spirit lives in him and rules him. And this nearness to God must express itself, irrespective of the severity and withdrawal of the ascetic, in a burning love for one's brethren (*cf.* Isaac of Nineveh, Hom. 48), in prayer for one's brethren, and in their service. Consequently, individual mysticism represents only one aspect; it is necessary for it to be complemented by community mysticism.

3. The Mysticism of the Russian Church

The mysticism of the Russian Church grew out of the same spiritual premises and is heir to the same spiritual tradition. A characteristic feature of it is the activity of the *staretz*, which is the loving service of one's neighbour carried out for the spiritual welfare of one's neighbour, to which the mystic (after he himself has obtained a firm inward control), joyfully and humbly submits himself, seized as he is by inward joy, the measureless joyful love which flows out over his fellow men. The *staretz* Seraphim (during the first thirty years of the nineteenth century), who was perhaps a characteristic representative of the mysticism of the Russian Orthodox Church, greeted the innumerable people who came to him with the joyful greeting: 'Christ is risen, you are my joy.' This greeting expresses the way in which he was mystically apprehended by the overpowering force of the eternal life that has appeared in the world, and it is typical of the profound nature and the deep roots of this mysticism. Another great representative of the Russian tradition of the *staretz* was Tychon of Zadonsk (second half of the eighteenth century), a figure whom Dostoyevsky had in mind when he portrayed Zosima in *The Brothers Karamazov*, who casts an ascetic and mystical illumination upon the world from his burning inward love for the incarnate Son of God. The nature of the mystical experience of the Church has also been expressed with particular force and clarity in the writings of the great Russian philosopher Khomiakov (1804–60). A prominent figure who continued the ancient mystical tradition was Bishop Theophanus, who produced a Russian redaction of the mystical compilation mentioned above, the *Philocalia*, in the middle of the nineteenth century. One place in particular where this tradition was maintained up to recent times was the monastery of Optino, in the southern part of the province of Kaluga in Russia, now abolished by the Communists, while up to the present day it is still maintained in part on Mount Athos, in the person of the hermits there. Furthermore, the bloody persecutions carried out by the Bolshevists have brought about a powerful renewal of the mystical life in the Eastern Church in Russia.

NIKOLAY SERGEEVICH ARSENIEV

V*b* CATHOLIC MYSTICISM IN THE WEST

1. The Middle Ages

A history of the Catholic mysticism of the Middle Ages can neither be independent of the development of Church life and thought, as though mysticism and scholasticism represented independent or even opposed tendencies, nor can it be seen simply as another aspect of these developments (as was done by A. von Harnack), as though the history of mysticism were simply to be equated with that of Catholic devotion. But to decide its exact significance, and to give a detailed account of its varied forms, would require a more lengthy study than this. All we can do here is to mention a few particularly characteristic manifestations and periods in the history of medieval mysticism.

a. The starting point of medieval mysticism is to be found in John Scotus Erigena. But the Neo-Platonic philosophy which he (and Augustine) taught, with its mystical doctrine, was not adopted and incorporated into the Church's thought until the eleventh century. The son of the Count of Saxony, *Hugh*, who founded a school in *St. Victor* near Paris, laid the foundations of the Neo-Platonic mysticism of the centuries that followed. Clearly drawing upon Augustine, but going beyond him, Hugh regards contemplation as elevated above the world, its ceaseless movement, and the vanity of human exertion. The soul turns away from the love of transitory things, which distract and destroy it, and is gathered into itself; it realizes its own worth, and the danger which threatens it of being lost in what is alien to it. In meditation on the mysteries of the divine work of salvation it finds the way through itself to God. In the contemplation of the truth it attains the truth, and partakes through reason in the blessedness of God. But the Church's means of grace are necessary as a previous preparation for this; God can only dwell in the soul that has been transformed by grace.

Bernard of Clairvaux constantly impressed upon the Pope who was his disciple (Eugenius III) that piety demanded, far more than all the ecclesiastical tasks to which he himself turned with such burning zeal, that one should be devoted to contemplation, without which one's life was lost. But although like Hugh he was concerned for the love of God, for him this was kindled in the first instance by the human person of Christ. The distinctive feature

379

of Bernard's mysticism is the contemplation of the actual figure of the historical Jesus. Contemplation of the Passion arouses pain for the sin that caused suffering, and evokes a feeling of thankfulness and love in return for the divine love manifested in the Passion. Again, the nuptial mysticism of Bernard represents Christ as the fairest among the children of men, who as the bridegroom of the soul leads it home. The most forceful expression of the effective and fervent character of this love for Jesus is found in his sermons on the Song of Songs.

Italian mysticism, especially that of Bonaventure, represents a union of themes from Hugh of St. Victor and from St. Bernard. Descriptions in contemplative terms are united with portrayals of the life of Jesus and of the future joy of heaven to impress certain sensations upon the soul. The formation of the will and the life of the mystic is carried out by means of the imagination and the affections. Contemplation leads along the prescribed path to the goal of human life in the love of God, while the very lucid scheme does not permit any speculation upon obscure mysteries or any striving for new experiences.

German mysticism, which owes its historical origin to the placing by the Pope of the pastoral care of nuns in Germany, in the hands of the Dominican Order, consisted in the first instance of the presentation of the basic principles of the Thomist system in German, but from the very beginning, in *Meister Eckhart*, presented an independent elaboration of the earlier mysticism (*cf.* I, 2 above). Conscious of the difficulty, but also of the value of the ideas, Eckhart addressed himself to a spiritual aristocracy. Though what he was striving for was a transformation of the course of the Christian's life, yet he disdained to work upon the will except by way of an insight into the nature of things. From this point, however, undistracted by secondary aims, the path to be followed by human activity also becomes clearly defined. Withdrawal from material things, the return into one's own soul, and detachment even from oneself lead to union with God; the birth of God in the depths of the soul is the aim of the history of salvation and the meaning of Christianity. *Tauler* was simpler and, in spite of all the criticism he received, closer to the Church than Meister Eckhart, but he shares his sentiments and aims; he described his mystical experiences in measured and earnest language to small groups of listeners (the Friends of God). He deepened the Mendicant ideal of poverty, and his earnest ethical teaching, the concern he showed for a personal Christianity, and his high regard for lay piety make him to some degree a forerunner of the Reformation. Following the lines laid down by Eckhart, but also influenced by Bernard of Clairvaux, *Suso* (*cf.* I, 2 above), sought to 'set on fire once again the name of Jesus, which has grown cold in men's hearts'. The union of severe asceticism, veneration of Mary, and enthusiastic devotion to the suffering Christ, the bridegroom, and the child Jesus, was maintained above all in convents of *nuns*, which in the fourteenth century were frequently places of high intellectual culture and an intense, sometimes excessive mystical devotion (*cf.* St. Mechthild and St. Gertrude).

Ruysbroek's ingenious *Ornament of the Spiritual Marriage* followed Eckhart in making its highest aim that of 'opening out into the essential emptiness', the 'dark and inscrutable abyss of God', while the *Dutch mysticism* which followed him was more concerned with the *conditions* of contemplation. Its most widespread work, the *Imitation of Christ* by Thomas à Kempis, makes the modest claim: 'Since I am not capable of comprehending incorporeal truth, I turn with greater assurance to the deeds and words of Thy humanity'. Although this only implies a shift of emphasis towards the mysticism of St.

Bernard—a movement which gradually but continually increased in force—it also introduces a new element, the method of the quietist disciplining of the will. This, which is already a subsidiary theme in Eckhart, was given its first extended expression, and a metaphyscial basis, in the *German Theology*, published by Luther, and widely disseminated in the form of a Protestant devotional work. God is regarded as attaining to consciousness and love of himself in the creation, which he brought into being to this end; consequently, man must let God work within himself unhindered, and become the instrument of God without any will of his own. While the home of the earlier mysticism was in the monasteries and convents, in the fifteenth century it found much wider acceptance among groups of laity (though in the case of the Brethren of the Common Life, in a life of retreat still closely resembling monasticism, and in close association with the Church).

A much later disciple of the mysticism of Eckhart, who was, however, also influenced by the Spanish quietism of Maria of Escobar, was Angelus Silesius (*cf. Vc.*, 2 below). *b.* The mysticism we have described so far almost always takes for granted the position of the institutional Church and the indispensability of its means of grace, even though the historical Jesus sometimes falls into the background, and the importance of the external aspects of Christianity is somewhat discounted; is regarded the possibility of attaining the highest goals as entirely dependent upon these means. But there are other forms of mysticism. The *German Theology* developed its ideas in opposition and conflict with the so-called *Free Spirits*. According to its account the consciousness of union with God which these mystics possessed convinced them that they had passed beyond the stage where they were subject to the same conditions as other men. They regarded themselves as sharing in divine knowledge, and their actions as being guided by the divine will. Thus they regarded themselves as exalted above other men, no longer restricted to the law and the ordinance of the Church, and independent of Church worship and the sacraments. They no longer had any obligation to do penance, or to imitate the serving and suffering Christ; without any mediation they had become one with God. The ideas of this mysticism which were hostile to the Church were not written down by those who held them, and consequently are only available to us in the accounts of them given by their opponents. Their dissemination varied in extent; that of the Amalricans (Amalrich of Bena) was probably quite small, while that of the Beghards (only some of whom broke with the Church) and of the Brethren and Sisters of the Free Spirit was wider; the extent of the influence of the Spanish Alumbrados, with whom Ignatius of Loyola and Teresa of Avila at first came into contact, is uncertain.

2. *The Post-Reformation Period*

a. The understanding and ideals which helped to prepare the way for the Reformation in North Germany also laid the basis of a restoration of devotion among Catholics. The great *Spanish* saints, who played the principal part in inspiring the Church with a new spirit, as well as in the foundation of the Society of Jesus, and to whom the leaders of the Catholic restoration looked up, continued the lines laid down by the Dutch mystics.

Even Ignatius of Loyola owes the impulses which were decisive in his life to German mysticism; his method of schooling the will (the *Exercises*) is a continuation of their practice for obtaining self-discipline. But although the *Exercitia Spiritualia*, which have been immeasurable in their effects, are indebted to mystical writings, yet they cannot be regarded as part of the history of mysticism. It was not the Society of Jesus, but the other Spanish

Counter-Reformation order, the Carmelites, reformed by St. Teresa of Avila, and, under her influence, by St. John of the Cross, who developed and spread the new type of mysticism, *quietism*, which later spread principally in France, the spiritual centre of the Catholic world in the seventeenth century. The classical expression of this mysticism (not the first—Osuna's *Abecedario*, etc., preceded it) was that of *Teresa*. In her Autobiography, *The Way of Perfection*, and the *Castle of the Soul* she describes the four stages which lead to God. The first stage is the 'prayer of recollection' ('prayer' is a general term for all turning to God in thought, feeling, and the direction of the will), a powerful renunciation of all concern for the world, through the recognition of sin, the contemplation of the Lord's suffering, and everything that is capable of leading the soul to inward recollection. Here again the final stage (as in medieval mysticism) is the 'prayer of rapture' a condition of unconscious ecstasy of short duration, the *Unio mystica*. But the terminology here is not entirely consistent, and also the whole emphasis is laid on the two intermediate stages, which are scarcely distinguished from one another, the prayer of 'peace', and that of 'union', where the will, or the will and the understanding, are united with God. This is a condition of exaltation which is already supernatural, but which persists. In contrast to the alternation of 'spiritual consolation' and 'dryness' found in earlier mysticism, we have here a constant union of the will with God, which must never lead to an inactive enjoyment, but is wholly compatible with pious activity and the service of the Church, and can even be regarded as an unequalled inspiration to these tasks. For guidance in following this path of prayer, the soul is entrusted to a director, whose advice must be followed, without regard to one's own insights.

b. Like the Spanish mystics of the period that followed

(John of the Cross), *St. Francis de Sales* took St. Teresa as his example. In his *Traité de l'amour de Dieu*, he accords to the will a dominant position as the natural sovereign of the life of the human soul. Consequently Christian perfection consists of the perfection of the will through the love of God, both affective, receptive love, and productive and active love. The purpose of this book is to describe the origin, growth, power, and activity of this love. The importance of Francis de Sales is that he made what had previously been a monastic piety accessible to the laity, took away its supernatural and enthusiastic features, and incorporated it into the spiritual movement of his age, while his disciple, Jeanne de Chantal, introduced this new mysticism into the Order of the Visitation which she founded. Thus in close association with the Church's sacramental order, and in subjection to spiritual directors, there arose in educated circles at the court and in the great cities a lay piety which formed a closed group and relied upon its own experience.

c. Although Teresa, who had the advice of Jesuits, did not fall prey to it, there was a danger hidden in pietism— at least in the eyes of the Society of Jesus. This danger was that its adherents, with their self-sufficient devotion, should find themselves able to dispense with the Church's means of grace. In 1687 *Miguel de Molinos*, whose influence was widespread in Rome and elsewhere, was imprisoned and his *Guida spirituale* condemned. Like Teresa before him, Molinos exalted daily communion, the constantly renewed experience of the miracle of God's incarnation, as the most powerful support of devotion. He teaches even the acceptance, in uninterrupted contemplation, of periods of abandonment by God and of temptations due to one's own lower nature, as the will of God, so that the peace of the soul is not disturbed by them. But Molinos himself had not gone to confession for many years, and his influence was felt in the neglect of the rosary, of images of the saints, and of relics and other means of devotion typical of the very ecclesiastical piety taught by the Jesuits. It was felt that a consequence of this mode of thought would be a separation from the Church's doctrinal system and an underestimation of the force of sin, and therefore, it was feared, an ultimate collapse of moral discipline. Consequently, the favour he had originally been shown by the Pope was unable to prevent his fall.

d. The fate in the Church of *French pietist mysticism* was also involved with this process. *Madame de Guyon*, in numerous writings, described the essence of the love of God as *l'amour désinteressé*, abandonment to the divine will, representing a complete renunciation of one's own desires, even pious desires, as the purest form of self-abnegation. *Fénélon* also emphasizes the propriety, from the Church's point of view, of this mysticism, with its subjection to the judgement of the bishop and its close dependence upon the Church's means of grace. But the opposing party saw in 'holy indifference' a threat to Christian hope and the value of the sacrament of penance. Personal rivalries were also involved; Bossuet and Louis XIV succeeded in obtaining in 1699 a papal condemnation of twenty-three statements by Fénélon. The history of quietism as a distinctive school of mysticism thus came to an end in the Catholic Church; it found a modest refuge in German pietism.

HERMANN DÖRRIES

Vc PROTESTANT MYSTICISM

1. The rich thought of German medieval mysticism (*cf.* V*b.*, 1 above) was not only taken over by the Reformation movement in an extremely unbalanced tradition, but besides, only a few of its main principles were further

developed by Protestantism. The widest influence was
exercised by one of its most attractive features, the pre-
eminence it gave to a powerful everyday morality over
the carrying out of ecclesiastical devotions. Not only did
Luther take up this theme in all the profundity of his
doctrine of vocation, but the Anabaptists, Müntzer,
Schwenckfeld, etc., also turned the demand for a genuine
renewal of man into a criticism of the Lutheran doctrine of
justification. The *mysticism of the Spirit*, the doctrines of
the 'inner word', which from the time of Müntzer and
Karlstadt was opposed to a literalist faith and the 'Church
built with bricks and mortar', and which was associated
with the doctrine of the renewal of man, continued to be
held only by small groups. Finally, what Tauler had
preached as the *mysticism of temptation and the cross* only
took root where it was a product of personal experience.
Luther found himself portrayed in these descriptions,
and Thomas Müntzer united a belief in the spark of the
Spirit in man with a passionate mysticism of the cross.
On the other hand, the notable decline of the *Christ
mysticism* of St. Bernard is no doubt due to its close association with late medieval forms of ecclesiastical devotion,
and to the fact that Luther clearly rejected it at a very
early period; only Schwenckfeld learned anything from
it. Luther himself stimulated mysticism in many ways,
with his concepts of the activity of the spirit, the power
of the word, the fellowship in Christ of the faithful, and
the invisible Church. But from the time when he had
been passionately attracted to the mysticism of Bonaventure in the monastery, but had found no peace in it,
he rejected it with increasing firmness (*cf*. Vol. III,
Luther 3*a*.).

Of this whole complex of living ideas, it was the mysticism of the 'inner word' which had the greatest future.
Only at the beginning, when the inner voice was understood as an answer to 'deprivation' and 'weariness', was

it genuinely mystical in nature, and as early as *Sebastian Franck* had faded into an individualistic and idealist piety full of rationalist elements. In his thinking, and even more among those whose attention was directed towards natural philosophy, it became associated with the veneration of nature and the anthropological and cosmological theories of *Paracelsus*. Moreover, in this association the feeble humanist concept of God replaced the powerful and living concept held by Paracelsus. Through Franck and Paracelsus, and the long pre-history of these ideas in medieval and Renaissance mysticism, Neo-Platonic principles survived and continued to be influential. After the death of these two great leaders, mysticism and spiritualism in the second half of the sixteenth century survived only in little groups of followers of Schwenckfeld and Paracelsus, among whom it was increasingly assimilated with secular speculation about nature. Only *Valentin Weigel* succeeded once again in gathering the complex variety of these traditions into a definite system, which for all its complexity clearly reveals certain influences peculiar to itself, especially in the field of the theory of knowledge, as well as its link with Franck and Paracelsus; and in the ultimate principles of its concept of God and the world, it clearly manifests its ancient Neo-Platonic heritage. When his writings were published after his death, they were not unjustifiably regarded as the crown and consummation of the mysticism of the sixteenth century; from this point on, his name was associated with the principal heretical groups. At the same period nature mysticism had already emerged as an eschatological movement, through its assimilation of the apocalyptic dreams which were derived from the astrology of the sixteenth century (Carion, Lichtenberger, etc.) and from the prophecies of Joachim of Floris; by the turn of the century, partly under the influence of the conjunction of certain planets, it reached a high pitch. When the expectation of the end gradually faded away, there remained an association of mysticism and striving for secret knowledge which gave itself the title of *pansophism*.

2. From this movement, living entirely upon the past, there emerged the creative spirit of *Jakob Böhme*. Although he was fully acquainted with the tradition of Paracelsus, and was himself a disciple of the spiritualizing criticism of the Church and the orthodox doctrines of justification and predestination, he represents a new departure. He underwent himself the experiences of the medieval mystics, was the first person since Paracelsus to feel the problem of nature in its whole profundity, and solved this through his own distinctive understanding of the basic principles of the Protestant concept of God. As in the case of Paracelsus, this, his most valuable contribution, was not taken up by others. Those who followed him were involved from the first with the pansophist reforming groups who under the name of Rosicrucians looked forward to a new reformation, and in widely scattered places tried to build up secret fellowships, or at least were connected by a loose literary association and by correspondence. Of all the groups in Swabia, Hesse, Nuremberg, North Germany, (especially Lübeck and Danzig), etc., the Silesian group, centred on Böhme's biographer, Abraham von Frankenberg, was the most genuine and the most important. It taught an amalgam of a devotion to Christ based on that of Schwenckfeld, Rosicrucian longing for reform, speculation on nature following Böhme and the Paracelsists, and the longing for a pansophist universal wisdom. At the same time, the boldest thinkers of this group, Daniel von Czepko and his great disciple Angelus Silesius, made the profoundest encounter with the German medieval mystics since the time of Müntzer and Sebastian Franck.

3. Although the mysticism of the adherents of Böhme

was carried on outside the Church, German mysticism, after the gradual penetration of Protestant devotional literature by mystical and even Catholic material, at least succeeded in touching the fringes of the official Lutheran Church in *J. Arndt* (*cf.* also P. Nicolai), although it was favourably regarded by very few (J. Gerhard). The orthodox doctrine of the *unio mystica* was no more than a pale reflection, deprived of its richer content; but it was sufficient to imply a dangerous threat to the doctrine of justification. The main stream of mysticism continued to flow outside the Church, but became increasingly influential in *educated circles*. Baroque poetry was felt to be spiritually akin to a mysticism which was learning to play with emblems and imaginative experiences, and was developing religious erotic and pastoral poetry. Spanish mystics such as John of the Cross and St. Teresa were just being translated; an interest in the Cabbala (*cf.* III above) was a literary passion. Prophets from the lower classes combined speculations on the lines of Böhme, usually almost empty of content, with eschatological expectations. But particularly during the Thirty Years War and afterwards, Germany was swarming with enthusiastic visionaries, of whom only a few were acquainted with more than the outward shell of mysticism (Engelbrecht, Gifftheil, J. Werner, and later Daut).

4. The influence of German Protestant mysticism, especially that of Böhme, first produced powerful *new movements* outside Germany. In *Holland*, where Böhme's works were first printed, they took root in a ground already prepared by the Mennonites, Coornheert, the Arminians and the Rhynsburger Collegiants, and lived on these and other newly formed groups (e.g. that of Gichtel). From there it travelled to *England* among numerous adherents of Böhme (Bromley, Pordage, Jane Leade, etc.). George Fox was seized by his ideas. The

Quaker movement, at first only a society of the 'inner light', also came under the influence of theosophical and Cabbalistic tendencies in the second generation (Keith).

At the same time, the mysticism of Böhme constantly reasserted its influence upon *Germany* from Holland. German poets such as Angelus Silesius associated themselves with Collegiants. Certainly, this influence only became significant when the Protestant mysticism of Holland was combined with the more radical, more ascetical, and psychologically more acute mysticism of Spanish and French quietism (*cf.* V*b.*, 2 above). For *Reformed Church pietism* Labadie replaced Böhme. Nevertheless, the poems of *Tersteegen*, the purest expression of quietist mysticism, leave Baroque literary forms far behind, and show the influence of the typically German expression of the love of Jesus in the poetry of Angelus Silesius. The more Lutheranism was seized by the mystical and pietist movement, the more Böhme returned once again to prominence. This is true of *Gottfried Arnold* who, in addition to his richly erotic poetry of devotion to Christ, also attempted to elaborate mysticism into a theoretical contemplation. From mystical literature he drew the material and the impulse to portray the decline of the Church since the days of its 'first love', from which pure mystical teaching had been handed down only in secret. In this way, he provided pietistic mysticism with a view of history, while *Poiret* sought to provide an epistemological basis for this 'mystical theology'.

From these poetic and theological resources, pietism created a devotional literature sensitive in its tone, but not always truly mystic. Only a few true mystics stand out from the rest; in the first generation particularly *J. W.* and *J. E. Petersen*, who turned to an increasing degree towards mysticism, and incorporated the thought of Böhme in their eschatological scheme, although without the decisive element of his dualism. By contrast, the emotional sensitivity of non-speculative Christ-mysticism reached its highest point in *Zinzendorf*, and allowed full scope to the erotic expression which accompanied it. Pietistic mysticism reached a wider audience only among the Herrnhut Brethren, in the conventicles of the followers of Tersteegen, and Württemberg. These circles were the meeting place not only of leading theologians such as *Oetinger*, who renewed the thought of such different spirits as Swedenborg and Böhme, but also of great enthusiasts of peasant origin such as M. Hahn. But in general, pietism drew deeply on the Reformation ideas, the indwelling of Christ, the urge for fellowship and the desire for sanctification that typified the preceding period of mysticism.

In spite of the fact that pietistic devotion was full of mystical themes, its *theology* was largely untouched by them. It was in the early works of Schleiermacher that mysticism first sought entrance into Protestant theology; and it was German idealism which first took up again the philosophical concerns of its leading spirits, especially Böhme. Among those who were influenced by Schleiermacher (*cf.* VI, 5 below), mysticism has since penetrated deeply into the very foundations of their theological thought (E. Troeltsch, R. Otto, P. Tillich). It is also present in a watered-down form in the associated devotional literature, and in many offshoots of the pietistic movement and its literature.

HEINRICH BORNKAMM

VI MODERN MYSTICISM

1. The end of the nineteenth century brought a change in German intellectual life, from materialism and naturalism to a new inwardness, from atheism to religion,

or at least to religious longing, and from superficiality to profundity. This new apprehension of life turned at once towards romanticism, symbolism, and mysticism, although mysticism here is not automatically nor in all cases to be understood in its full meaning of the union and unity of the soul with God. In the plays which *Ibsen* wrote in his later years, beginning with *The Master Builder*, the brief words of his realistic dialogue no longer merely proclaimed the unspoken depths of the soul, but revealed a mystery of life, a creative presence in the heart of things. In the dramas of *G. Hauptmann*, from the same period, the same phenomenon occurs, and he also introduces ancient religious material, such as the apocalyptic themes in *The Assumption of Hannele*, the hope of the kingdom of God in *The Sunken Bell* (the Third Empire, already proclaimed by Ibsen, became a slogan of the period; *cf. Arno Holz*), the legends in *Poor Henry* and even certain ecstatic and miracle stories from the gospels in *Emmanuel Quint* (1910, since when, however, Hauptmann has turned to a new 'paganism'). On the whole, however, these themes are introduced in a symbolic sense, and not as a result of religious faith. But even in the realistic lyrics of *Liliencron* and *Dehmel* such themes are present, even to the point where they approach the occult, though in Dehmel's poem 'The Harp' native mysticism, which was a growing force, is a stronger and more genuine theme. These themes recur in a finer and more beautiful form in the neo-romanticism of *Hugo von Hofmannsthal* and *Maurice Maeterlinck*, who portray with terrifying power, in a few quiet words, the passage from what the senses can perceive to what is beyond them (e.g. *L'intruse, Les Aveugles*). Both consciously sought a link with earlier mysticism. *Alfred Mombert*, whom Dehmel saw as completing his work, and *Stefan George* must also be mentioned here.

A second school of thought came from the pantheism

393

of the *monist* movement, and expressed in a more profound and more living form the very rationalist attempt of Haeckel and the *Monistenbund* (Monist Society) to work out a 'reconciliation of science and religion' (which among other things had plans for worship in newly built chapels with scientific 'miracles of life' and displays), turning into a truly religious *nature mysticism* with a new Church. This movement was almost as artificial as the first, but those who took part in it were serious in their intentions, and sought to live on the basis of their new faith. In the books of *Bruno Wille* (esp. the *Revelation of the Juniper Tree*, 1895, and *The Living Universe*, 1905), in Julius Hart's confession of faith *The New God* (1899), in W. Bölsche's *Mystery of Nature* (1905), *Hours in the Universe* (1909), and even in *Faith in Life* (1927), a clear and impressive expression was given to this new mysticism. The imaginative and courageous publisher *Eugen Diederichs*, first in Florence and Leipzig, and then in Jena, joined the movement, published its writings, helped it to spread through its fine and artistically designed publications, and began to hold nature festivals on the Jena mountains, for which he aroused great enthusiasm among the students, especially the *Freideutschen* ('Free Germans'). This movement involved not merely a profound veneration for nature and a communion with the 'living universe', but also a new feeling of redemption and a new morality ('new ethics'), and even more than this, a new faith in eternity: 'All life is a dying, and all dying is a becoming . . . he whom the universe has swallowed up, has himself drunk of the whole universe . . . wait, but a while, and you shall see him again, rising like a strong giant over my head, casting his shadow over the ocean meadows . . .' (J. Hart). An important influence in the same direction was also exercised in Germany by the books of *R. W. Trine*, which had sold millions of copies in America; he was a follower of *Emerson*, and was influenced by the latter's mystical apprehension of nature (*cf. Thoreau's Walden*, which was also several times translated into German at the same period); he was still close to the firm piety of the Puritans, and was a forceful preacher of a pantheist and mystical faith as a redemptive and healing power ('mind cure').

A third school of thought is represented by the *revival of earlier mysticism*, which was also taken up by Diederichs' publishing firm, and after him, by the firm *Inselverlag*. In particular, Meister Eckhart and the *German Theology* (as 'the book of the perfect life', both published by Hermann Büttner), followed by this slim volume of selections published by the *Inselverlag*, had an extensive influence. Bölsche (*cf.* above) also published Novalis and Angelus Silesius. This revival of earlier mysticism went back to the most recondite monastic piety and even to Plotinus; but Lao-tse also appeared at this period in a whole series of editions. Admittedly, this was more a literary activity than a genuine restoration of their works to a living use. But for the German mystics at least their re-publication under Romantic and popularist influences also represented a genuine revival, especially among wide circles in the youth movement, which also reintroduced the singing of their hymns in honour of the Virgin Mary.

2. These three movements were the beginning of a process which reached its consummation in genuine new mysticism, centred on God, and of great tenderness and beauty, which appeared in *Rainer Maria Rilke's Stundenbuch* (Book of Hours) published in 1906. Because it was genuine and profound, it exercised a great influence on the devotion and the poetry of the last generation. Rilke's inherited Catholic piety, the sight of the noble sacred art of Italy and the dreaming monasteries set about with cypresses, into which his 'young brothers in soutanes went', and finally, Tolstoy and the mystical spirit

of Russia, produced a profound effect upon him. But none of this explains why after hundreds of years a mystical piety once again burst forth in a human soul in all its beauty, though also with all its dangers, and grew to a mysterious flowering. Ultimately, Rilke is a completely individual and a completely modern person. The God with whom his soul is united is neither the supersubstantial One of the ancient mystics, nor the soul of the world working itself out in natural laws, the 'roundelay of the soul' described by the disciples of Haeckel, but the profound and obscure life, the 'dumb one who grows and yet remains a show, the constantly changing figure which always rises up alone out of destiny'. He is the 'old man, whose hair is scorched and burned with soot', and also the 'future, the great light of dawn shining over the plains of eternity'. He is also the God of the warm and intimate life from which modern intellectual man has so far removed himself, and to which he is nevertheless mysteriously and sensibly close in everything: in the early morning he is the 'cock-crow after the night of time, the dew, the matin prayer and the young maid'; and when the day declines towards the evening, then 'his kingdom rises like smoke from every roof'. Whoever becomes aware of him for the first time becomes lonely: 'He is troubled by his neighbour and the time of day. Only later does he grow close to nature and feel the wind and the distances . . . .' Here someone is really living again in the presence of God and in unity with God, though it may be asked whether he is really living in that poverty which is 'a great light shining from within'. Here too, however, the danger of all mysticism can once again be seen, that man may exalt himself to become God. This danger is doubly great for modern man, through the temptation which pantheism offers to all our devotion. 'What will you do, O God, when I die? I am your vessel, what will you do when I break? When

I go you lose your meaning.' The gospel of Nietzsche sounds an equally dangerous note, with the confusion found in all mystical redemption from the self and in all 'escape from being'; 'Let everything happen to you, beauty and horror!'; 'Sent forth by your senses, go to the very limits of your longing!' Can he really be totally and ultimately serious, when in a book on poverty and death he sounds the notes of a bitter criticism of civilization and of longing for the end of his life with all its richness?

3. The effects produced by Rilke's *Stundenbuch* can be traced particularly in *expressionism*, which contains a note of the weariness of civilization often adopted by Bolshevism. The first I would mention, very close to Rilke, though much more crude, is *Jakob Kneip* (*Bekenntnis* 1900; *Der Lebendige Gott—The Living God*, 1900), who like Rilke came from a Catholic environment, and as an altar boy was steeped from the first in the mysticism of sacramental rites, but passed through all the doubts of modern life, finally to make a partial return; very close to him is the worker-poet *H. Wohlgemuth* (*Aus der Tiefe*, 1922), who encountered the voice of God coming to him from the darkness of his mind, and another worker-poet, *Alfons Petzold*, who became known in the war. Then there is also *Paul Zech*: 'I sense you, I feel you, yes, O mighty force, you are truly there and greater than I believed . . .' *Karl Otten*: 'I cannot say your name, mountains of thoughts cast the mantle of their strength about you . . .'; *Ernst Stadtler*: in posing the question of God, which seems to have found a powerful fulfilment, he suddenly realizes like Rilke, that it is his own soul which is questioning and which answers. The voice of this mysticism speaks most powerfully in the poems of *Kurt Heynike* (Gottes Geigen, 1918) and in a number of poems and writings of *Franz Werfel* (*Aus den drei Reichen*, 1919; *Spiegelmensch*, 1920; *Spielhof*, 1921). The mystical tendency of the modern period can also be clearly seen in the plastic arts,

as in the work of *Barlach*, or the biblical paintings of *Noldes*; cf. O. Beyer, *Religiöse Plastik Unserer Zeit*, 1925.

4. Mysticism was always associated with occult phenomena, beginning with the intuitive vision of the supernatural and the hearing of voices from another world, through all kinds of ecstatics and visionaries to 'mediums' pure and simple. Thus in the spiritual movement towards mysticism, since the beginning of the century and at the present day, we constantly encounter clairvoyants and telepathy, spiritualism and the theosophy of *Annie Besant*, much of the substance of which is taken from the utterances of mediums. The war increased this aspect of the spiritual atmosphere of the present day. A wave of prophecies and apocalyptic visions passed through the world, even penetrating educated circles, in a profound foreboding of the '*Decline of the West*' (the title of Spengler's work). Spiritualism flourished, because people wanted to remain in contact with relatives lost in the war. The anthroposophism of *Rudolf Steiner*, who was hitherto almost unknown, and who claimed to give a methodical experience of higher worlds, became an intellectual fashion. Admittedly, like the astrology and cosmological speculation of which there has also been a revival, it was more a pseudo-science than a religion, until *F. Rittelmeyer* brought to it a sacramental mysticism and a part of the legacy of a religion of faith properly speaking, and made it the devotion of a new 'Christian Community'. Yet another change was related to the experience of the war: the optimism of nature mysticism, with its joy in life, turned into rejection of the world, though the effect of this was not essentially a world-denying mysticism of union with God, but led to the 'theology of crisis' or dialectic theology.

5. The movement towards mysticism never went very far in *Protestant theology*. It is true that the harsh attitude of Albrecht Ritschl and his early disciples was regarded

as going too far, and much more place was given to the
ideas suggested by Schleiermacher, especially in his
Discourses (Troeltsch, Wobbermin, Emil Fuchs); but for
the most part the religion of faith was strictly maintained
(*cf.* VII below). Rudolf Otto was more strongly influenced by mysticism; he came upon mysticism by way
of Schleiermacher and Fries, and not only revealed the
Indian idea of the love of God (*Vishnu-Narayana*, 1917;
The Indian Religion of Grace and Christianity, 1930) and
described the mysticism of union with God in the writings
of Sankara, in comparison with that of Meister Eckhart
(*West-östliche Mystik*, 1926), but also, in his principal
work, *The Idea of the Holy*, drew important material from
primitive people as well as from mysticism, to describe
the nature of religion, and maintained that the vision of
God and divination, as well as faith, formed a constituent
part of religion and offered an understanding of the truth.
He too, however, also laid a powerful emphasis on justification by faith, on the will and on action. Mysticism
affected more powerfully a number of active churchmen,
who, moreover, by the power of their thinking and teaching, influenced not only lay people, but also the rising
generation of theologians: *J. Müller*, for whom faith was
still the essential element of religion; *Paul Eberhardt*
(*Das Buch der Stunde*); *A. Bonus*, who, however, tended to
restrict himself to popular modes of thought; *Albert
Kalthoff*, whose piety drew its burning inspiration from
Nietzsche, from socialism, and from nature mysticism—
he also became the president of the Monist Society—
and especially *Karl Jatho*, whose truly good and Christian
personality, popular preaching and homely pastoral
care made him probably the best and most effective
representative of this movement. Before the war, this
kind of devotion could be called the 'secret religion of the
educated' (*C. von Satsrov*, 1914), and the great success of
the novel *The Saint and her Fool* by *Agnes Günther* (1913),

399

essential features of which were romanticism and mysticism (and also the occult), was a sign of the times. But, as we have said, the war completely changed the position. On the one hand, it brought with it anthroposophy, and on the other hand the theology of crisis. Karl Barth began his conflict against 'experience', to the point of explaining faith as a 'vacuum'; Emil Brunner annihilated Schleiermacher on account of his 'mysticism'. But the pendulum has already swung as far as it can in the opposite direction, and is ready to swing back.

6. We go on to a brief glance at *Catholic theology*, in which a place has always been found for mysticism as a necessary complement to the religion of the law (the religion of faith falling into the background), and where it has always been firmly established. But even there, it had retreated before the intellectual flood tide of the end of the last century. But in Catholicism, too, it underwent a revival with the new flow of ideas. It can be seen in the first instance in the modernist movement, and, to some extent mediated by *J. H. Newman*, in the mystical 'modernism' of *Baron von Hügel* and *Tyrrell*. It then passed to France, where one school of thought wanted to fling wide the door to the Church by way of mysticism (*Saudreau, Les degrés de la vie spirituelle*, 1896). But a reaction set in against this school, in favour of the older view, which regarded mysticism not as the highest stage in all (Catholic) devotion, but as a special gift of supernatural visions and phenomena (*Poulain, Les grâces de l'oraison*, 1901; *Maumigny, L'oraison extraordinaire*, 1905, translated into German in 1928 by *Richstätter*, who also provided a valuable introduction). The liturgical movement (*cf.* Vol. III *The Liturgical Movement*) and the movement to bring the Ignatian Exercises into wider use are also significant. Other important works have been produced by *J. Zahn, E. Krebs*, and *M. Grabmann*, and in particular, among modern Catholics, by *Joseph Bernhart*.

F. Heiler also came from this circle. In present-day Catholic literature hidden streams of mysticism are everywhere at work; special mention must be made of *Joseph Wittig*, and the delicate poems of *Felix Timmèrmann*.

HEINRICH WEINEL

VII THE FUNDAMENTAL RELATIONSHIP BETWEEN CHRISTIANITY AND MYSTICISM

1. The Argument Concerning the Religious Value of Mysticism

The dispute concerning the religious value of mysticism finds some thinkers completely excluding it from the sphere of true religion, while others consider that religious devotion only reaches its perfection in mysticism; they may be thinking directly of the spiritualized form of mysticism (*cf.* I above) as this culminating point of devotion, or else, changing the meaning of the concept, they may have in mind a profound and close personalist relationship to God, which they term mystical. Finally, mysticism and the religion of prophetic faith are regarded as the two opposite poles of religion.

2. Mysticism as True Religion

Those who *radically reject mysticism* are fond of equating mysticism and magic, which is made easier for them by the practical methods employed by primitive mysticism in particular (*cf.* I, 1 above), though they ignore the ultimate intentions, especially of the more spiritual form of mysticism. But all mysticism claims to be a relationship between man and ultimate reality; and it goes on to assert that if the error of degrading the divine into the instrument of human purposes is to be avoided, this relationship must be regarded as valuable in itself, and seen as the highest and ultimate aim which man not only can reach, but ought to strive for. But if this is so, then in this respect at least mysticism is not an error, but *true religion*. The disappearance of the distinction between God and man (*cf.* I, 2, 3 above) is also condemned as an error in mysticism. But we must distinguish between a mysticism which develops a philosophical view of the world to the point of a real doctrine of the unity of all things, monism in the true sense (*cf.* I, 3 above), and another form in which the unity which is sought remains something beyond this world, which can therefore only be reached by turning away from the world (as in Plotinus). If this is so, then it is premature to make the previous negative judgement a general condemnation. Finally, the protest against the evaluation of mysticism as compatible with genuine religion can be based on the thesis that true religion demands a *personal* divine power, and the possibility of a personal relationship and dialogue between man and God. This thesis depends in part upon the observation that, even where strong *pantheist* mystical tendencies are evident, popular belief still clings firmly to the personal character of the deity to whom the highest honour is paid, or turns back for help to other personal forces (as in Hinduism and Buddhism). But questions of religious principle cannot be decided from empirical observations in this way. The motives at work in this phenomenon may well be regarded as 'elementary'; but this alone does not mean that they can provide a criterion for religious judgements. Again, this thesis and the consequent rejection of mysticism from the sphere of true religion can simply be an expression of the exclusive religious claim of theistic faith, which is no longer even capable of acknowledging that other forms of religious devotion are true religion in their own way; it is an outright condemnation made without any serious attempt to test it against the facts.

3. *Mysticism and Theistic Religious Devotion*

The problem of mysticism and theism is not merely concerned with the attempt to assess the religious value of one against the other. The fact that mysticism has found a place within exclusively theistic religions (*cf.* III, IV, V above, and also Sufism in Mohammedanism) demands an explanation of the relationship between mysticism and theistic devotion. The mere fact that in numerous places they are found together does not necessarily mean that they exist side by side with no fundamental tension; the course of history is full of the association of incompatible ideas. It is perfectly obvious that a mysticism which explicitly proclaims the *unity of all things* is quite incompatible with theistic faith. But the links between theistic faith and the mysticism of the transcendent are not so simple. Yet here too we find that where the dominant aspect of the relationship to God is a clear *personalism* it comes into conflict with the mystic approach. For a theistic devotion which is fully conscious of its true nature, the highest and ultimate goal is that of a personal relationship which continues to maintain a clear distinction between 'I' and 'you'. On the other hand, mysticism strives towards forms of experience in which for the subject of the experience, the worshipper, these limits and distinctions are lost in a true union. This mysticism seeks not merely to fear, love, and trust God; it seeks to partake in his supernatural being as a matter of experience. This it can only do if the clearly convinced and sovereign personal God fades away into the abstract substance of the Ultimate. Of course the appearance of mysticism in theistic religion can also be a reaction against a tendency that may have manifested itself to make God extremely remote, thus denying a true intimacy with God and the possibility of his close presence. In this situation, mysticism offers itself as a substitute for a religious need which the theistic belief is not satisfying.

There is another way in which mysticism can obtain an entry into the realm of theistic devotion. Theism also recognizes a manner of being enveloped by God and of being intimately indwelt by him, which tends to break down the sober distinction between two separate persons. At this point it is very easy, at least in the language used to describe the situation, for the boundaries between this indwelling and mysticism to disappear. When a powerfully effective abandonment to God leads to genuine ecstasies of the inner being, as in the case of the Hindu Bhakti devotion, the limits actually do break down. Such devotionalism is alien to Christian theism, in which even the profound consciousness of union with God maintains the *diastasis*, the distinction between God and man, and holds firmly and clearly to an ethical relationship. Even where the Christian knows that he is enveloped by the power and loving kindness of God, the relationship between two distinct persons is not really broken down, as in the mystical experience of union. Furthermore, this certainty is of the close presence and the coming of God to be with man, and not of the apprehension in experience of an original unity which was there from the start, or of an emotional union brought about by man. Thus there is a clear distinction between the mystical experience of the unity and the intimate relationship with God of Christian theism. The question of *personality mysticism* belongs in this context. If this means the intimacy and closeness of the personalist relationship with God that is acknowledged by Christian faith, then it is probably acceptable to say that even theistic devotion is only consummated in such 'mysticism'. But the use of the word 'mysticism 'is not appropriate here (*cf.* I, above), and the clear distinctions that it makes possible are blurred. The other, emotional union with God may, of course, be denoted by the term 'mysticism' in this intermediate sense. But this is not

what is meant when mysticism is described as the ultimate and profoundest point reached by all religion.

4. Conclusion

Thus mysticism and an intimate theistic relationship to
God—Christian faith—are two *distinct* phenomena different in nature. Both are the highest form of the religious outlook they represent, in that both are concerned
with a profound relationship between man and the
ultimate reality, and both regard this relationship as the
highest and ultimate aim and obligation of man. We
may ask whether it is possible at this point to give a *final
evaluation* of the one against the other. Such judgements
are regularly given from both sides, in each case to the
advantage of the position adopted and to the disadvan-
tage of the other. One point of view argues from its own
presuppositions against those of the other. In such a
situation, the task of a theological evaluation can only
be to isolate themes which give a proper basis for a
reasonable judgement in one direction or the other on the
part of a thinking person. Thus it is necessary to attempt
this evaluation as far as possible by weighing against
each other the central principles of the two opposed
phenomena. The true glory of mysticism is this. It
pursues its way through broad regions of intellectual
activity: the mystic is involved in theoretical speculations extensive in their scope, and practises a strict concentration of thought; he disciplines his senses, and
represses all egocentric desires and emotions; but this is
only a way to the ultimate goal; mysticism, having
achieved its goal, leaves all this behind and, reaching
out beyond everything that in any sense can be called
the sphere of the human mind, is directly present in the
absolute beyond of the ultimate and eternal.

The decisive question with regard to mysticism is what
is the true situation with regard to this alleged surpassing

of all spiritual and intellectual concerns. There is reason to suppose that in reality it is not a matter of something which is the ultimate and highest goal above and beyond the most profound concerns and attainments of the human spirit and intellect, within the limits of which a theistic relationship to God remains, as an intimate trust in God, and a surrender to God through ethical obedience, but is in fact something of a quite different kind, but on the same level. It is certainly no accident that in addition to the spiritual and intellectual discipline—which is all that is in fact really involved—it is possible for mysticism to recommend artificial and mechanical practices as a means of obtaining its goal. And what is attained through one method or the other is in itself completely unaltered; the sublimation obtained by spiritualized mysticism only lies on the way to the goal and looks out towards it from the point it has reached. But ultimately all spiritual endeavour reverts to a condition which could have been attained, even without such preparation, by means of purely mechanical and unspiritual measures. But what is attained through these means is simply a distinctive kind of psychosis. This means that mysticism, however close a connection it may come to have with human intellectual and spiritual activity, and however much it may be enriched in its content from this source, is ultimately not what it claims to be, something that surpasses human thought and activity, but a parallel route which leads to something lower.

THEOPHIL STEINMANN

BIBLIOGRAPHY

Arseniev, Nikolay Sergeevich. *Mysticism and the Early Church*. Translated by Arthur Chambers. London: S.C.M. Press, 1926.

Baeck, Leo. *The Essence of Judaism*. Revised edition. London: Bailey Bros. and New York: Schocken Books, 1948.

Baillie, John. *The Idea of Revelation in Recent Thought*. Oxford University Press and New York: Columbia University Press, 1956.

Bartsch, Hans Werner. *Kerygma and Myth: A Theological Debate*. With contributions by Rudolf Bultmann and others. Translated by Reginald H. Fuller. London: S.P.C.K., 1953 and 1964, and New York, Harper & Row Torchbooks, 1964.

Brunner, Heinrich Emil. *Dogmatics*. 3 vols. Translated by Olive Wyon. London: Lutterworth Press and Philadelphia: Westminster Press, 1950–62.

The Mediator. Translated by Olive Wyon. London and Redhill: Lutterworth Press, 1942.

Revelation and Reason. Translated by Olive Wyon. London: S.C.M. Press, 1947.

Clemen, Carl. *Religions of the World: Their Nature and Their History*. In collaboration with Franz Babinger and others. Translated by A. K. Dallas. London: G. G. Harrap, 1931.

Dibelius, Martin. *Jesus*. Translated by Charles B. Hedrick and Frederick C. Grant. London: S.C.M. Press, 1963 and Philadelphia: The Westminster Press, 1949.

Heim, Karl. *God Transcendent: Foundation for a Christian Metaphysic*. Translated from the 3rd German edition by Edgar Primrose Dickie. Welwyn: Nisbet, 1935.

Leeuw, Gerardus van der. *Religion in Essence and Manifestation*. Translated by J. E. Turner, London: Allen & Unwin, 1964 (2nd edition) and Torchbook edition. New York: Harper & Row, 1963.

Macquarrie, John. *Twentieth Century Religious Thought: The Frontiers of Philosophy and Theology, 1900–1960*. S.C.M. Press, 1966 and New York: Harper & Row, 1963.

Ogden, Schubert. *Christ Without Myth: A Study Based on the Theology of Rudolf Bultmann*. 1st edition. London: Collins, 1962 and New York: Harper, 1961.

Outler, Albert C. *Psychotherapy and the Christian Message*. 1st edition. New York: Harper, 1954.

Tillich, Paul. *The Protestant Era*. Translated and with a concluding essay by James Luther Adams. Welwyn: Nisbet, 1951 and Chicago: University of Chicago Press, 1948.

Systematic Theology. Welwyn: Nisbet, and Chicago: University of Chicago Press, 1957. 3 vols in 1. Edited by James Luther Adams. Vol. 1. New York: Harper & Row, 1967. Pp. 71–159.

Troeltsch, Ernst. *Christian Thought: Its History and Application*. Edited by Baron F. von Hügel. London: University of London Press, Ltd., 1923.

Wach, Joachim. *Types of Religious Experience, Christian and Non-Christian*. Chicago: University of Chicago Press, 1951.

Wobbermin, Georg. *The Nature of Religion*. Translated by Theophil Menzel and Daniel Sommer Robinson. New York: Thomas Y. Crowell Company, 1933.

Index of Names

Aaron, 32
Abelard, 189
Abraham Abulafia, 367
Adoptionism, 102
Aetius, 113
Alexander, Bishop of Alexandria, 108, 109, 110
Alexander of Hales, 217
Alexandria, Council of (A.D. 362), 114
Alexandrine theologians, 94, 95
Alumbrados, 383
Amalrich of Bena (and Amalricans), 383
Anabaptists, 129, 387
Anaximander, 262
Ancyra, Council of (A.D. 358), 114
Aner, Karl, 25
Angelus Silesius, 357, 382, 389, 391, 395
Anhomoians, 113
Anselm, 157, 189, 219
Antioch, Council of the Dedication (A.D. 341), 112; Synod at (A.D. 344), 112
Antiochenes, 115, 116
Apologists, 94, 95, 98, 99, 100, 101, 102, 103, 214
Apostolic Fathers, 96, 214
Appar, 166
Apollinaris of Laodicea, 115
Apollinarianism, 117
Aquinas, Thomas, 190, 217, 312
Arausio, Synod of (A.D. 529), 217

Arian Dispute, Arianism, 106, 115, 116, 135
Arimanum, Council of, 114
Aristotle, 242, 267
Arius, 103, 108, 109, 110, 111
Arles, Synod of (A.D. 353), 113
Arminians, 130, 194, 390
Arndt, J., 390
Arnold Gottfried, 391
Arseniev, Nikolay Sergeevich, 25
Artemon, 103
Athanasius, 109, 110, 111, 112, 113, 114, 189
Augsburg Confession, 190, 191
Augustine, St., 110, 120, 121, 187, 188, 189, 190, 195, 214, 215, 216, 217, 233, 265, 266, 365, 379
Aulén, G., 331
Avenarius, R., 236

Baeck, Leo, 25
Baius, M., 193
Balla, Emil, 25
Banez, 221
Barlach, 398
Barsanuthius, 374
Barth, Karl, 15, 19, 400
Basil the Great, 114, 115
Bauke, Hermann, 25
Baumgarten, S. J., 130
Baur, F. C., 136
Beghards, 383
Berggrav, E., 331
Bergson, 284, 288

409

Index

71 72 73 74   12 11 10 9 8 7 6 5 4 3 2 1